PRISON MANAGEMENT

PRISON MANAGEMENT
PROBLEMS AND SOLUTIONS

Dr. Madhavarao Mahaworker

Publications

KALPAZ PUBLICATIONS
DELHI - 110 052

Prison Management: Problems and Solution

Rs. 750

ISBN : 81-7835-314-8

Published in 2006 in India by
Kalpaz Publications,
C-30, Satyawati Nagar,
Delhi-110 052
Email : kalpaz@hotmail.com

Lasertype Setting by: Tact Computer Graphics, Delhi
Printed at: Salasar Imaging System, Delhi

Contents

Preface

"World History is Nothing but the History of Universal Anarchy".

"In the Universal Age, the institution of prison and imprisonment is found throughout the world". This is the first research work on "PRISON MANAGEMENT: PROBLEMS AND SOLUTIONS", with special reference to Universal State. A research work on important topic like, "PRISON MANAGEMENT: PROBLEMS AND SOLUTIONS", in the Global Age, will prove a milestone towards world peace, liberty, equality, fraternity, justice, development and rationality. Because, the "Supreme Human Aim is becoming a Universal Being". Prison is dynamic. This book is a scholarly exposition of a difficult subject and confidently expected to provide reliable guidance to all those engaged in the research on "Universal Rationalization of Prison Administration". The aims and objectives of this work is to develop a global movement to replace the institution of prison by alternatives to prison and imprisonment.

This book has been divided into seven chapters. Chapter I contains institution of prison and imprisonment is universally found in all the sovereign states and confined up to modern state system. Prison and imprisonment is the monopoly of the Ruler but penal power is shared by the Ruler, Caste (Religious) Head and Capitalist. Yet, crimes are committed from local level to global level. Prison Administration being a global problem, requires global remedies.

Chapter II deals with Prison System in India, Modern prison system originated in 1835 from the Minute by T.B. Macaulay. In the Constitution of India, Prison has been included in the State List. Prisons are nationalized. Day-today administration of prisons rests on principles incorporated in the ante-diluvian Prisons Act of 1894 and Prisoners Act of 1900. Prisons are an agency to maintain law and order.

Chapter III contains regarding the Organisation, Classification and Control of Prisons in Karnataka, from 1956 to 2001. Karnataka

Prisons Rules were implemented from 1974 onwards. The IG Prisons exercises general control and superintendence over all prisons. Prisons have been unscientifically organized, classified and controlled.

Chapter IV deals with Prison Management in Karnataka. Prisons are owned and managed by the Government. The officer in charge of a prison receives and detains all persons duly committed to his custody. Newly admitted prisoners are subjected to quarantine. Prisoners Panchayat Board is constituted in each jail. All prisons are co-prisons. Men prisoners are separated from women prisoners. The Prison Management is a "Lock-in and Lock-out and Neglected Management".

Chapter V is concerned with Prison Reformation in Karnataka. It commenced with the establishment of the Central Prison at Bangalore in 1863. In 1940, "Mysore Jails reforms Committee" was appointed and most of its recommendations were implemented. Men's Open Air Prison was commenced at Koramangala. 'Prisoner's Transformation Project', 'prisoners Families and Children in Distress' schemes etc. were commenced. To train prisoners, there is Prison Training Institute. Yet, prison reformation has corrected neither prisoners nor staff.

Chapter VI deals with Contemporary Prison Scene in Karnataka. "Prison Reformation which commenced with the establishment of the Old Central Jail of Bangalore, reached its peak with its shifting to the New Central Jail, Bangalore in 2001". Prisons Department is a "Lock-in and Lock-out Department" in all fields. The ailings are budgetary constraints, shortage of staff, increase in the number of prisoners especially under trials, overcrowding, domination of traditional prison system, ante-rationalisation and scandals are common. Common. Rehabilitation measures are very few.

Chapter VII is concerned with Summing and Conclusions with reference to Future of Prison Administration is Karnataka. Formulation of National Prison Policy on the basis of World Prison Policy. "Prisons as old institutions were detention centers, as new institutions are punishment centers and in future should become rationalist centers in the Age of Rationality".

Dr. M. B. Mahaworker

1
Origin of Prison and Objectives of Study

1. Conceptual Framework

Meaning of Prison

Gaol or Jail, a prison, the two forms of the word are due to the parallel dual forms in Old Central and Norman respectively, jaiole or jaole, and gaiole or gayolle. The form "gaol" still commonly survives in English and is in official usage, e.g., "gaol delivery". The spelling "jail" is used in American.[1] Prisons, were first used in England for punishment during sixteenth century.[2]

The word Prison and Gaol derived from the Latin words which respectively to 'seize' and 'cage'.[3] The word prison means different things to different people. To the law abiding it is the place where criminals end up. To the criminal it may be a vague hazard or unavoidable indignity often exercised. To the World Governmentist, it is an instrument of the power system or it is an instrument of the anti-World Governmentist.

Regarding the meaning of prison, there is no unanimity among the writers. According to the prevailing usage in India, the term "Jail" is a generic term which applies to penal institutions housing both prisoners awaiting trial and prisoners committed to sentences. Consequently, the jails perform the function of remand institutions and prisons.[4] Prison traditionally defined, is a place in which persons are kept in custody pending trial, or in which they are confined as punishment after conviction.[5]

According to the Oxford English Dictionary, prison is a "a place properly arranged and equipped for the reception of persons who by legal process are committed to it for safe custody while awaiting trial or for punishment".[6] Jails intended as places of 'safe keeping' for persons awaiting trial, are at the same time utilized (deliberately or otherwise) as rehabilitation facilities for convicted offenders. Prison is that part of the penal system where criminals are held in custody for varying lengths of time determined by the courts as punishment for offences.[7]

Punjab Police Chief P.C. Dogra, recently put it "Jails are emerging as the new co-ordination centres for militancy".[8] Any place can be converted into jail. Penal institutions are places where persons whose liberty has been curtailed by law are continued to assure the successful administration of justice or the application of penal treatment.

Whatever may be the official definition of prison as jail, work-house, reformatory, penitentiary, state prison, house of correction or whatever else, it is a place where the punishment of imprisonment is executed. The prison is the manifestation of people's tireless efforts towards the discovery of curative and regenerative processes.[9] Terms popularly applied to what is more correctly but more cumbersomely classified as custodial treatment.[10]

2. Origin of Prison

It is not possible to provide the exact historical evidence to prove when and where the prison first arose. Punishments in society are as old as civilization itself, though imprisonment in its present form was not always in use. As places of detention prisons are old institutions; as places of punishment they are however comparatively modern. The instances of the former use may be found as early as twentieth century B.C.[11] Prisons in the shape of dungeons had existed from times immemorial in all the old countries of the world. In his book *The Future of Imprisonment*, Norval Morris refers to punitive imprisonment used extensively in Rome, China, India, Assyria, and Babylon and firmly established in Renaissance Europe.[12]

In Ancient Rome those convicted of crimes were only confined until such time as punishment, chastisement, torture or execution–

could be meted out. Death by hanging, by hurling over the tarpeian rock, crucifixion, beheading and drowning in the sack, exile, beating with rods and forced labour were the older forms of punishment. Imprisonment at that time was not the common form of punishment. In their origin prisons are certainly to be considered only as places of detention.[13]

The idea that attempts should be made to cure enemies of society of their anti-social tendencies by confining them for a period regulated by the seriousness of their offences. One of the first institutions for the reform of offenders was that built for women in 1593 by the Protestants of Amsterdam. Forty years earlier a prison for vagabonds and loose women had been established in Bridewell London. This use of the prisons as places of detention has continued up to this date.

3. Purpose of Imprisonment

Indeed it was not until the nineteenth century that imprisonment began to constitute an important sanction and not really until the eighteen fifties, that with the abolition of transportation, it moved into first place.[14] Prison is neither a power nor a power within the power. Prison itself is not a social system. It is a means of the social system. "Prison is neither above nor beyond but within the social system".

It is not an autonomous body. It is an instrument of the state, shaped by its social milieu and by stage of social, political and economic developments. It treats to and is acted upon by the society as various struggle to advance their interests.[15] Prison is a means to an end and not an end in itself. Prison is for the protection and it interests by down grading the prisoner, rather than protecting his social status.

The primary objectives of prison are the protection of society against criminal aggression by anti-social elements. The objective is defeated if any anti-social individual is allowed to return to society without being reformed. "House of Correction", the earliest prison in Britain was designed to be a place where the anti-social individuals could be reformed into a useful member of the society. In those days too much stress was laid down on deterrence and the prisons were made places of horror so as to deter anti-social individuals from indulging in crime.

This ancient view has been found to be wrong and has given place to the modern view that ultimate purpose is of imprisonment and rehabilitation. Mahatma Gandhiji states, "Criminals should be treated as patients in hospitals and jails should be hospitals admitting such patients for treatment and cure. The outlook of jail staff should be that of physicians in hospitals. The prisoners should feel that the officials are their friends. No one committed crime for the fun of it. It was the sign of the diseased mind. The cause of a particular disease should be investigated and removed".[16]

Crimes are committed for fun also. Five youths set alight a 45 year old Indian man in the Brazilian Capital Brasilia, just for fun. The students poured methylated spirits over Galdino Jesus Dossantos while he was in a sleepy mood in a bus shelter, then set him ablaze with a cigarette.[17]

Crime is fun for children of officials.[18] Delhi teens steal cars for joy rides.[19] Some children commit crimes because, for them crime has become child's play.[20] Some people commit crimes so that they can enter jail and get food, clothing, shelter and security. The institution of jail is also considered by some as a means to draw public attention. To draw the attention of the society towards their demands, some people have voluntary programmes like 'Fill Jail'. Jail is also a means to emerge as a leader and enhance their popularity. Going to prison is also a trial of strength of supporters.

Some people volunteer to prison. A twelve year old boy held his class and teacher at gun point reports Reuters from Lisbon, Ohio. This sixth grade student later told he pulled gun because his biological mother was in jail and he wanted to join her.[21] Jails are also glorified. Penal institutions are also converted into historical monuments. Prison is an institution of social control and symbol of legitimate coercion. It is no more a resting ground in the legal process where death penalty, banishment or life imprisonment, transportation may be the verdict.[22] Rather the institution of prison has imbibed and is influenced by the conventional norms, ideals and assumptions of humanitarianism, enlightenment, and the welfare state. It not only carries the bearings of the ideals of the period, but also impregnated with the expediencies of organizational science.[23]

4. Theories Relating to the Objectives of Imprisonment

In ancient and medieval times, prisoners were simply confined in the prison for trial. Punishments were given to them outside the prison. In the modern age imprisonment emerged as the primary method of punishment. Due to the growth in civilization changes have taken place in the penal system. The important theories dealing with the objectives of imprisonment are as under:

Vindication

It means the imposition of punishment for wrong doing, simply means the restoration or reassertion of the law protected values, which the perpetrator has destroyed. In a purely objective manner– the wrong must be righted by imposition of yet another detriment. The roots of this theory may be have to be found in the sacrifice which primitive and archaic man had to bring in order to appease the gods who had been outraged by the evil-doer. A few philosophers have espoused vindication as strongly as Kant, particularly in the hypothetical example of a political island society that wishes to dissolve itself with mutual consent.

Retribution

It is the oldest theory. It justified punishment as an end in itself. As per this theory, punishment is inflicted because a crime has been committed. Kant held the opinion that the punishment is a must in proportion to the offence. In contemporary society the retributive theory appears to be outdated, because the modern theory emphasizes on (1) future of an offender than the past (2) dealing with the offender than with the offence.

Penitence

The penitentiary movement of 19th century Pennsylvania and New York, was dedicated to the proposition that a law breaker need the opportunity to make peace with himself, to search his soul and to come to terms with his creator. The penitence system which became known as the separate, solitary or Pennsylvania system was based on Howard's cellular system. But, it advocated strict separation of the prisoners by day as well as by night. The reformative virtues of this system were held to lie in complete absence of contamination, in religious instruction and silent contemplation.[24]

Penitence as an ingredient of modern corrections has been severely attacked by criminologists and lay men alike, mainly for reasons of the supported incompatibility of a prison environment with the vision of the hopefully adjusted personality of a successful penitent. Little data is available from which to draw inference as to the extent of the existence of a penitence craving. Hence, penitence does not seem to play a significant role in our modern prison system.

Neutralization

This theory is sometimes put forth as another justification for imprisonment. The theory of neutralization argues that, by putting a man in prison, society physically removes him, from its bosom and, for the period of his incarceration, makes it physically impossible for him to commit further crimes. This theory has been criticized on ethical and utilitarian grounds. Restraint has an incapacitating effect. Even in the non-punitive system, society's right and obligation to incarcerate dangerous offenders is generally conceded. Naturally, the principle of utility would dictate that, no force should be employed than is necessary for the preventive purpose. Imprisonment may serve the objective of neutralization in its widest sense.

Deterrence

The principal and most established ground for corrections is that of deterrence. In recent years, it has frequently been designated as prevention. The term deterrence refers to the employment of terror as such a stimulus. When mankind was so brutal and uncouth that only drastic demonstrations sufficed as stimuli against proposed crime. But, now it is accepted that excessive terror back fires in many ways. Terror has vanished from the idea of deterrence. What is left is the anticipation of a detriment to be avoided, such detriment is the loss of freedom.

These are the conclusions of the effectiveness of a prison and parole system, a study, incidentally, which received worldwide public acclaim at the Third United Nations Congress, in Stockholm, Sweden, in August 1965. The institution of prison has to be continued which has proven its effectiveness particularly,

(a) By abandoning its use in categories and cases not requiring and imprisonment and this would seem to constitute a considerable percentage, and

(b) By making the best of the time of determination through efforts at rehabilitation.

5. Characteristics of Prison

The following are the characteristics of the prison system:

(i) Prison is an instrument of the power system. It helps to quench the power thirst of the people. It continues so long the power system continues. Prison is transitory. So far, it has served the world society. With the change in the world system, prison also dies.

(ii) Prison has a unique position in the society in which organizations compete either for economic resources or for the loyalty and support of group members. It is non-competitive in the sense that no other organization challenges it directly.

(iii) It is relatively an isolated system.

(iv) It is a closed or protected system. Members of the larger society (except for the relatives of the inmates and official and non-official visitors) have no direct stake in the prison in terms of ownership, goods, services or reciprocal relations of any kind. Thus, the prison is relatively protected from outside scrutiny.

(v) There is use of force. The use of force is the static power of tool-proof steel cells.

(vi) This authoritarian system is regimentation and depersonalization, life is routine.

(vii) The incorrigible unit (prison) has the ever present eye of authority.

(viii) The unresponsiveness of the governing authority.

(ix) There is uncertainty and indefiniteness.

(x) At present, prison system is confined to nationalism. Prisons are found only within the national boundaries. Prison is universally found in all nations. There is only "National Prison System". There is no "International Prison System". Because, nations can be punished but cannot be imprisoned. The National Prison System failed to spread itself to the International Prison System.

(xi) Finally, in the primitive age prison was not there. In the ancient, medieval and modern systems prison is there. In the World Age it is not required. Because, the "World Government" stands for the abolition of prison itself. Already we are on the road to the World Government and all roads must lead to the World Government only. Therefore, prison is a transitory institution.

The word prison means different things to different people. To the World Governmentist prison is an instrument of the power system to quench the power thirst of the people. To the powerist it is an instrument to maintain the power system. To the anarchist it is a waste institution and is a burden on the society.

To the modernist it is a means of social control. To the internationalist prison is an instrument of the nation system to serve national and international interests. To the law abiding, it is a place where criminals end up. To the criminal, it may be a vague hazard or unavoidable indignity often experienced. To the social inadequate, it may be a shelter. To the politician, monk and businessman, it is a place which serves their interests.

Punishment is as old as civilization itself. First, the penal system originated. Later on, the institution of prison originated. Prison is artificial. In the primitive system there was no state, religion and wealth concentration. Man was a roaming animal from place to place. He led a nomadic life. He had mixed nature i.e. social and anti-social in global sense. There was no power system. Hence, there was no institution of prison.

Ancient System

Two epochs may be distinguished in the history of penal institutions. During the first which lasted towards the end of the eighteenth century A.D., penal institutions were chiefly dungeons of detention rooms in secure parts of castles or city towers which were to detain prisoners awaiting trial or execution. Death by hanging, by hurling over the tarpeian rock, crucifixion, beheading and drowning in the sack, exile, beating with rods and forced labour were the older forms of punishment. Ex-communication, dismissal of workers etc. were also other forms of punishment. Imprisonment at that time was not the common form of punishment. In their origin prisons are certainly to be considered only as places of detention.

The second epoch was of universal adoption of imprisonment as a substitute for virtually all corporal or capital penalties. It came to be realised that the process of imprisonment, involving in isolation from family and community, under not so pleasant conditions, could itself be considered as a convenient mode of punishment to replace the old corporal punishment, most countries readily took it. Imprisonment as a principal method of punishment is a comparatively modern method of dealing with offenders, though it's roots run back to the earliest societies. It was adopted by the Church and used quite extensively and then common jails and special prisons for the criminals arose.

It may be noted here that John Howard made no suggestion that jails should be used as places of punishment. It was the cessation of transportation to America that forced the leaders of the prison reform to consider the building of national prisons. It was the spread of nationalism from Europe to America, which led to the National or Modern Prison System. In the meantime, however, to take care of the prisoners who had been formerly transported to America, England resorted to the use of 'hulks' or floating prisons. It was also decided to transport prisoners to Australia.

Howard was not a rationalist. Even he never claimed himself as a citizen of the world. He was a deeply religious man and politician. He cannot be considered as a humanitarian in today's global sense. He was a humanitarian according to his times.

Man being a social and anti-social animal in the global sense, stopped nomadic life and started a settled life. Gradually, people created the power system. According to the power system, there were three kinds of power: Religion, State and Wealth Concentration. This marked the replacement of the primitive system by the ancient system.

It is impossible exactly to locate when and where first the prison arose. Definitely, it can be said that, with the creation of the religion, state and private property, prison is created. All these powers are artificial. Prison is an instrument of the power system. It was created to serve the interests of the ruler, caste head and wealth concentrator.

In the struggle for supremacy of one kind of power over another kind, prison was monopolised by the ruler. But, penal power was shared by all the three kinds of power i.e. Caste (Religious) Head, Ruler and Wealth Concentrator. Caste Head is empowered to excommunicate his followers, the ruler is empowered to punish the ruled and the wealth concentrator punishes his workers.

As soon as firm Government established in the world, men began to realize that crime is harmful not only to an individual, but to the state as well. The state imposed certain duties upon its citizens and in turn it was bound to protect their lives and their property. It was therefore the duty of the state to arrest, judge and punish him.[25]

In preliterate societies imprisonment was rarely used as a penalty. The penalty of imprisonment hardly ever occurred in early Greece.[26] Imprisonment was not at all used in the Roman Republic, but was used for minor offences in the Roman Empire.[27]

Locking up criminals in dungeons and jails is a practice that goes as far back as recorded history. Such confinement was largely reserved for suspected offenders awaiting trial or for convicted criminals awaiting the lash or the hangman's noose.[28] Only in contemporary recent times has word prison come to the common penalty, for acts harmful to the community both grave and petty which the law forbids. In the old Roman Law, carcer or prison was used only as the place for holding, not for punishing offenders.[29]

As places of detention prisons are old institutions; as places of punishment they are however comparatively modern. The instances of former use may be found as early as twentieth century B.C. With the commencement of the ancient system the formation of the prison system commenced. It was firmly established in this age only. Since the beginning of the recorded history there has been allusions to prisons.[30]

Medieval System

In the Medieval times also the old system of punishment continued. The penalty of imprisonment was either forbidden in law or rarely awarded. The ancient Roman idea that "Prison ought to be used for detention only, but not for punishment" was an accepted legal principle in most of Europe in the Middle Age.

Even in the later Middle Age, imprisonment as a penalty was either unknown or used only for very restricted groups of offenders. In France, for example, the last code of laws prior to the Revolution was enacted in 1670 and contained no mention of imprisonment as a penalty.[31] Even as late as 1771, the French Jurist Jousse stated that prison was used only to hold criminals before trial and not to punish them for their crimes.[32] In Frankfurt, on the other hand, it was ordered in the first part of the sixteenth century that for certain offences "the criminal shall be imprisoned and forgotten for a time".

Nevertheless, imprisonment was sometimes used in France and other Western countries either as a means of securing the payment of fines or as a commutation of death penalty when mitigating circumstances were found. In medieval England, when Henry de Bracton wrote treatise on English Law, De legibus et Consuetudivibus Angliae, he referred to prisons as places "where men remained only until it had been decided whether they should be punished or freed".

Nevertheless, imprisonment as a form of punishment was some what commoner in England than on the Continent, where legal systems were based more closely on Roman Law.[33] Henry II, for instance, provided imprisonment for one year for perjury in a grand assize; Henry III provided the same penalty for breaches of the forest law; and the Statute of Westminster of 1275 punished rape with two years imprisonment .

Incarceration was used in medieval England as a means of enforcing the payment of fines. In 1241, for example, some Jews convicted of circumcising a Christian child were ordered either to pay twenty thousand marks or else be kept perpetual prisoners.[34] These few exceptions apart, "Medieval Anglo-Saxon society, with its wide use of capital and corporal punishment, had little use for imprisonment" and even up to the middle of the twelfth century, "some counties (in England) were without public jails or prisoners cages, and Henry II commanded their construction at the Assize of Clarendon, in 1166". These jails were, in the beginning, administered under the fee system.

The sheriff and magistrates of the English counties did not assume any direct responsibility for the maintenance of jails or for the treatment of occupants. This "unpleasant chore" was turned over to the private keeper as a concession. The keepers were not paid any salary. Their income came from fees exacted from the prisoners or their friends and relatives.

Naturally, the fees that they charged were so high as to enable them to operate prisons with profits. In these gaols the "prisoners and their families were kept at their own expense for months or years awaiting the time of trial, well-fed if they had means, but perhaps starved to death if they were poor. At a later date, the prisoners hung collecting bags out of their windows on Sunday mornings".[35]

This fee system continued in England for several centuries without much criticism in official circles until the time of the great prison reformer, John Howard. Imprisonment, however, came into extensive use in the later half of the thirteenth century during the reign of Edward I. But even in this period, it was used primarily as "squeezer" or means of securing fines.

The keep or dungeon of the lord's castle was usually the place of detention pending the payment of the fine or the execution of the sentence. Growth of population and the consequent increase in the number of offenders made it necessary to make special provision for their care; in 1166, the Assize of Clarendon directed the building of gaols in all counties and boroughs.

While these gaols were for the most part under local authority, the king's courts at Westminster had from times immemorial, maintained their own prisons of the king's bench, Marshalsea and the Fleet, almost entirely for debtors and others confined as a result of civil processes or for contempt of court.[36] Some institutions akin to the prison existed at an early date such as Delte Stinche in Florence in 1300 A.D.[37]

In general until about the last part of the thirteenth century in England and probably a little later in some of the continental countries, imprisonment as a punishment was used only for very restricted groups of offenders. Von Bar has stated that "The penalty of imprisonment was almost unknown in France in the later Middle Ages".[38]

Prisons in the shape of dungeons had existed from times immemorial in all the old countries of the world. In 'Future of Imprisonment', Norval Morris refers to punitive imprisonment used extensively in Rome, Egypt, China, India, Assyria, and Babylon and firmly established in Renaissance Europe.[39] The prison came into existence largely as an interim house of detention of an offender pending his trial and punishment.

Modern System

Italian political philosopher Niccolo Machiavelli (1469-1527), through his famous book *The Prince* written in 1513 while he was in prison, advocated the replacement of the medieval system by the modern system by imposing the supremacy of the state over religion and wealth concentration.

There is a link between Machiavelli's Prince and prison reformation. Because, the book originated in jail. It means the modern age originated in prison. Consequently, in future, there were chances for the replacement of the formation of the prison system by the reformation of the prison system. The establishment of the modern system continued in the sixteenth century. Machiavelli did not advocate new prison system. He was not a prison reformer. Yet, "Experiment with imprisonment as a form of punishment" commenced in sixteenth century itself, in Europe.

Until the middle of the sixteenth century prisons were dungeons or strong rooms used merely to detain persons awaiting trial or imposition of sentence, usually death, mutilation or banishment. Punishment of crime by imprisonment was unknown.

With the breakdown of feudalism, the fencing of the pastures and the general economic upheaval of the middle age, a new class of petty criminals arose who obviously could not be punished so cruelly. The court sentenced these petty thieves, vagabonds, beggars and prostitutes to hard labour in work houses, which were later to become the houses of correction of the sixteenth century. The principal objective of jail administration in most of the European countries in the Middle Age and even thereafter was only to detain the offenders awaiting trial or execution of sentence and to squeeze them for payment of their fines or debts which incidentally yielded good profits to the keepers of the jails.

(a) Experiment with Imprisonment as a Form of Punishment

After the collapse of feudalism, Western Europe in the sixteenth century was swarmed with paupers, mendicants and roving outlaws. Majority of rural population who had been forced to leave their lands and estates and the mercenary armies and soldiers left by the feudal barons were all congregated in the towns and cities and created an acute socio-economic problem for the whole of Western Europe.

It was to solve this problem that the City of London established a workhouse in 1557 in a former royal palace at Bridewell which had given to it for this purpose by Edward VI in 1553 under the influence of Sir Thomas Lever and Bishop Ridley. This was the first house of correction, and the term Bridewell came to be applied to other similar institutions that sprang up in England soon after. By an Act of 1576, the British Parliament provided that every county should have a house of correction, and in 1609 such institution became mandatory in every English county.

The earliest of the house of correction was the Bridewell in London, which served as a model for other parts of England and also for the colonies. In many localities, however, the difficulty of making them self-supporting caused the authorities to continue the barbarities of the stocks, the pillory, the branding iron, and the whipping post.[40]

The London 'Bridewell', the Amsterdam Rasphius and Spinhuis founded respectively in 1557, 1595 and 1597; Francis 'Florentine Hospice' established about 1677; the Reformatories for Boys and Women in St. Michale's Hospice in Rome founded in 1704 and 1735 and the Ghent Work House established in 1775, were the most important institutions of this time. This period of experimentation lasted up to the close of the eighteenth century when imprisonment was universally adopted as a substitute for most of the corporal or capital penalties.

Most of the elements of penal institutions were brought into general use towards the end of the Eighteenth century. It may be said that prisons as such were built only in the sixteenth century in European countries. Originally, the major purposes of the administration of these institutions were to correct idleness and vagrancy on the one hand, and to make profits on the other, by compelling sturdy beggars, and vagabonds sent there to do hard and unpleasant work. Later, these institutions also came to be gradually used for imprisoning minor offenders.

In 1630, by an order of the Privy Council, houses of correction were located next to the jails so that misdemeanants could be put to work instead of being confined idle in the jails. In 1711, by an Act of Parliament, the maximum term of imprisonment in these institutions was fixed at three years. By subsequent legislation, the number of offences for which persons might be confined was largely increased. And through this process, the English houses of correction gradually lost their original correctional function and became regular jails for convicted persons.

However, the establishment of Bridewell House of correction in 1557 marked the beginning of a new era in the history of the evolution of the European penal institutions. It was an era "of experimentation with imprisonment as a form of punishment for certain types of offenders".[41]

In other parts of Europe, houses of correction on the pattern of Bridewell were started by the Dutch. They established a house of correction in Amsterdam in 1595. Following the Dutch pattern, houses of correction were later established in Germany, Switzerland and many other countries in Europe. The ultimate object of the administration of these establishments was the reformation of offenders. But this end was sought to be fulfilled by wrong means of strict discipline of punishment and hard labour with little touch of human sympathy.

There was little emphasis on the classification of inmates according to age, sex or other principles. The most striking was the deplorable conditions of these institutions which "soon produced widespread agitation for further changes in methods of handling criminals. Leading agitators included Montesquieu, Voltaire, Thomas Paine, Diderot, Adam Smith, Bentham, Sir Thomas Romilly, John Howard, and Elizabeth Fry. These leaders painstakingly exposed and publicized the conditions of filth and immorality that prevailed in these houses which, they charged instead of reforming their inmates, actually fostered crime and disease".[42]

As regards the set up, the earlier prisons were not very different from the ill-ventilated and ill-provided dungeons of old. These prisons were managed by private persons trying to make profits which resulted in corruption and cruelty.[43]

(b) History of Prison Reformation in England

The history of prison reformation in England dates back to the year 1557 when the old Royal Palace of Bridewell in London at the behest of Bishop Ridley was turned into a house of correction partly to provide employment opportunities to the needy poor and partly to punish, correct and reform by labour of a diversified nature minor offenders of the class of petty prostitutes and sturdy beggars and vagabonds. The historical background of the new development was the social upheavel and spiritual movement of the Age of Reformation. The first results were highly satisfactory.

(c) Prison Reform Movement in the United States

In the USA, the prison reform movement was pioneered by the Quakers of Pennsylvania, under William Pen's leadership. They had brought with them to their new home "a mixed heritage of experiences and ideas. In England they had been persecuted for their heterodoxy and in their exile in Holland they learnt about the work houses of that country. Their religion made them humane towards their errying and suffering fellow men and the work of their co-religionalist-John Howard, made them conscious of their own crime problem and opened their eyes to the lives of their own congregate Jails".[44]

Through the Philadelphia Society for Alleviating the Miseries of Public Relations, the citizens of Philadelphia in 1790 obtained the passage of a law which marked the beginning of the penitentiary system in the United States. The Act established the principle of solitary confinement of felons with productive work and strict discipline.

The Walnut Street Jail in Philadelphia was remodelled and became the first American experiment with segregation of the more dangerous criminals in solitary cells, the grouping of mis-demeanants, and witnesses in larger rooms while engaged in productive indoor and outdoor work at equitable wages and with reasonable hours of work.

Pennsylvania or Separate System

By 1820, the Walnut Street Jail and its imitaters fell into disrepute. The Quakers of Pennsylvania became the leaders of prison reforms after the Revolutionary War. Imprisonment was substituted for corporal punishment and the death penalty was restricted only to murder. To reduce the evils of congregation the so-called Pennsylvania system was experimented upon in the Walnut Street Jail at Philadelphia. This system was established with the purpose of obtaining "reformation by introspection, meditation and penitence".

This was the first cellular confinement in America which the humanitarians of the day felt would put the prisoner on the path of reformation. However, after a few years the Walnut Street Prison steadily deteriorated and became a failure. Consequently, the system was replaced by the Auburn System.

Auburn or Silent System

The Auburn system employed solitary confinement only for short periods and allowed the prisoners to work in association during the day-time under a rule of silence. The prisoners were separately confined at night. These two systems of prisons, the Pennsylvania or the Separate System and the Auburn or the Silent system, were not so radically different. After a controversy between the two systems the Auburn system won the day.

International Scene

International Standard Minimum Rules on Prison Reformation

Growing problem of crime control in contemporary world has proved that no country can deal with its crime problem effectively without participation, of the whole world. It also requires broader public participation in programmes and activities of social defence aiming at prevention of crime and treatment, reclamation and rehabilitation of criminals.[45]

The international society is an anarchical society. There is no super governmental system over the modern governmental system, which can regulate the global relations. The UNO is not the World Government. At the same time, some efforts to replace the modern governmental system by the World Governmental System are also found. This emerged as a movement for the World Government.

Professor Laski, a political philosopher pleaded for the creation of a World Federation, which is also for him, the next stage in the evolution of the State. C. Streit in his book *Union Now* also visualises a federal union of various democratic nation-states and outlines the scheme and method of a World Government of the federal type.[46] Sri Aurobindo, an Indian political philosopher said, "The idea of One World is natural and organic and not an adopted child of the speculative and the forecasting mind of the thinker."

Albert Einstein in 1946 said, "Everything that is done in international affairs must be done from the viewpoint of it will advance or hinder the establishment of the World Government". The movement for the World Government was further encouraged when a Preliminary Draft of a World Constitution was framed by Chicago University in 1948. Reinhold Nebuhar in his essay 'The Myth of World Government' has emphasized the necessity to curtail the absolute sovereignty. "They are rightfully concerned about the fact that unbridged national sovereignty is a principle of anarchy in an interdependant world. Their answer to this problem is to call for a Constitutional Convention of the World .... which will abridge the sovereignty of nations."

Ram Manohar Lohia, another Indian political philosopher (1910-67), said: "Peace can come only via World Government and this can come only via new world views".[47] Jaya Prakash Narayan, another Indian political philosopher, also expresses the necessity for the establishment of a World Government. To him, "A day might come when the national communities might federate together to form the world communities". In the Cold War, Professor Arnold Toynbee said: "If we do not now abolish War, War is going to abolish us.... abolishing war would involve setting up atleast a rudimentary World Government". He categorically said: "One World or None".[48]

Gradually, the movement for the World Government became weak and the international system under the leadership of the UNO continued to strengthen further. UNO, as a global association of nations, has made some efforts towards prison reformation throughout the world.

(i) UN-Standard Minimum Rules for the Treatment of Prisoners

Perhaps, the first record of a concrete proposal to an international body to consider minimal "rights" for all "deprived of their liberty by a judicial decision" is the one offered to the meeting of the International Penal and Penitentiary Commission held at Berne in 1926. Eventually, a set of fifty-five rules was presented to the next IPPC Congress, held at Prague in 1930. After further studies, a first international draft was produced in 1933 and endorsed by the League of Nations in 1934.

Berne was again the scene of the IPPC meeting place in 1949 to consider a revision of the rules to bring them upto date. The culmination of these efforts was the adoption of a new set of ninety-four Rules by the First United Nations Congress on the Prevention of Crime and the Treatment of Offenders, held at Geneva in 1955. The Economic and Social Council, in 1957 approved the Standard Minimum Rules for the Treatment of Prisoners and invited Governments to give favourable consideration to their adoption and application.[49]

In this respect, the Universal Declaration of Human Rights, 1948, containing inter alia, several fundamental human rights in criminal justice has undoubtedly served as the springboard for concrete initiatives. The principles enunciated in the Declaration have subsequently been elaborated in the International Covenant on Civil and Political Rights and over thirty specific crime prevention and criminal justice standards.

Under it's Technical Assistance Programme, the UNO helping the Member Nations in suggesting progressive programmes for the scientific care and treatment of offenders. It urged the member nations to modify their national practices accordingly. This helped all the nations to join the international mainstream in prison reformation.

The Standard Minimum Rules for the Treatment of Prisoners are not intended to describe in detail a model system of penal institutions. They seek only, on the basis of the general consensus of contemporary thought and the essential elements of the most adequate systems of today, to set out what is generally accepted as being good principle and practice in the treatment of prisoners and the management of institutions.[50] These Rules are not aimed at the establishment of the prisonless world.

The Standard Minimum Rules had gradually influenced the policy on prison administration all over the world in a steady manner. These Rules were more an expression of policy in the treatment of prisoners and universally accepted as such and the calling for the periodic report every five years by the Secretary General of the UN served the useful purpose of reminding the nations of the job still unfinished.[51]

In this respect, the United Nations Standard Minimum Rules for the Treatment of Prisoners in 1955, accompanied by the Recommendations on the Selection and Training of Personnel for Penal and Correctional Institutions have set the tone for global action.

The UN Standard Minimum Rules for the Treatment of Prisoners provides a rationale to the use of imprisonment as an important component of the criminal justice process. Despite an apparent Western bias of its provisions, the underlying principles continue to have a universal appeal and to form a basis for all countries to act upon. It has clearly been accepted that in view of the great variety of legal, social, economic and geographical conditions of the world, not all of the rules are capable of application in all places and at all times.

Undeniably, the Rules are of a profound value in the development of prison management and custodial treatment policies. In the first part, all the essential aspects of registration of prisoners, separation of categories, accommodation, personal hygiene, clothing and bedding, food, exercise and sports, medical services, discipline and punishment, instruments of restraint, information to and complaints by prisoners, contact with the outside world, books, religion, retention of property, notification in case of death, illness, transfer etc., removal of prisoners, institutional personnel, and inspection are included.

The second part, covers special categories of prisoners, including those under sentence, insane and mentally abnormal, prisoners under arrest or waiting trial, civil prisoners, and persons arrested or imprisoned without charge. For prisoners under sentence, the Rules dwell upon guiding principles, treatment, classification and individualisation, privileges, work, education and recreation, and social relations and aftercare. In order to ensure a vigorous follow up of the provisions, an annexure has been added detailing out the procedures as adopted by the Economic and Social Council in 1987.

Thus, the rules symbolise an international movement towards the rationalisation of penal policies from the viewpoint of all such human rights of prisoners as are not inconsistent with the conditions of incarceration itself.

In many countries, prisons are even today deemed as a system created merely to maintain law and order. It has yet to be viewed as an essential means of preserving and raising the quality of human life. By and large, investment on prisons is still considered as non-developmental. Public attitude is generally ambivalent. As most of the prisoners in developing countries are themselves a victim of stark deprivation and of forced induction into criminogenic culture, they hardly have an advocacy of their own or on their behalf. As a consequence, prisons receive the lowest priority within the criminal justice system in most of the countries.

Obviously, this United Nations instrument cannot be said to have a complete answer to all the problems that the prison systems are currently faced with. The newly emerging trends and forms of criminality, especially those which are perpetuated by men of means and organised syndicates within and across the borders and which endanger the well being, safety and survival of vast populations, pose a challenge to some of the very basic assumptions that the Rules are based on. The future course of action would inevitably involve constant invocations and rationalisation in the existing approaches.

In fact, international efforts to fill in the gaps projected by UN Standard Minimum Rules for the Treatment of Prisoners have gained momentum since the adoption of another instrument on juvenile justice in 1985. The Beijing Rules, as these are popularly known, are now proposed to be supplemented at the United Nations Congress by the Draft Standard Rules for the Protection of Juveniles Deprived of their Liberty.

While the proposed instruments stand out on their own merit, of a far-reaching significance is the exercise underway on the preparation of the UN Standard Minimum Rules for Non-Custodial Measures (The Tokyo Rules). For the first time in the history, an effort is afoot to pave the way to a progressive refinement of the penal system which seems to have over relied on imprisonment as a remedy for crime.

The Draft Tokyo Rules aim at evolving a set of principles to regulate the use of non-custodial measures, and to administer programmes for offenders dealt with through alternatives to imprisonment. These intend to secure a greater involvement of the community in the treatment of offenders as well as to develop among them a sense of social responsibility. The objective is not to denounce prisons but to re-establish their primary function of serving as one of the inevitable modes of the treatment of offenders.[52]

(ii) UN Body of Principles

Body of Principles for the Protection of All Persons under Any Form of Detention or Imprisonment; Standard Minimum Rules for the Treatment of Prisoners; and Basic Principles for the Treatment of Prisoners provide a comprehensive set of safeguards for the protection of the rights of persons who are detained or imprisoned.

The Body of Principles was adopted by The General Assembly in December 1988. The Standard Minimum Rules were adopted by the First United Nations Congress on the Prevention of Crime and the Treatment of Offenders, held in Geneva in 1955. The Basic Principles adopted by the General Assembly in December 1990, complete the set of safeguards with eleven point form standards.

The content of these instruments forms the basis for organizing any prison regime. In sum, they provide that all prisoners and detainees must be treated with respect for their human dignity, with regard to the conditions of their detention, treatment and discipline; contact with the outside world; health; classification and separation; complaints; records; work and recreation; and religion and culture.[53]

(iii) UN-Standard Minimum Rules for Juvenile Justice

The adoption of The Standard Minimum Rules for the Administration of Juvenile Justice by The Seventh United Nations Congress on the Prevention of Crime and the Treatment of Offenders in 1985, represents a milestone in mankind's quest for protecting the rights of the child in distress. The rules symbolise a concerned response to the rising trend of juvenile delinquency in the contemporary world. It is a clearly defined guidelines for the national governments to evolve progressively their juvenile justice systems on universally cherished human values. Doubtlessly, the formulation of the rules fulfill a long standing demand voiced by the international community at the earlier Congresses to have minimum standards for juvenile justice on the lines of those for the treatment of prisoners.[54]

The Convention on the Rights of the Child entered into force in September 1990 and now has more than hundred States parties. It provides for certain special rights for juvenile offenders, in recognition of their special vulnerability and societies interest in rehabilitating them. In particular, the Convention sets out a prohibition on life imprisonment of juveniles, as well as protecting them against capital punishment and torture. Imprisonment of juveniles must be a measure of last resort and when imposed, must be for the shortest possible period of time.

In every case, the Convention requires that juveniles in conflict with the law be treated with humanity and respect for the dignity of the human person, and in a manner which takes into account the child's age and the possibility of rehabilitating him or her.

UN Guidelines for the Prevention of Juvenile Delinquency (Riyadh Guidelines); UN Standard Minimum Rules for the Administration of Juvenile Justice (Beijing); and UN Rules for The Protection of Juveniles Deprived of their Liberty; these three instruments, together with the Convention on the Rights of the Child, form the basic standards relevant to the administration of juvenile justice.

Like the Convention, these instruments (adopted by the General Assembly in December 1990, November 1985 and December 1990, respectively) require that national legal systems must take into account the special status and the vulnerability of juveniles who have come into conflict with the law. They deal with both prevention and treatment, on the basis of the central principle that the best interests of the child are to guide all action in the field of juvenile justice.[55]

(iv) Open Penal Institutions

The Open Prison, or 'prison without bars' or minimum-security prison as they are called was a very late development within the prison system. The movement of open penal institutions got momentum with the 12th International Penal and Penitentiary Conference held at the Hague in 1950. One agenda of the Conference was "To what extent can open institutions replace the traditional prisons". In the Conference an attempt was made to draw out the principles of open prisons after conducting a survey of 14 European countries and their systems in open institutions.

According to United Nations Seminar on Prevention of Crime and Treatment of Offenders (1955), an open penal institution is characterized by the absence of physical or material precautions (such as walls, locks, bars and armed guards) against escape and by a system based on self-discipline and inmate's sense of responsibility towards group in which they live.

The open prisons differ from the closed prisons in its philosophy of administration, discipline, enforcement of orders, assessment of problems and models of tackling them. The new pattern of administration is based on trust, tolerance, truth and totality. The ideas of reformation and rehabilitation of the prisoner is given prime importance. The positive outcomes of this type of penal institution are self-help, constructive work, social usefulness, sense of dignity, positive change in attitudes and behaviour of the prisoners.[56]

Nowadays, open prisons are increasing in number, which is a healthy trend. Because lighter and easier punishments like extreme punishments would have the same psychological effect. In many cases a lenient punishment would also eliminate much of the hatred and bitterness against the world that are common to all inmates of prisons.[57]

Till today, the open prison has failed to eliminate the traditional prison throughout the world. At present traditional prison is the dominant prison. Yet, traditional and open prisons are found throughout the world simultaneously. Because, open prison is an extension of the traditional prison.

Why Prisons Exist and What They are Meant to Achieve

Prisons have existed in some societies for many centuries. Usually, they have places where men and women were detained until they underwent some legal process. They might be waiting to go on trial, or for execution or exile, or until a ransom, a fine or a debt was paid. Occasionally, individuals who posed a particular threat to the local ruler or state might be deprived of their liberty for a long period. The use of imprisonment as a direct punishment of the court was introduced to Western Europe and North America in the 18th century. It has spread gradually to most countries, often as a result of colonial oppression.

(i) Arguments for the Continuation of Imprisonment

Developing institutions and the repealing old ones for enforcing the laws of society is a relatively modern practice. Confinement before the seventeenth century was simply a form of detention, and no other reason to justify its existence was needed.

During the period of the development of the Philadelphia and Auburn prison systems many theories have evolved that were intended to support the idea of the penitentiary. To some it was evident that prison system had become society's white elephant and even more justification for its existence was necessary. Today, the arguments for imprisonment usually include one or more of the following:

(a) Imprisonment deters others from committing crimes; it makes the potential perpetrator of a crime think twice.

(b) Imprisonment provides the means by which criminals may repay society for the damage done to society or to its individual members.

(c) Imprisonment provides a place where the idle, the vagrants, those who do not contribute to society's well being may find labour and thus they may become beneficial to society and to themselves.

(d) Prisons are essential to punish the wrongdoers for their anti-social acts.

(e) Imprisonment is simply a hospital for the socially sick person and serves to cure him.

(f) Prisons exist in order that the process of rehabilitation or re-socialization can be most efficiently accomplished by society.

(g) Prisons exist in order to protect society from people who are violent or destructive.

(h) Imprisonment is necessary in order to protect the criminal from becoming brutalized by his fellowman in an eye-for-an-eye-attitude.[58]

(ii) Penal Systems Today

According to a recent UN survey of member nations, data indicate that about two-third of the member nations responding to the survey are maintaining adequate and humane prison systems and are treating their inmates according to a recommended standard of rules. These rules include the provision for adequate medical services, adequate clothing and bedding, a healthy diet, education and recreation services, certain opportunity for resocialization and other items.

The responses to the survey by member nations does not tell us much about successful work programmes, vocational training, work or leave programmes, or any alternatives to prison that may be supported by the prison system. These are difficult to find and in many cases do not exist.

Prison abolition and prison alternatives continue to be exciting concepts supported in only a few nations. Innovation of resocialization programmes is lacking in most of the world's prison programmes. There appears to be little evidence that any great change will take place in the near future unless some radically different philosophy of social deviance and correction develops throughout the world.

The obstacles to the implementation of even basic rules as recommended by the UN is caused by legislative inaction, lack of adequate funding, shortages of facilities, and insufficient number of qualified personnel. In many nations the slowness and complexity of the legal machinery prevent implementation of furloughs and work release programmes, temporary home leave, programmes of increased compensation for prison labour and programmes of parole or probation with concurrent alternatives applied over-crowding of prisons now a more serious problem.

Prison programmes continue to depreciate in many nations because inadequate funding necessitates the hiring of unqualified personnel, even after training, to work in the system. Low wages earned by prison staff discourage qualified persons from even applying for the many jobs that need to be filled. Specialists such as psychiatrists, psychologists, medical doctors, and social workers are almost non-existent in many prisons. This condition only underlines the need for a stronger demand for alternatives.

Whatever the cause, crime from local to global level, increasing at an alarming rate. Methods of punishment or prevention are simply not working. The judicial systems in many nations are so much overloaded that they have reached a point of collapse. Law itself is the reactor rather than the anticipator and it will continue to fall behind in providing appropriate measures for coping with the rapidly changing norms from modern society to global society.

Some nations have already begun to develop this new model of corrections. The recent conference of the European Ministers of Justice on the subject of alternatives to short-term imprisonment held in Zurich, Switzerland and other similar meetings that the concept of alternatives to prison has come into its own and is no longer simply a theory presented by reformists.

Third and Last Epoch

Rationalisation of Prison Reformation

Today, we are entering a third and last epoch of institutional development. The contemporary society, which has increasingly reliant on the use of prison as a major method of conflict resolution is not required.

(i) Prison Abolition Movement

From John Bartlow Martin to Jessica Mitford a popular prison abolitionist, literature has grown. This is a fairly new force, a demand for abolition of prisons by an influential segment of the population. While this group is small and most of its members are located in the United States, it is growing at a comparatively rapid rate. The seemingly normal system of corrections and imprisonment is now being challenged, and the arguments for abolition are many.

Part of the efforts of the abolitionist centres around the argument that a new public viewpoint about imprisonment must be developed. This viewpoint is that imprisonment is abnormal and represents an idiosyneracy of civilization.[59] Nowadays, enough evidence is available to support the assumption that prisons are not needed in the future. Alternative methods of resocialization and changing penal sanctions have accomplished a move towards prison abolition in several countries. Alternatives have already been quite successful in the Netherlands, Sweden, Canada and in some states of America. Reductions in prison population in the Netherlands and in Sweden have not upset the national order.

A nation with the desire to rationalise its systems of corrections must take global interests into consideration. There appears to be a correlation between low prison populations and encouraging attitudes towards abolishing prisons. This occurs when a humanitarian, egalitarian and rational attitude is the core of the philosophy of corrections administration. This attitude is predominant in Sweden.[60]

Offenders do not always receive the same sentence for the same crime in court systems throughout the world today. This points to the fact that penal codes should be reconstructed, and the national governments must be made aware that new social and legal controls should be written and old laws expunged. Prisons must be, in fact, the very last resorts.

The value of short-term sentencing is becoming increasingly evident. The United States experimented with programmes of short-term incarceration several years ago and found useful in terms of deterring crime. In addition, short-term sentencing of six months or less has reduced prison population and also the disabilities that longer sentences promote.

(ii) The Present Environment for Change

In today's world the problem of prisons is the prison itself. The role of the prison must be limited to a place of confinement only for the most dangerous social deviants. Even in this role, prisoners subjected to prison confinement should be sentenced to determinate sentences at the end of which he is released. Prisons cannot serve as treatment centres. If incarceration is necessary, the main goal of imprisonment should be to enhance the offenders chances for achieving satisfaction in legitimate activities after release from incarceration.

If these goals are sought, then the need for prisons in the future will be minimized and prospects for a world without prisons will be realized. Now, the social scientists have opined that only punishment cannot solve the problem of crime and criminal in society, because all criminals are not of the same type. They differ socially, politically and economically in many ways. Also since the criminals differ in their background, it also becomes necessary to give them different punishment.[61] It is not the severity of the punishment that ensures that justice is done, but surety of it.

(iii) The Future of Imprisonment

The fiasco of the prison rationally requires a contraction of the prison, and an eventual abolition of it. In 1985, the notion of a freeze on prison construction was introduced in a plenary sub-session of the VIII United Nations' Congress on the Prevention of Crime and the Treatment of Offenders. The background was the mounting prison figures and huge construction projects, in many countries.[62]

It may be concluded that, while The United Nations is doing its best within its limitations in criminal policy matters, many modern governments while adopting its recommendations, seldom implemented them. The most glaring case is the still limited effectiveness of the Standard Minimum Rules for the Treatment of Prisoners adopted in 1955. Curiously, the international society has not been able to produce a better global system and the failure explains the continuity of obsolete penal systems. The fact is that fear of crime, is one of the main features of contemporary society and that feature will be accentuated in the near future if global criminal justice order is not set up.

In many respects, the emergence of the prison as a major penal sanction could be attributed not just to the social, economic and political needs of the period, but also to the rise and fall of those alternatives, which were initially designed to control offenders by diverting them from gaol, corporal and capital punishment. In the case of alternatives and their refined intentions, the prison was presented as a unique opportunity to reform, contain and deter its inmate populations as well as acting as a form of general deterrence to outsiders.

The enactment of penal policy does not take place in a vacuum. From the Bridewell, the workhouses, the hulks, transportation, impressments to prison and beyond, the social forces behind the expansion of controls show a remarkable affinity: what to do with criminals and how to avert the social consequences of a rising crime rate.[63] Now, the global forces are towards the abolition of prisons. Consequently, a movement for the abolition of prisons should start at the world level.

References

1. Mohanty Amarendra and Hazary Narayan: *Indian Prison System*, Ashish Publishing House, New Delhi, 1990, p. 7.
2. Jeanne Hearsch: *Birth Right of Man*, UNESCO, 1968.
3. *Encyclopaedia Britannica*: 14th ed., Vol. 10, 1939, p.18.
4. *Concise Dictionary of History*: ed. by Callum Brines, Tiger Books International, London, 1993, p. 333.
5. Jonna Kelley: *When The Gates Shut*, Longman, London, 1967, p. 7.
6. Mohanty Amarendra and Hazary Narayan: *op. cit.*, p. 2.
7. *Encyclopaedia Americana*: Vol. 22, Connecticut, 1980, p. 619.
8. *Oxford English Dictionary*: Vol. III, Oxford University Press, Kolkatta, 1979, p.1385.
9. *Cambridge Encyclopaedia*, 1994, p. 895.
10. *The Indian Express*, 9th August 1998, Bangalore.
11. Sykes, M. Gresham: *The Society of Captives—A Study of Maximum Security Prison*, Princeton University Press, New Jersey, 1958, p. 8.
12. Wolff Michael: *The Penal Institutions of Britain—Prisons*, Borstals, Detention Centres, Approved Schools and Ramand Homes; Eyre and Spoil's Woode, London, 1977, p.13.

13. Bhushan Vidya: *Prison Administration in India* (with special reference to Uttar Pradesh), S. Chand and Company, New Delhi, 1970, p. 1.
14. *Indian Journal of Public Administration;* Indian Institute of Public Administration; New Delhi; XXV; January-March, 1979, p. 124.
15. Bhushan Vidya: *op. cit.*, p.1.
16. Fitzgerald, P.J.: *Criminal Law and Punishment*, Oxford, Clarendon Press, 1962, p. 233.
17. Singh J.: Indra: *Indian Prison—A Sociological Survey*, Concept Publishing Company, New Delhi, 1979, p. 16.
18. Mohanty Amarendra and Hazary Narayan: *op. cit.*, p. 3.
19. *The Indian Express*, 23rd April 1997, Bangalore, p. 1.
20. *Ibid.*, 4th December 1996.
21. *Ibid.*, 7th March 1998, p.1.
22. *Ibid.*, 29th April 1998.
23. *The Times of India*, National Daily Newspaper, 25th March 2000, Bangalore, p. 10.
24. Mohanty Amarendra and Hazary Narayan: *op. cit.*, p. 178.
25. Singh J. Indra: *op. cit.*, p.1.
26. *Encyclopaedia Britannica*: op. cit., p. 515.
27. Hugh, J. Klare: *People in Prison*, Pitman Publishing, London, 1973, p. 3.
28. Bhushan Vidya: op. cit., p. 1.
29. *Encyclopaedia Britannica*: Vol. 14,1977, p. 1103.
30. *Compton's Pictured Encyclopaedia and Fact—Index*: Vol. 11, Compton and Company, Chicago, 1956, p. 414.
31. Vinegradaff, P.: *Outlines of Historical Jurisprudence*, Oxford University Press, 1920-22, Vol. II, London, p. 190.
32. Datir, R.N.: *Prison as a Social System*, Popular Prakashan, Mumbai, 1978, p.1.
33. *Encyclopaedia Britannica*: 14th ed., Vol. 14, 1977, p.1098.
34. *Ibid.*, Vol.18, 1939, p. 514.
35. Sutherland H. Edwin and Cressey R. Donald: *Principles of Criminology*, Sixth ed., 2nd Indian reprint, 1968, p. 270.
36. *Encyclopaedia of the Social Sciences*, ed. by Edwin, R.A., Seligman, 15th Printing, 1963, Vol. VII, p. 616.
37. *Encyclopaedia Americana. op. cit.*, p. 606.

38. Cressey R. Sutherland: *op. cit.*, p. 270.
39. Roy, J.G.: *Prisons and Society*, Gyan Publishing House, New Delhi,1989, pp. 27-28.
40. *Encyclopaedia Britannica*, 14th ed., Vol.18, 1939, p. 514.
41. *Ibid.*, 977, p.1098.
42. Bar Karl I Von: *A History of Continental Criminal Law*, Boston Little Brown, 1916, p.191.
43. Indian Journal of Public Administration; *Prison Administration* by S.M. Diaz, XXV, (Jan.-March)1; 1979, New Delhi, p. 124.
44. *Encyclopaedia Britannica*, Vol.14, 1977, p. 1103.
45. *Ibid.*, Vol.18, 1967, p. 557.
46. *Indian Journal of Public Administration; op. cit.*; XXV; 1, Jan.-March, 1979; p. 124.
47. Mohanty Amarendra and Hazary Narayan, *op. cit.*, p. 18.
48. Bushan Vidya: *op. cit.*, p. 7.
49. Indian Journal of Public Administration; Roy, J.G.: Role of Voluntary Agencies in Prevention of Crime and Treatment of Offenders, 33(3); July-September, 1987, p. 654.
50. Gupta, R.L.: *Political Theory*, Sultan Chand and Sons, New Delhi, 1980, p. 79.
51. Prasad Chandra Deo: *Political Ideas of Ram Manohar Lohia*, Janaki Prakashan, Patna, 1989, pp. 210, 216.
52. Toynbee Arnold: *One World and India.*
53. Social Defence; Shah H. Jyotsna: Fourth United Nations Congress on the Prevention of Crime and Treatment of Offenders Report on "Standard Minimum Rules for the Treatment of Offenders in the light of recent developments in the correctional field"; Central Bureau of Correctional Services; Department of Social Welfare; Government of India, New Delhi, Vol. VI; Number 22; October, 1970, pp. 43-44.
54. Leonard Orlaud: *Prisons-Houses of Darkness*, Macmillan Publishing Company, Inc. New Yark, 1945, p.166.
55. Social Defence; Shah H. Jyotsna: *International Concern on Crime*; op. cit., Vol. VI; Number 22; October, 1970; pp. 5-6.
56. Social Defence; Hira Singh: *UN Standard Minimum Rules for the Treatment of Prisoners*, Vol. XXIX; Number 100; April, 1990, pp. 1-4, National Institute of Social Defence, Government of India, New Delhi.

57. Indo-British Training Project on Human Rights and Prison Management; Produced by Governance and Social Justice Unit; Published by Public Relations Unit; The British Council; New Delhi, 25th June 1999; pp.18, 19-20.
58. Social Defence; Hira Singh: United Nations Standards on Juvenile Justice, *op. cit.*, Vol. XXI; Number 84; April, 1986; p. 13.
59. Indo-British Training Project on Human Rights and Prisons Management; op. cit., pp. 17-18, 20.
60. Ghosh S., *Open Prisons and the Inmates*; Mittal Publications, New Delhi, 1992, pp. 8-10.
61. Darrow Clarence: *Crime*, George G. Harrup and Company, London, 1992, p. 165.
62. Dodge R. Calvert: *A World Without Prisons*, Lexington Books, D.C. Heath and Company, Lexington, Massachusetts, Toronto, 1979, p. 8.
63. Mathiesen Thomas: *Prison on Trial*, Sage Publications, London, 1992, pp.1, 10-13.

2

Prison Administration in General

1. Prison System in Ancient India

It is essential to deal briefly with the evolutionary stages of prison system in India. The social environments and the stages of societal developments helped to shape the penal institutions. For a systematic description of jails, the indirect reference to the judicial aspect of state craft, will help to know something about the prison system and its evolution.

The ancient Indian society exhibited all the characteristics of ascriptive social system. Many crimes and wrongs were sins and entailed secular punishments and also religious sanction. In Vedic period, administration of justice did not form a part of the state duties. Offences like murder, theft and adultery are mentioned but there is nothing to indicate that the king or an authorized officer as a judge, either in civil or criminal cases, passed any judicial judgement. Some critics have suggested that Sabhapati of the later Vedic period may have been a judge.

Usually, the aggrieved party had itself to take such steps which could redress him. Distraint of the defendant or the accused by the plaintiff, his sitting before the latter's house and not allowing him to move out till his claim was satisfied or wrong righted was a well established practice in Vedic India.[1] Yet, in reality weaker sections of the society were helpless. Because, it was a socially graded society.

During the Rig Vedic period the idea of a divine cosmic order existed. Riti, the regularity of the universal process was the process of law and it was the Sabha or Popular Village Assembly rather than king who tried to arbitrate when it was feasible to do so. This helps us to conjure that there was no prison in the Vedic period, but the house of the accused served the purpose for jail and he was practically imprisoned in his own house till he managed to compensate the plaintiff.

The Dharma Sutras and the *Dharma Shastras* (the earliest is that of Manu and other important *Dharma Shastras* are those of Yagnavalkya, Vishnu and Narada), reveal a more or less full-fledged and well-developed judiciary. Law or dharma was not a measure passed by legislature in Ancient India, it was based upon *Shrutis* (hearings) and *Smritis* (remembrance). It was enforced by social approval or the dread of hell and not by the force of the state. King was at its head and it was his pious duty to punish the wrong-doers; if he fails from discharging it, he would go to hell.[2] *Sutras* and *Shastras*, we rarely come across the words "prison" or "jailor" (in Arthashastra the word Bandhanagaradhyaksha is used for jailor).[3]

The notable factor in *Dharmasutras* (religious scriptures) in prescribing punishment was "caste preference". All castes were not treated alike. The Varna (class) of a person (Brahmins, Kshatriyas,Vaisyas and Sudras) was given much importance while prescribing and awarding punishments; Brahmins were given the highest advantage and the Sudras the lowest advantage.[4] Examples of the caste preferences are mentioned in the History of Dhamasastra by P. V. Kane and Kautilya's Arthashastra by R. Shamashastry.

As regards punishments during ancient period: (i) death, (ii) mutilaton, (iii) banishment (iv) branding (v) fines in lieu of mutilaton, and (vi) fines were the principal forms of *danda* (punishment).[5] Ex-communication, dismissal of workers etc., were other forms of punishment. Fine was the most common and condemned person who could not pay his bill to bondag: until it was paid by his labour. Fines for the murder of a Brahmin were 1000 cows, for killing a Kshatriya 500 cows, for a Vaishya 100 cows and 10 cows for a Sudra or a woman of any caste. Mutilation of hand and other limbs were often inflicted upon the thieves. Generally, death sentence was imposed upon murderers, traitors, dacoits and persons guilty of heinous sex offences.[6]

In India, the early prisons were only places of detention where an offender was detained until trial and the execution of the latter. Among the various types of corporal punishments—branding, hanging, mutilation and death, the imprisonment was the most mild of penalty in penology. Imprisonment occupied an ordinary place among the penal treatment and this type of corporal punishment was suggested in the Hindu Scriptures. The evil doer was put into prison to segregate him from the society.

The main aim of imprisonment was to keep away the wrong-doers, so that they might not defile the members of social order.[7] These prisons were totally dark dens, cool and damp, unlighted, and unwarmed. There was not proper arrangement for the sanitation and no means of facility for human dwelling.[8] The Indian law-givers had a little description of jail life. A few Smriti writers supplied some information concerning jail. Yagna Valkya had narrated that a person who was instrumental for the escape of a prisoner had to undergo capital punishment. Vishnu suggested the penalty of imprisonment to a person who hurted the eyes of a man.

Kautilya prescribed the jail should be constructed in the capital and provide separate accommodation for men and women. This ascertains the fact that the principle of classification of men and women was in existence in the jails during ancient period. The entrances were well guarded. Kautilya had discussed the problems of prisoners' life and their welfare. He held the opinion that every fifth day some prisoners should be made free who pay some money as fine or undergo some other mild corporal punishment or promise to work for social uplift.

He has also suggested general amnesty on the birth of a prince or coronation of a royal heir, social festivals, birthday of the ruling monarch who inspects prison, old prisoners, sick persons in the jail or orphans undergoing imprisonment. Kautilya has further described the duties of the jailor who always keeps eyes on the movement of the prisoners and the proper functioning of the prison authorities. If a prisoner by chance moves out of his cell he was fined twenty four rupees and the warden who was in league with the prisoner was fined the double amount. In case the warder disturbs the prison life, the higher authority imposed a fine of five hundred rupees.

Sometimes the prisoner was put to death by the warder so the penalty in this case was the highest i.e. one thousand rupees. Kautilya has gone deep to jail life and opines that the prisoner escaping after breaking the prison walls, must be put to death. This shows that the jail authority called *Bandhanagaradhyaksha* was always vigilant and alert and no evil action could escape his eyes.

In the early years of Ashoka, there was an unreformed prison in which most of the traditional fiendish tortures were inflicted and from which no prisoner came out alive. But from his moral edicts which belong to his later period of his rule when he was influenced by Buddhism were taken. Professor Ram Chandra Dikhitar in his book entitled *Mauryan Polity*, has suggested that Ashoka was familiar with the Arthashastra, for Ashoka speaks of as much as twenty-five jail deliveries effected by him in the course of twenty-six years, since his Coronation.[9]

In the post-Mauryan age, the Jatakas give a picture of the society and supply information regarding crime and imprisonment. Seyya Jataka relates that, king having fettered an officer put him in jail. But, when the king was informed of his guiltless action, the king released the officer from prison. The other Jataka (No. 201) narrates about the fettered prisoner while another Jataka (No. 427) described the release of the political prisoners at the time of war and commissioned them in the army.

From Harshacharita it appears that the condition of the prisoners was far from satisfactory. The life of Hiuen-Tsang recorded that prisoners generally received harsh treatment. They were not allowed to shave. They had hairy faces and matted beards. There were, however, occasions when prisoners were released.[10] The officers of the jail were known as *Bandhanagaradhyaksha* and *Karaka*. The former was the superintendent of jail and the latter was one of his assistants. The jail department was under the charge of Sannidhata, who was to select sites for their location and build necessary buildings.

2. Prison System in Medieval India

The legal system in Medieval India resembled that of ancient India. The contemporary Muslim sovereigns seldom attempted to tamper with the day today administration of justice. During Mughal period sources of law and its character were essentially Quaranic. The crudeness and insufficiency of the judicial systems were aggravated by the fact that only law recognized by the emperor and his judge was the Quaranic law, which had originated and grown to maturity outside India. Brahmanic Courts and Gentoc Code– a loose mass of Sanskrit legal rules and sacred injunctions–survived Emperor Akbar.[11]

According to Muslim idea of jurisprudence crimes were grouped into three categories, viz., (a) offences against God, (b) offences against State, and (c) offences against Private Property. Punishments for these offences were of the following types: (i) hadd (ii) tazir (iii) qisas and (iv) tashir. Hadd was the punishment which was supposed to be the right of God and cannot be altered by any human judge. Tazir was punishment imposed to reform the culprit and depending on the discretion of the judge; Qisas was the personal right of the victim or his next kin to inflict punishment; Tashir was public degradation.

These punishments included fines and confiscation, forfeiture of rank and title, subjecting to humiliations, banishment, whipping, mutilation of offending limbs, executions and other corporal punishments. The principal forms of punishments during Mughal period were: (i) capital punishment, (ii) mutilation, (iii) flogging, (iv) banishment, (v) tashir, (vi) fines and (vii) imprisonment. The principal forms of caste punishments like ex-communication and class punishments like dismissal from work continued.

However, imprisonment was not resorted to as a form of punishment in the case of ordinary criminals. It was used mostly as a means of detention only. There were fortresses situated in different parts of the country, in which the criminals were detained pending trial and judgement. But, imprisonment not being the normal feature of the legal system, these fortified prisons did not present any problem for the administrators.

Although imprisonment was a very usual form of punishment in Mughal India, there were no specific rules fixed for it. The chief feature of the punishment was that no period was fixed for it. The quazi and the magistrate had a right to send any one to prison for the offence or crime for which punishment could be awarded and the accused had to show signs of repentance to secure his freedom. When the prisoners were taken to the prison they were usually "loaded with iron fetters on their feet and shackles on their necks". For temporary confinement, there were police lock-ups in the cities termed as Chabutra-i-Kotwali. The officer incharge of the Chabutra-i-Kotwali used to be Mushrif.

There used to be three noble prisons or castles in Mughal India. One was at Gwalior, second at Ranthambore and the third was at Rohtas. Criminals condemned to death punishment were usually sent to the fort of Ranthambore. They met their death two months after their survival there. Gwalior Fort was reserved for the noble offenders. To Rohtas were sent those nobles who were condemned to perpetual imprisonment, from where 'very few returned home'. Princes of Royal Blood were often sent to this place.

In such "Fort Prisons" there were no rules for recruitment of staff and no rules and regulations for treatment of prisoners. Prior to the arrival of the British in India, most of the punishments were meted out outside the prison, and there was no uniform code for all the members of the society. Punishments were awarded to persons taking into consideration of their castes and religion. Very few persons were imprisoned possibly the political prisoners.

Occasionally, the prisoners were transferred from one place to another. According to Muslim Law, the quazis were supposed to visit the prisons and inquire into the conditions there, and release those who showed signs of repentance. However, they neglected their duty. The only redeeming feature for the prisoners was that order for their release was issued on special occasions. These occasions were birth of crowned prince, recovery of the emperor or of his sons from long illness, or some occasional Royal visit to a prison fortress.[12]

To sum up, the features of the prison system prevailing in the pre-British were as follows:

(i) There were no prisons in the modern sense.

(ii) There was no description about the internal administration of prison.

(iii) Prison service was a part of police service.

(iv) There was no separation of prison service from civil service.

(v) Imprisonment was not the normal feature of punishment, and most of the punishments were meted out outside the prison.

(vi) Very few persons were sent to prisons (possibly the political prisoners).

(vii) Some forts were used for keeping certain types of prisoners (mostly political prisoners).

3. Prison System in British India

The Jail system in Western countries is commonly traced to the Poor Houses in England during the regime of Queen Elizabeth I. They housed not only the offenders but also paupers. The inmates were provided food and clothing and were also required to work. Within a short period of their existence, these institutions, however, greatly deteriorated and were severally criticised for their sub-human conditions. Eventually, separate institutions were organised for undertrials and convicts. The officials of the East India Company brought the system to the sub-continent.[13]

In sixteenth century during the regime of East India Company the prison conditions in India were terrible and inhuman. This was due to the fact that, deterrence was the only aim of the prison system. With the advent of the British the administrative structure in the country began to assume a new form. At first little alteration was made in the existing legal system. In 1773 was passed the Regulating Act which established the Supreme Court at Calcutta to exercise all civil, criminal, admiralty and ecclesiastical jurisdiction. It indicated the intention of the British to introduce English laws and English superintendence of law and justice. The imprisonment as a form of punishment (or the modern prison system) was first applied in India in 1773.[14]

In 1784, the British Parliament empowered the East India Company to rule India and since then some attempts were made to introduce reforms in the administration of justice. Infact, the jails were an extension of Mughal rule which were being managed by the personnel of the East India Company in their efforts to maintain peace and establish their trade. The prison institutions were run by district magistrates who were known for their indifference and reluctance to this aspect of administration, and hence conditions therein were extremely bad. No effort was being made to ameliorate the conditions of prisoners. They were just slave-labourers.

The directors of the East India Company were reluctant to spend money on jails and improve the state of affairs therein. There were 75,000 prisoners out of which 65,700 were engaged in the construction of roads and were given exemption from other works inside the prison. There are some references according to which it is known that only in two jails carpets were being manufactured.[15]

I

4. Second Epoch: Prison Reformation in Modern India

(i) First Committee on Prison Reformation

Macaulay's Committee

In 1835, there were forty-three Civil, seventy five Criminal and sixty-eight Mixed jails. Administrative structure for modern prison system originated from the Minute by T.B. Macaulay. Macaulay drew attention of the Government of India to the terrible conditions in the Indian Jails and on his suggestion, a Committee was appointed on 2nd January 1836, to look in to the conditions and report thereon. It submitted its report in 1838 criticising severely "The corruption of the subordinate establishment, the laxity of discipline and the system of employing the prisoners in extra-mural labour on public roads".[16]

The far-reaching recommendations of the Committee were:

(a) That Central Jails should be built to accommodate not more than 1000 prisoners each.

(b) That Inspector-General of Prisons should be appointed in all provinces.

(c) That sufficient building should be provided in all jails to accommodate prisoners comfortably.

In pursuance of the recommendations of the Committee, a Central Prison was constructed at Agra in 1846. This was the first Central Prison in India and was followed by construction of Central

Prisons at Bareilly and Allahabad in 1848, at Lahore in 1852, at Madras in 1857, at Bombay (Mumbai), Alipore, Banaras and Fatehgarh in 1864 and at Lucknow in 1867.

In 1844, the first Inspector-General of Prisons was appointed in the North-Western Province (present Uttar Pradesh). His appointment was made on an experimental basis for two years and was extended for another four years. In 1850, the Government of India made it a permanent post and suggested that each province should have an Inspector-General of Prisons. Punjab appointed the Inspector-General in 1852, Bengal in 1854, Bombay in 1854, Madras (Chennai) in 1854, and Central Provinces in 1862.

Upto 1860, the management of the District Jails had devolved on the Magistrate. But, it was found that, in the process of administration, these officials had been overwhelmed with multifarious business of all departments. Another agency was therefore, required and this was most suitably found in the Civil Surgeon.

Henceforth, in 1862 The North-Western Province employed civil surgeons as superintendents of district jails. The experiment proved so successful that the Government of India issued orders in 1864 that all provinces should employ civil surgeons as superintendents of district jails. The same course was introduced all over Bengal Presidency and also in Madras and Bombay.

However, the recommendations of the "Macaulay Committee" could not be implemented because, among other things, the East India Company rule was in 1858, replaced by the British Crown rule. The English Criminal Law came to be applied to Indians. The Indian Penal Code and the Criminal Procedure Code which had long been in preparation were enacted in 1859 and 1860 respectively. The Indian Penal Code defined each and every offence and prescribed punishment for it, while the Criminal Procedure Code laid the procedure for prosecuting the criminals.

The imprisonment as a form of punishment which was first applied in India in 1773 came to be applied on uniform basis throughout India in 1860. The institution of jail as understood these days, is of British origin and was introduced in India as a part of British Administration. Before the institution of jail, the system of punishment did not require any financial burden on the part of the Government. The Directors of the East India Company were reluctant to spend money on jails and although jails were modelled on British lines, there was not enough accommodation and there was inadequate food, clothing and medical attention for the prisoners. Thus, the conditions of jails were extremely bad.[17]

(ii) Second Committee on Prison Reformation

The Second Committee on Prison Reforms was appointed in 1864 to consider questions of jail management, because of high death rate in prisons and by other allied considerations. This Committee fixed a minimum space for each prisoner in jail, i.e. 54 superficial feet and 640 cubic feet per prisoner, recommended for improvements in diet, clothing and bedding and insisted upon regular medical inspection of prisoners.

It also recommended that every central prison should have cellular accommodation for fifteen per cent of its population and that juveniles be kept separate from other prisoners and that they should be given education. In India also cellular accommodation was considered most suitable for prison life, but this could not be adopted on account of huge cost involved.

A noteworthy feature of administrative structure of prison system in India, is participation of warders and night watchmen (promotees from prisoners) in the executive duties. This system was introduced by the British in 1864, in order to minimize expenditure on establishment, giving incentives to prisoners, and to implement the policy of ruling prisoners through prisoners only.[18]

In 1870, the Government of India passed the Prisons Act to amend the law relating to prisons in the country. It laid down that there should be a superintendent, a medical officer, a jailor and such subordinate officers as the local government thinks necessary. The superintendent was authorised to appoint, with the approval of the Inspector General of Prisons, the jailor and deputy-jailor.

The Act enumerated the duties of the superintendent. The Act made provision for the separation of prisoners of males from females, of children from adults, of criminal from civil. Civil prisoners were allowed to follow their respective trades and professions with the superintendent's permission. Prisoners sentenced to simple imprisonment also were allowed to work and no prisoner not sentenced to rigorous imprisonment was to be punished for neglect of work. The Act defined the list of prison offences and empowered the superintendent to punish such offences. The Act of 1870 tried to give effect to the recommendations of the Committee of 1864 and brought the prison administration in the forefront.

(iii) Third All India Jail Committee

The Third India Jail Committee was appointed in 1877. This Committee was composed entirely of officials actually engaged in prison work. It reviewed the jail management generally and mostly concerned itself more with the matters of detail in prison work than with the general aims and principles of administration.

(iv) Fourth All India Jail Committee

In 1888, was appointed the Fourth Committee on an all India basis. This Committee was expressly directed towards the routine working of the prisons. This report covered nearly the whole field of internal management of jails and laid down elaborate rules for prison management. The Committee recommended the separation of undertrial prisoners and the classification of prisoners into casuals and habituals. Most of the recommendations of the Committee were incorporated in the jail manuals of various provinces.

(v) Fifth All India Jail Committee

The work of the Fourth All India Jail Committee was supplemented by the next All India Committee of 1892. This was the Fifth All India Committee. It resurveyed the whole prison administration in India and drew up proposals on the subject of prison offences and punishment.

The Report of this Committee was accepted by the Government of India which passed the Prisons Act of 1894. This Act provided that the convicted criminal prisoners may be confined either in association or individually in cells or partly in one way or partly in the other. The Act fixed nine hours labour a day for a criminal prisoner sentenced to labour or employed on labour at his own desire. It further defined prison offences and prescribed punishments varying from a formal warning to separate confinement for any period not exceeding six months. Any two of the punishments could be awarded for any offence subject to certain exceptions.

The Prisons Act of 1894 was largely based on deterrent principles and reflected the contemporary English public opinion on the subject. The legislators were concerned more with prison working than with prison treatment and gave more consideration to prison offences and punishments than to its effects.

The British occupied the Andaman Islands. The first settlement was established in North Andamans in the year 1789. Attempts at colonisation were ultimately given up but the penal settlement survived. Then came the Revolt of 1857 in India. The British found that they had on their hands a large number of rebel convicts whom the Indian prisons of those days would hardly contain. The Andamans offered a readymade solution. It is estimated that between 1858 and 1860 some 2000-4000 Sepoy mutineers were sent to the Andamans. Many of them died. In 1882 the practice of sending prisoners to Andamans was stopped and they were kept in Central Prison, Bangalore. The construction of Cellular Jail was taken up in 1896. The construction itself was carried out by convicts.[19]

Reformatory Schools Act

The year 1897 was a landmark in the history of prison reform movement in India. In that year was passed the Reformatory Schools Act. The Act modified the prior legislation on the subject, which had remained more or less a dead letter, and directed the courts to send a youthful offender below fifteen years of age to a Reformatory School instead of a prison. Then the Prisoners Act of 1900 was passed.

Even though different commissions were appointed, the Indian prison system lagged behind on the reformative side of the prison work. It failed to regard the prisoner as an individual and conceived him rather as a unit in administrative machinery. It lost sight of the effort which humanising and civilizing influences had on the mind of the individual prisoner and failed to focus attention on his material well being and problems of diet, health and labour. Thus, it was mainly the idea of deterrence which influenced prison policy till the year 1919.

(vi) Sixth Indian Jails Committee

The First World War and Internationalism failed to bring revolutionary changes in the Indian prison reformation. Yet, emergence of internationalism further boosted the morale of the prison reformists. In order to bring about an over all change in Indian prison system, the Indian Jails Committee was set up in 1919 in which Sir Alexander G. Gadrew was the chairman. This was the Sixth All India Committee on Prisons. It submitted a comprehensive report in 1920 suggesting far reaching changes in the various aspects of prison system.

The Committee for the first time suggested two conceptual pivots—"prevention" and "reformation" for a more effective base for prison administration in India. "The aim of prison administration is the prevention of further crime and the restoration of the criminal to society as a reformed character",[20] stated the Committee.

The report contained a number of recommendations dealing among others with subjects as prison staff, separation and classification of prisoners, prison labour and manufactures, discipline and punishment, reformatory influences in prison, prison hygiene, medical administration, aid to the prisoners on release, probation and borstal treatment.

The publication of the report gave an immediate and great impetus to prison reforms throughout India. The Government of India took its strictures and recommendations seriously and issued instructions to all local Governments to study the report and implement the suggestions mentioned therein.

Not only were the prison departments affected but penal reform also received a great philip. The enactment of the Borstal Act, the Children's and the Probation Acts and the Punjab Good Conduct Prisoners' Provisional Release Act were undoubtedly the direct or indirect result of the general interest, aroused by the Report. The Report, it may be remarked, "laid the foundation stone of modern prison system in India".[21]

Unfortunately, the changes in the prison system in India received a sudden set-back due to the constitutional changes brought about by the Government of India Act, 1919. The enforcement of this Act effected the transfer of the jail department from the control of the Government of India to that of the provincial government. Prisons were placed in the reserved list under the dyarchical set up of the province and the prison reform movement was there upon thrown back for a decade.[22]

There is a close resemblance in respect of prison reforms in England and in India. In Great Britain interest in prison reforms was accelerated when a large number of educated, public-spirited, conscientious men and women were thrown into prisons due to an agitation for women suffrage. These prisoners severely criticised the prison system.

The years 1921-22 were the years of Non-Cooperation Movement in India in which freedom-fighters voluntarily courted arrest and imprisonment. They bitterly criticised the rotten prison conditions and forced the provincial governments to inquire into them. The committees appointed in different States were Punjab Jail Reforms Committee (1919 and 1948), Uttar Pradesh (1929, 1938 and 1946), Bombay (1939 and 1946), Mysore (1941), Bihar (1948), Madras (1950), Orissa (1952) and Travancore Cochin (now Kerala) 1953.

6. Government of India Act, 1935

In 1935 was passed the Government of India Act. Dyarchy was abolished in the provinces and the reserved subjects were transferred to the ministers' control. The Congress contested the elections and assumed power in seven out of eleven provinces. The penal reform movement again received an impetus and attention was focused on the hitherto neglected prison reforms.

The Congress governments went out of office on the issue of Second World War thus brining active penal reforms to an abrupt end. During the War no major legal changes were introduced in the prison system. The Indian Government was fully engaged with war problems and had no time to devote to prison affairs. In 1942, the Government of India faced Satyagraha Movement launched by the Congress. Thousands of Congressmen were locked in jails which were filled beyond their capacity. Due to over-crowding proper treatment could not be given to these Satyagrahis and the lot of the ordinary prisoners was even worse. This extraordinary situation continued till India secured its independence.

II

Prison Reformation in Independent India

Post-Second World War System

Soon after the Second World War, the whole world was divided into Capitalist Camp and Communist Camp. Both these camps were ever ready to fight the Third World War to establish supremacy of one over the other. In this Cold War, nationalism was still spreading along with internationalism.

In such an international dangerous environment, the Imperial Britain granted national independence to India on 15th August 1947, after dividing undivided India into India and Pakistan. Independent India, did not align to any camp. India joined the UNO before it secured independence and continued its membership after independence. Already India was a member of the International Prison Congress. Consequently, India was expected to follow the international standard in prison reformation.

Prison Reformation in Independent India

The leaders of the movement of the Indian independence and internationalism specially UNO repeatedly suffered incarceration at the hands of imperial rulers. Prison under foreign rulers was "The Gaol a place of dread". It was, therefore, legitimately assumed that rulers of India would accord highest priority to prison reforms by converting them at least from institution of horror to modern reclamation and correctional centres.

The independent India took some interest towards prison reformation. The Government of India passed the Exchange of Prisoners Act, 1948. In 1950, the Transfer of Prisoners Act was passed. This Act made provision for the removal of prisoners from one State to another. Even the Constitution of the Indian Republic has not prescribed the "Rationalisation of the Indian Prison

Reformation and Penal Systems" as one of its goal in near future. The rulers of the day were indifferent towards the fate of the prison administration

In the Constitution of India, Prison Administration has been included in the State List (Item number 4 in List II (State List) in the Seventh Schedule of the Constitution). As prison rules and regulations vary from one state to another the much needed co-ordination was lacking. However, it was realized soon after independence that the jail manuals of the States of the Union, based on the antediluvian Prisons Act of 1894, could not cope with the changing times. It was felt very strongly that some broad guidelines should be given with a view to co-ordinate the prison reform programmes of the different state governments.

The decade 1951–60 in India was a decade of enthusiasm for prison reforms. Local committees were appointed by some state governments (viz., Madras, Orissa, Uttar Pradesh and Maharashtra) to suggest prison reforms.

(i) United Nations Assistance

To follow international standard in prison reformation, India had requested the UNO in 1951 to send an expert in prison reformation under its Technical Assistance Programme, for imparting a training course to the selected jail officers and to suggest progressive programmes for the scientific care and treatment of offenders. Accordingly, Dr. W.C Wreckless came to India and in his report suggested many valuable changes, most of which were not, in essence, radically different from the recommendations of the Indian Jails Committee of 1919.

In 1952, the Uttar Pradesh Government started a new experiment in open prison under the name of Sampurnanand Camp. In some other states also open prisons were set up. Prison welfare officers were appointed in a number of states in later years. A few new ideas of prison reforms were introduced in the country during this decade. The prisoners could now avail of furlough and parole. They were granted wages, albeit nominal, for the workdone by them. In 1952, the Government of Bombay introduced the system of prison panchayats in the prisons.[23] The introduction of panchayat system led to some improvement in the living conditions of prisoners. Jail training schools were set up in some states.

(ii) All India Conference of Inspectors-General of Prisons

The year 1952 further witnessed a breakthrough in national coordination on correctional work. An All India Conference of Inspectors-General of Prisons was held in Bombay in 1952 which also recommended the setting up of a committee to draft a skeleton Model Jail Manual. The Central Government passed Prisoners (Attendance in Courts) Act, 1955. Whipping was abolished in 1955 and the Probation of Offenders Act was enacted in 1958. The UN Standard Minimum Rules for the Treatment of Prisoners further strengthened the international minimum standard of prison reformation. India was expected to follow the UN Standard Minimum Rules for the Treatment of Prisoners.

(iii) All India Jail Manual Committee

In pursuance of the recommendations of Dr. Wreckless and All India Conference of Inspectors-General, the Government of India appointed an All India Jail Manual Committee in 1957.

This Committee of 1957-59 studied the problems of crime and delinquency from a very progressive angle and poignantly observed that the solutions to these problems do not lie only in prisons but in the larger socio-economic fields as well. It felt, that, these problems can be solved neither by making punishment more deterrent nor by making the system of punishment too weak and diluted. The Committee wanted prisons to be transformed into correctional institutions.

In consonance with its radical approach to the problems of crime and delinquency and to the prime objective of correctional administration, this Committee furnished a detailed report containing necessary principles of modernization of prisons together with a Model Prison Manual in 1960 on a broad guideline for the States to revise their outdated prison manuals.

Among the various recommendations of the Committee, the following are the important ones:

(a) The Correctional Services, i.e. the prisons, probation, after-care and institutional services for children should be integrated under a Director or Commissioner of Correctional Administration and be under the control of the Home Department.
(b) An O&M Division should be established to devote exclusive attention to the orderly growth and dynamic development of the organization.
(c) The Deputy Inspectors-General should be incharge of various divisions and there should be a separate Deputy Inspector-General for health services in prisons.
(d) The probation system should be used on a more extensive scale than at present in order to reduce the pressure on prisons.
(e) There should be a well arranged network of diversified institutions.
(f) A Central Bureau of Correctional Services should be organized at the Union level.
(g) A Central Advisory Board should be set up by the Government of India and there should be a Research and Planning unit in each state.
(h) An All India Correctional Services should be set up.
(i) There should be a separation of executive and clerical function and of executive and accounts functions.
(j) There should be a State After Care Organization in each state.
(k) The Jail Manual should be revised periodically.
(l) Classification of prisoners should be dynamic.

(iv) Central Bureau of Correctional Services

Another development was in pursuance of the recommendations of the All India Jail Manual Committee, the Government of India set up a Central Bureau of Correctional Services in 1961 (It was reconstituted in 1975 as the National Institute of Social Defence) as a central technical advisory body. Its main functions are to coordinate and develop uniform policy, to standardise the collection of statistics on a national basis, to exchange information with foreign government and the UN agencies and to promote research, training and studies and surveys in the field of prevention of crime and treatment of offenders.

During the decade 1951-60 the Central and State Governments took the task of prison reforms with spirit and enthusiasm. But, this did not last long. The valuable recommendations of these committees were not implemented effectively. Official apathy and bureaucratic bungling continued. Even after the end of another decade (1961-70) the general state of prison administration in the country was described by an official committee as "depressing".

Our jails were terribly over crowded. In 1961, there were 1,176 prison institutions in the country and these included 52 central jails, 180 district jails, 919 sub-jails, 2 juvenile jails, 9 Borstals, 3 women's jails and 5 open jails. By 1970 the total number of institutions had come down to 1,170 and yet admissions to jails in 1970 were 13,78,657 as compared to 11,05,896 in 1961.

During this period the number of undertrials also rose. In 1960, there were 5,93,398 undertrials as against 4,12,498 convicts. In 1970, there were 9,38,598 undertrials as against 4,40,059 convicts. Thus, while the convict admission rose by 7% only, the admission of undertrials rose by 58%. As the total accommodation remained the same it had led to more and more undertrials living with convicts.

The huddling together of a large number of undertrials with convicted prisoners and the mixing together of old and hardened criminals with young first offenders tend to promote in the minds of all inmates feelings of criminality instead of remorse and regret for their previous conduct and a desire to reform. Apart from the overcrowding in jails, the general manner in which the rituals of the daily life inside the jails were rigidly administered and enforced tends to dehumanise the prisoner who is cowed down by oppressive atmosphere around with all its brutalities, stench, degradation and insult.

Instead of functioning as a reformatory house to rehabilitate the criminal to reform him and make him see the error of his ways and return a better and nobler man, the ethos inside our jails was tragically set in the opposite direction, making it practically difficult for any reformatory process to operate meaningfully.[24]

(v) Working Group on Prisons

In 1972, the Government of India appointed a Working Group on Prisons. This Committee recommended for:

(a) The establishment of a Research Unit at the headquarters of the Inspector-General of Prisons in each State;

(b) The setting up of a training institute in each State as well as of Regional Training Institute;

(c) Diversification of the institutions, accommodation and other connected matters etc.

The most remarkable recommendation of this Working Group was that it recommended the inclusion of prisons in the Five-Year Plan and a provision of Rs.100 crore. It thought that a prison administration could not be streamlined unless the Government of India and the State Governments made available more resources for developing every aspect of the existing system. As a follow up of this report, the Ministry of Home Affairs initiated efforts for the improvement and modernization of jail administration by making a grant of Rs. two crore in the budget for 1977-78 and of Rs. four crore in the budget of 1978-79.

The Working Group on Prisons emphasized the need for a National Policy on Prison and Correctional Administration. It discarded the traditional prison-based policy. The report of the Group identified the main elements of proposed National Policy. To bring desired changes in the prison administration as a whole, the Group recommended that the top priority was to be given to the adoption of the National Policy on Prisons as suggested by them along with the inclusion of certain aspects of the prison administration in the Five-Year Plan, to include the subject of prisons and allied institutions in the Concurrent List, the enactment of suitable legislation by the Centre as well as by the State, and the revision of the State Prison Manuals.[25]

To help the State Governments in their efforts to undertake jail reforms, the Central Government formulated a scheme in 1977 to give financial assistance for prison reforms. Accordingly, the Seventh Finance Commission had recommended allocation of Rs. 48.31 crore to 11 states in the form of grants-in-aid for five years (1979-84) for upgradation of standards of jail administration including upkeep of prisoners. Priority was accorded by the Commission to ensure adequate direct expenditure on food, clothing and medicines for prisoners, to improve basic amenities like water supply, sanitary facilities, electrification, etc., and to develop additional jail capacity in States.[26]

(vi) All India Committee on Jail Reforms

Several reports and articles appeared in the press about the conditions of jails, particularly in Tihar Jail, Delhi, and most of the jails in Uttar Pradesh and Bihar where a number of undertrial prisoners were confined without trial for over 10 years. The Supreme Court of India in various judgments had brought out the shortcomings in the prison administration in the country and pointed out the inadequacy of prisons to function as centres of reformation.

The Government of India therefore appointed a committee viz., the All India Committee on Jail Reforms headed by Justice A.N. Mulla (retired) in April 1980 for making a comprehensive review of prison administration in the country and suggesting suitable measures for its improvement. This committee submitted its final report in 1983.

According to the All India Committee on Jail Reforms, 1980-83, there were 76 Central Prisons, 250 district prisons, 822 sub-jails, 27 open jails and 20 special jails in 1980. The total capacity of all these institutions was 79,544, 63,654, 26,057, 6,640 and 4,626 respectively. There were also 6 institutions for women offenders, 8 juvenile jails and 11 Borstal Schools with an inmate capacity of 975, 1,827 and 2,102 respectively. Out of a total of 1,59,692 prisoners, 92,276 were undertrials. Thus more than half of the total prison population were undertrials.

While commenting on the problem of overcrowding, the Committee observed, "Overcrowded prisons tend to be unmanageable on correctional lines. In some of the States, prison barracks were so much overcrowded that inmates had to sleep in shifts. Under such conditions custody of inmates became the primary and probably the only, concern of the staff and even the care and welfare of inmates was neglected. The frequent influx of large number of agitators further worsened the situation and aggravated the problem of prison management".

It noted with profound regret that the Standard Minimum Rules for the Treatment of Prisoners were not being generally observed in several States and Union Territories in India and that the conditions of prisons in the country had deteriorated and had reached a point of crisis. One of the main reasons for this general deterioration, according to the Committee, was the lack of national commitment arising out of a national consensus on the goals and objectives of prison administration and modalities of achieving them.

The Committee had, therefore, formulated the draft of a National Policy on Prisons and recommended for its adoption by the Government of India in consultation with the State Government and Union Territory Administrations. The goals and objectives of prisons in India, according to the proposed National Policy on Prisons, were to protect society and to reform and reassimilate offenders in the social milieu by giving them appropriate correctional treatment.

The Committee, however, felt that, crime being a social problem cannot be tackled merely through legislation or pronouncement of laudable objectives. It therefore recommended that a regular plan aiming at creating a favourable rehabilitation culture in the society should be drawn up and implemented by prison administration.

Among the important suggestions made by the Committee were:

(a) Directive Principle of National Policy on Prisons had to be formulated and embodied in Part 4 of the Indian Constitution.

(b) The subject of Prisons and allied institutions were to be included in the Concurrent List of Seventh Schedule of the Constitution.

(c) Provision of an uniform framework for correctional administration by a consolidated, new and uniform comprehensive legislation to be enacted by the Parliament for the entire country.

(d) Revision of Jail Manuals should be given top priority.

(e) Suitable amendment of Indian Penal Code.

The follow up action on the report had been initiated by the Ministry of Home Affairs in consultation with concerned ministries and department of the Central and State Governments.

(vii) Committee on Women Prisoners

The Government of India further constituted a Committee on Women Prisoners in May 1986 with retired justice of Supreme Court V.K. Krishna Ayer as the chairman. The Committee submitted its report in 1987. The major recommendations of this committee were:

(a) Provision of a national policy relating to the women prisoners in India.
(b) Formation of new rules and regulations relating to their punishment and conduct.
(c) Maintenance of proper coordination among the police, law and prison for providing due justice to women prisoners.
(d) Provision of legal-aid for them.
(e) Construction of separate prisons for women prisoners.
(f) Proper care of the baby born in jail to a woman prisoner and provision of nutritious diet for the mother and the child.[27]

(viii) Juvenile Justice Act

With a view to providing a uniform pattern of justice to juveniles throughout the country, the Juvenile Justice Act, 1986 was enacted by Parliament in December 1986 replacing children's Acts in various states and union territories, and it came into force in 1987 throughout the country. It provides for care, protection, treatment, development and rehabilitation of neglected or delinquent juveniles and adjudication of certain matters relating to, and dispose of, delinquents.

It laid down a uniform legal framework so as to ensure that no child under any circumstances is lodged in jail or police lock-up. Juvenile welfare boards and juvenile courts have been established to provide for a specialised approach towards neglected and delinquent juveniles respectively.

During the pendency of any enquiry regarding the juvenile, be sent to an observation home or a place of safety. After the completion of enquiry neglected and delinquent juveniles be sent to an observation home or a place of safety. After the completion of enquiry neglected and delinquent juveniles be lodged in juvenile home and special homes respectively. The Act represents a blue print for fair, equitable and just treatment of juveniles with due emphasis on the rights of child.[28]

In order to effectively implement this Act, Union Ministry of Welfare implemented a Centrally-sponsored scheme for prevention and control of juvenile maladjustment since 1986-87. Under this scheme, assistance was provided for setting up/upgradation of observation homes, juvenile homes, special homes and after care-facilities as well as training of functionaries. Expenditure is shared between Central and State Governments equally.

There was a dearth of after-care organisation for the rehabilitation of juveniles who have no one to back upon after their release from the correctional institutions. As Professor K.S. Shukla points out, "After-care schemes were started in the last decade of the 19th century, but they have not shown signs of growth numerically or structurally. Although they have an unenviable role in the rehabilitative process and are important for a released juvenile, yet, except in Maharashtra, Tamil Nadu, U.P., West Bengal and Delhi, they have not been able to assume systematised and concrete shape. Both official and non official agencies may have to share the blame for inadequate attention to this sccheme".[29] Thus, special efforts will have to be made to make up this deficiency in States which lack these facilities.

The Juvenile Justice Act, 1986, was envisaged to provide a distinct system, independent of the criminal justice system, to deal with children with emphasis on protection rather than penalisation. But the Act is far from exclusive and relies heavily on the administrative machinery like the police and the magistrates.

Table 1 Institutions for Juveniles in 1996-97

(i)	271	Juvenile Welfare Boards
(ii)	189	Juvenile Courts
(iii)	280	Observation Homes
(iv)	251	Juvenile Homes
(v)	36	Special Homes
(vi)	46	After-care Organisations
(vii)	24,000	Children were under Government-Care

Table 2 Juvenile Deliquency in 1996

(i)	19,098	Children, 26.3 per cent of them girls, apprehended (in 1996)
(ii)	23.5	per cent admonished or advised
(iii)	12	per cent placed under parental/guardian-care
(iv)	4.2	per cent (795 children) sent to 'fit institutions' (as specified by the Act)

(v)	18.5	per cent (1623 children) to Special Homes
(vi)	7.9	per cent acquired
(vii)	80	per cent of the children were illiterate.[30]

The Supreme Court in May 2000 has clarified a major ambiguity in The Juvenile Justice Act by ruling that a Juvenile would be tried by a regular court if he was arrested after crossing the age of 16 years.[31]

(ix) Open Prisons

After independence, open prisons flourished with enthusiasm and with the advancement of knowledge about human behaviour and psycho-social environment to modify criminal behaviour. The policy of repression, vengeance, deterrence and inhuman attitude was replaced by a policy of protection through corrective and preventive measures aiming at constructive rehabilitation of offenders. Of all the measures undertaken by the Government of India in the area of prison reform, employment of prisoners in open conditions has proved to be most successful.

(x) Role of National Human Rights Commission

The Universal Declaration of Human Rights, 1948 was adopted by the Government of India, in 1993. Unfortunately, without rationalising the Universal Declaration of Human Rights, the Government of India simply accepted and implemented it. According to the Protection of Human Rights Act, 1993, the National Human Rights Commission (NHRC) has been established. Since its inception, the NHRC has been playing an important role in prison reform. It has made the following major recommendations.

Section 12(c) of the Protection of Human Rights Act, 1993, provides that the "Commission shall visit, under intimation to the State Government, any jail or institution under the control of State Government where persons are detained or lodged for purpose of treatment, reformation or protection to study the living conditions of the inmates and make recommendation thereon."

The NHRC in its annual report of 1994-95 had recommended that the Indian Prisons Act of 1894 be revised to reform the prison system and a new all-India jail manual be prepared to serve as a model. It concluded that the prison system is "seriously in need of reform, nationwide. It is mired in attitudes and practices that are antiquated at best, but that often border on the intolerable."

"Reliance on the century-old Act of 1894 is symptomatic of the lack of vision or progress in this area", the Commission Chaired by Justice Ranganath Misra, felt. The report said that many such as Tihar Jail in Delhi were overcrowded. Yet, others like the open jail in Hyderabad were underutilised. In some jails, it said, "callousness prevailed, prisoners were seen in shackles, mentally disturbed inmates-regardless of whether they were criminal or otherwise were incarcerated with others, with no real effort being made to rise above the very minimum required for the meanest survival".

Where prisoners worked, their remuneration was often a pittance, offering scant hope of savings being generated for future rehabilitation in society. The Commission during its visits saw many jails which are squalid, such as the newly constructed central jail in Patna. In yet others, it said the diet was inferior, and the management was denounced by the inmates as brutal and corrupt, often within a single State, conditions varied from one jail to another.

The Commission which had in the past expressed deep concern over overcrowding, lack of sanitation, poor medical facilities and inadequate diet in prisons, the core of the problem is the apathy and lack of priority accorded to prison conditions. What lies at the root of the difficulties was the apathy towards the rights of prisoners and undertrials, said the Commission, which has already expressed dismay at reports of the delay in the disposal of cases and mismanagement in the administration of prisons.

The Report of the NHRC, on the state of jails in the country served as yet another reminder of the urgent need to improve the country's prison system and the conditions in the prisons. However, the situation has only progressively deteriorated and every ill of the jail system had in the past only became worse or grew bigger in spread and magnitude.

The Human Rights Commission's report also detailed them and proposed changes in laws and attitudes, adoption of measures by Government and creation of public awareness to rectify the situation. What was needed was the willingness and where withal to translate the proposals and decisions that emerge out of such meeting into concrete measures. The conditions in our jails help only to perpetuate criminal conduct and to make inmate a life-long outlaw. The situation will not change as long as jails continue to be centres for punishment as opposed to these for reforming errant individuals.

The NHRC in 1997 and in 1999 had stressed the need[32] for setting up State Human Rights Commissions (SHRC) in States as expeditiously as possible. But, only eight States in the country had set up SHRCs[33] It said, the New Prison Act of 1996 was finalized and further action on its implementation was to be taken soon. It also pressed the State Governments to set up State Human Rights Commissions and Human Rights Courts at the district level.

The NHRC in December 1997 ruled that an undertrial cannot be put to hard work. It asked the Uttar Pradesh Government to pay an interim compensation of Rs. one lakh within a month to the parents of Ashoka Kumar, an undertrial in Roorkee sub-jail who succumbed to injuries on August 28,1996, while carrying a load at the behest of the Roorkee sub-jail authorities.[34]

The NHRC headed by M.N. Venkatachaliah condemned in a report on increasing criminality among the police. Referring to the NHRC's experience, it said, "there can be no substantial improvement in the human rights situation in this country unless those whose duty was to protect such rights, cease to predators themselves". He said 60 per cent of all the arrests made by the police were 'unnecessary and unjustifiable". At least 43 per cent of the prison's total expenditure was incurred on accommodating the innocent persons arrested, without evidence.

The NHRC further claimed that of all the arms of the state, it is the police in which the average citizen has the least confidence. Indian criminal justice system suffers from substantive and procedural deficiencies, once a citizen is arrested, even if on a relatively minor charge, he could be held in custody for years before his case comes up for trial. Often, prisoners serve more time in jail waiting for their day in court than they would if convicted for the crimes they have been accused of. The result: convicted offenders are vastly out-numbered by undertrials.

The NHRC, drew attention to the very low rate of convictions secured by the police for heinous crimes. Nearly 80 per cent of such cases end in acquittals, it is clear that the police are not doing their job properly. Either the wrong persons are acquitted or incomplete and ham-handed investigations are conducted, which ensures that the offenders get off scot-free. The National Commission for Women also concurred with the views of NHRC concerning women prisoners.

From time to time, the Supreme Court addresses itself of the plight of undertrials and has issued directives to lower courts for the speedy disposition of cases against those accused of minor charges and yet, these cases drag on. In its annual report, the NHRC has made specific recommendations for the reorganisation of the criminal justice system.

Those who are affluent are still able to negotiate their way around the numerous obstacles that lie on the road to justice. But for the ordinary citizen, an encounter with the law is very much the stuff of nightmares[35]

(xi) Modernisation of Prison Administration

The Central Government is administering a scheme for "Modernisation of Prison Administration". The 1st phase of the scheme was implemented during the period from 1987-92 and an amount of Rs. 45.08 crore was released to various state governments for modernisation of prisons. Under this scheme during the Eighth Plan period (1993-97). The Central assistance was released to the state governments on 75 per cent basis for strengthening on security and communication arrangements and on 50 per cent basis for other items like repair and renovation of old buildings, medical facilities, vocational training, modernisation of prison industries, facilities to women offenders, development of borstal schools, staff training etc.

In addition, Central assistance on 100 per cent basis is provided to Regional Institutes for Correctional Administration (RICA), Vellore, Chandigarh for various developmental activities. During the period from 1993 to March 1997 the grant of Rs. 50.44 crore has been released to various state governments/RICAs.

In addition to the Central assistance under the scheme of Modernisation of Prison Administration, the 10th Finance Commission has also recommended an amount of Rs. 41.44 crore for repair and renovation of jail buildings and Rs. 24.87 lakh for medical facilities in jails. The above grants were released to the state governments during 1996-2000.

Under the ongoing scheme for modernisation, Central assistance is provided for strengthening of security and communication arrangements, repair and renovation of prison buildings, medical facilities, vocational trainings, facilities for women offenders etc. Assistance is also provided for a few selected states for construction of high security enclosures for accommodating hard-core terrorists. During the period from 1993 to March 2000 a grant of Rs. 72.78 crore was released to various State Governments.[36]

(xii) Contemporary Scene

"In the twenty first century also India has not made any attempt towards the rationalisation of prison reformation, internally and externally". Today, our prisons are governed by the antediluvian Prisons Act of 1894. It is because, in the opinion of the Government of India and the State Governments, this Act suits to the Indian Jails even in the twenty-first century also. But, this Act has failed to bring prison reformation and there is no chance to lead to the rationalisation of prison and allied subjects in future also.

Though, "Liberalisation, Privatisation and Globalisation" national policy is in practice, fortunately, the Government of India, till today has continued the nationalisation of prison and retained it in the State List. The Constitution assigns the custody and correction of criminals to the states and union territories. Day-to-day administration of prisoners rests on principles incorporated in the Prisons Act of 1894, The Prisoners Act of 1900, and the Transfer of Prisoners Act of 1950.

Some prison administrators concede that the prevailing conditions of poverty in Indian society contribute to recidivism because a prison sentence guarantees minimal level of food, clothing and shelter. Despite this overall view, Indian prisons are seriously overcrowded. Prisoners are given better or worse treatment according to the nature of their crime and class status. Sanitary conditions are poor. Punishments for misbehaviour while incarcerated have been known to be particularly onerous.

Prison conditions vary from state-to-state. Women prisoners are mostly incarcerated in segregated areas of men's prisons. Conditions for holding prisoners also vary according to classification. India retains a system set-up during the colonial period that mandates different treatment for different categories of prisoners. Under this system, foreigners, individuals held for political reasons and prisoners of high caste and class are segregated from lower class prisoners and given better treatment.

This treatment includes larger or less crowded cells, access to books and newspapers, and more and better food. Despite laws that mandate egalitarian treatment of Dalits (See Glossary), members of Scheduled Tribes (See Glossary), a rigid class system that circumvents the spirit of these laws exists within the prison system (See Varma Caste and other Divisions,Chapter 5).

The press and human rights groups periodically raise the subject of prison conditions, including problems of overcrowding, the plight of prisoners detained for long periods while awaiting trial, and the proper treatment of women and juvenile prisoners (children are often incarcerated with their parents). Reports have also surfaced alleging that torture, beatings, rape, sexual abuse and unexplained suicides occur on many occasions in prisons.

Because of a shortage of mental institutions, "non-criminal lunatics" are imprisoned, often under conditions worse than those afforded criminals. The Government concedes that problems exist, but insists that its attempts at prison reforms have suffered from a paucity of resources.

The Indian prison reformative system has failed to correct the hardcore criminals who have treated jail term as just another temporary relocation of workplace, in the age of cell-phone. The prison terms are no deterrent for hardcore criminals. There is growing evidence that some of the most crimes are now being planned and monitored from within the country's 584 odd high-security prisons. There are confirmed reports of prisoners having easy access to cell-phones, their choice of cuisine delivered right into their cells, and of jail barracks turning into fertile recruitment grounds for prison lords.

More alarmingly "jails are emerging as the new co-ordination centres for militancy". The trend is the blatant use of muscle power and money power in prisons. Instances of coordinated crimes are increasing and inmates appear to be having too comfortable a time. The other debilitating factor, is the complicity and corruptibility of the prison staff. A parallel economy is flourishing inside the precincts of prisons. Clearly the idea of shutting away the perpetrators of crimes against humanity in solitary confinement for reformation seems to have boomeranged. With a population of over two lakh in India alone, a whopping 77 per cent of whom are undertrials, they find themselves in conducive company and environment to plot more of the same.[37]

There are different types of jails—central jails, district jails, sub-jails, open jails, institutions for young offenders and jails for women. Administrative set up of jails in states is headed by the Director General/Inspector General of Prisons.

The Union Ministry of Welfare has recently formulated a scheme for welfare of prisoners for providing counselling and guidance to prisoners and setting up of rehabilitation homes for facilitating reintegration of offenders within the community. It is a Centrally-sponsored scheme where expenditure is equally borne by State Governments and Central Government. Objective of the scheme is to identify cases of institutionalised offenders who need prolonged care, protection and assistance in the community, on their release.[38]

In a series of sweeping directions, the Supreme Court on 8th January 1997 gave jail authorities in the country six months to make "Our Prisons, houses of reforms", by ending over-crowding, torture, ill-treatment and neglect of health and hygiene of inmates of over a thousand jails all over India. The Court directed the concerned authorities to take a decision on the recommendation of the Law Commission regarding congestion of undertrials, apply their mind to the Mulla Committee Report on streamlining the remission system and premature release (parole) and examine the question of framing a model All India Jail Manual.

The judges also directed the authorities to deliberate about enacting of a new Prisons Act to replace the century—old Indian Prisons Act, 1894, and as a first step, all states should consider amending their own enactment (if any) in harmony with the all India thinking in this regard.[39] But, nothing has been done so far.

The NHRC, in September 2000 rightly demanded amendment in the existing Prisons Act, which is not very relevant to the present criminal justice system. The Commission, which sent its draft on legislation on prisons to the Home Ministry a few years ago, has also framed guidelines for the prisons reforms, which is considered as an important area for the promotion of human rights.

In the same month, it further recommended a National Prison Policy (NPP) to ensure uniformity of standard prison administration and treatment of about 2.5 lakh prisoners in various jails all over the country. Stressing that prison reforms and other segments of criminal justice system should go hand in hand, NHRC said, "It should include the rationalisation of sentencing policy and legal reforms, with a view to reducing over-crowding of undertrials in prisons". It asked for an alternative to imprisonment and institutionalisation of the successful experiments of open prisons.[40]

Overcrowding in prisons is a common problem in India. The contemporary India has the fourth largest prison population in the world, according to Worldwatch Institute.[41] There is shortage of prisons. Within a prison there is scarcity of cells. But, irrationality is found in all the Indian prisons, which is in existence in the form of worshipping places, i.e., mandirs, masjidis, churches, gurudwaras, caste literature etc. In a word, irrationality is the dominant philosophy in the Indian Prison Reformative system.

Exclusive Courts in Jail Premises

The Central Government had advised the States and Union Territories on January 31st, 2001, to set up exclusive courts in the jail premises for disposal of petty offences involving undertrial prisoners. Such a measure would go a long way in decongesting jails. Special courts will be held once or twice a month.

The States and Union Territories had been advised to set up legal aid cells, in all the jail premises to provide legal aid and advice to the inmates. The Central Government had suggested that the concerned district administrations and jail authorities should forthwith be asked to cooperate by providing space in the jail for the special court and legal aid cell and infrastructure in the form of staff and office equipment.

The Central Government had further advised that State legal authorities should continue panel of advocates who would be assigned to the legal aid cells in the jails to advice the inmates once or twice in a week. The presence of lady advocates on the panel was also mooted to win the confidence of woman inmates.[42]

In March 2001, thirty-four lakh cases were pending in the High Courts and about two crore cases were pending in subordinate courts around the country. It's not just the courts but sometimes the law itself is the biggest impediment in the course of justice.[43] The Common-wealth Human Rights Initiative, an NGO, stated in its 1999 report that the criminal justice system has been on the verge of total collapse.

According to the latest figures of the National Crime Records Bureau (NCRB), there is abysmally low rate of conviction. It is a sharp indictment of the criminal justice system. Of the total cases registered by the police, only a small fraction ends up in the accused being convicted. An overwhelming majority of the cases fall by the wayside: they are not investigated or they are not tried. From the criminal justice point of view, it is a serious flaw in the system, because, in the ultimate analysis, it is the certainty of punishment and not its severity that deters crime. The Bureau has suggested a sharp reduction in the trail period of criminal cases to restore the people's faith in the system.

The police have a point that the court procedures are so cumbersome and time consuming that, hard pressed as they are for time, they are unable to cope with the demands. The finding of the NCRB is quite startling: in nearly fifty per cent cases, it takes five years for the court to dispose of a case from the time it is registered. Unless, rationalisation is made to ensure that no criminal escapes punishment, people will loose their faith in the criminal justice system.[44]

The one thousand seven hundred thirty-four "Fast Track Courts" set up by the Government to reduce a huge back log of over 2.35 crore cases came into existence from 1st April 2001. The courts will first deal with criminal cases pending for two or more years and those of undertrials in jails. These "Fast Track Courts" have started functioning from 4th April 2001 in Maharashtra State. As on 3rd May 2001, a budget of Rs. 500 crore has been sanctioned and 488 out of the proposed 1,734 fast track courts have already been established.[45] India was yet to ratify the UN Convention on Torture in June 1999 after signing it.

In India, prisons are even today deemed created merely to maintain law and order. It has yet to be viewed as an essential means of preserving and raising the quality of human life. Investment on prisons is still considered as non-developmental. Indian's attitude is greatly ambivalent. As most of the prisoners in India are themselves a victim of stark deprivation and of forced induction into criminogenic culture, they hardly have an advocacy of their own or on their behalf. Rationalisation of prison reformation is not seen any where in India. As a consequence, prisons received the lowest priority within the criminal justice system in India.[46]

The nexus between criminals, politicians, priests, businessmen and jail officials is commonly found. Prison officials are engaged in custody oriented rather than reformative functions. By and large they are irrationalised.

The foregoing study clearly reveals that our policy makers lack theoretical awareness of the objectives and principles of rationalised prison administration. They are also lacking in progressive will and initiative to bring the desired rationality in conformity with the global knowledge. The Indian official efforts of prison reforms have so far been confined primarily to the appointment of commissions or committees without implementing their recommendations. Even the Government of India, failed to appoint a Commission for the Rationalisation of Prison Reformation. The NHRC and the Supreme Court have not followed the policy of rationalisation. The New Prisons Act of 1996, which had been finalised by the NHRC, itself is not a rationalised act.

From the years 1836 to 2000, i.e., more than 150 years, India failed to reform prison. India is still following the prison reformation policy, which is outdated. The Indian prison conditions are so much worst that any rationalist who enters prison becomes an irrationalist.

References

1. Altekar A.S.: *State and Government in Ancient India*, Jainendra Press, Delhi, 1958, p. 245.
2. Basham, A.L.: *The Wonder That Was India*, Macmillan Company, New York, 1959, pp.113, 247.
3. Singh, J. Indra: *op. cit.*, p.18.

4. Kane, P.V. : *History of Dharmasastra* (Ancient and Medieval Religions and Civil Law), Bhandarkar Oriental Research Institute, Poona, 1946, pp. 400-02, 405.
5. Indian Journal of Public Administration, Nagla, B.K.; *op. cit.*, XXXV; October-December 1989, p. 1013.
6. Basham, A.L.: *op. cit.*, p. 256.
7. Journal of Correctional Work, Prakash, S.: *History of Indian Prison System*, XXII; Lucknow, 1976, p. 89.
8. Basham, A.L.: *op. cit.*, Fontana, Calcutta, 1975, p.119.
9. Singh J. Indra: *op. cit.*, pp. 20-21.
10. Das Sukla: *Crime and Punishment in Ancient India*, Abhinav, New Delhi, 1977, p. 74.
11. Sarkar Jadunath: *Mughal Administration in India*, Calcutta, 1935, pp.114-17.
12. Social Defence; Satya Prakash Sangar, *Crime and Punishment in Mughal India*; XX, 79, January, 1985, pp.12, 36-37.
13. Trivedi, B.V.: *op. cit.*, p.1.
14. Madan, G.R.: *Indian Social Problems*, Vol. I, Allied Publications, New Delhi, 1997, p.126.
15. Singh J. Indra: *op. cit.*, p. 23.
16. Bhushan Vidya: *op. cit.*, p. 17.
17. Madan, G.R.: *op. cit.*, pp. 126-27.
18. Nagla, B.K., *op. cit.*, p. 1017.
19. Manorama Year Book, 1994, pp. 695-99.
20. Mohanty Amarendra and Hazary Narayan: *op. cit.*, p. 26.
21. Barker, F.A.: *The Modern Prison System in India*, London, 1944, p. 4.
22. Bhushan Vidya: *op. cit.*, p. 25.
23. Nagla, B.K.: *op. cit.*, p. 1019.
24. *Encyclopaedia of Police in India*. Vol. III, ed. by Ghosh, S.K., Ashish Publishing House, New Delhi, 1997, p. 2217.
25. Roy, J.G.: *op. cit.*, pp.18-20.
26. India 1983; Ministry of Information and Broadcasting; Government of India; New Delhi, 1983; p. 450.
27. Mohanty Amarendra and Hazary Narayan: *op. cit.*, pp. 28-30.
28. India—A Reference Annual, 1990, *op. cit.*, pp. 229-30.
29. Encyclopaedia of Social Work, Vol. II, ed. by Shukla, K.S., Ministry of Welfare, Government of India, 1987, p.141.

30. *Indian Express*, 18th April 1997, Bangalore.
31. *The New Indian Express*, 15th May 2000, Shimoga, p. 9.
32. *Deccan Herald*, 28th, 29th and 27th August 1995 and *The Indian Express*, 2nd October 1997, Bangalore.
33. *The Hindu*, 6th March 1999, Bangalore, p. 5.
34. *The Indian Express*, 9th February 1996 and 19th February 1998, Bangalore.
35. *The Times of India*, 15th March 1999, Bangalore, p.12.
36. India 1998—A Reference Annual; *op. cit.*, p. 534, India 2001, *op. cit.*, p. 634.
37. *Indian Express* by Unni Rajen Shankar and Hussain Zaidi, 9th August 1998, Bangalore.
38. *Indian Express*, 1997, Bangalore, p. 8.
39. India—A Reference Annual, 1990, *op. cit.*; p. 231.
40. *Indian Express*, 9th January 1997, Bangalore.
41. *New Indian Express*, 15th September, p. 9., 20th September 2000, p. 6.
42. *Ibid.*, 28th May 2000, Shimoga, p. 1.
43. *Ibid.*, 1st February 2001, Shimoga, p. 11.
44. *The New Sunday Express* by Manoj Mitta, 25th March 2001, Shimoga, p. 26.
45. *The New Indian Express* by Narayankar B.D., 24th March 2001, Shimoga, p. 5., and also see 28th May 2001, p. 8.
46. *Ibid.*, 2nd April 2001, p. 9, 5th April 2001, p. 6, and also see 4th May 2001, Shimoga, p. 8.

3
Reformation of the Prison System in British India

The second epoch was of universal adoption of imprisonment as a substitute for virtually 'all corporal or capital penalties'. It came to be realised that the process of imprisonment, involving detention in isolation from family and community, under not so pleasant conditions, could itself be considered as a convenient mode of punishment to replace the old corporal punishment, most countries readily took it.[1] Imprisonment as a principal method of punishment is a comparatively modem method of dealing with offenders, though its, roots ran back to the earliest societies. It was adopted by the Church and used quite extensively and then common jails and special prisons for the criminals arose.[2]

1 (i) Outside (Caste) Influences

A strongly religious content was introduced when imprisonment first became acceptable as an alternative to hanging or transportation in the early half of the nineteenth century. Not only was prison regarded as a more Christian form of punishment, solitary confinement and the treadmill notwithstanding, but religion was for long the sole means of rehabilitation for the prisoner. Besides, the ministry to those in is one with which the Church is specifically charged, and to neglect it—'Lord, when we saw thee in prison and did not minister unto thee'—is grievous indeed. The arrangements made for religion in prison are, as a consequence, for more elaborate than the standing of the Church outside would seem to warrant.[3]

Every prisoner on reception has to declare his religious denomination or if he is prepared to argue the point, his last of one.

Inevitably, as in the case of all such censuces (like in the services) a high proportion of those put down as 'C of E' (about two-thirds of a typical prison population) are labelled thus only because the prisoner himself has failed to make a more positive selection. Once registered, a prisoner cannot change his religious classification except with the opproval of the Visiting Committee (or Board of Visitors) whom he must convince of the 'good faith' of his application for a 'change of religion'. Quite apart form discovering frivolous applications, there is evidence to sugest that the Visiting Committee use their powers to delay the official implementation of a genuine decision made by the prisoner but which the Visiting Committee may feel was made under unfavourable circumstances: at a time of emotional stress and uncertainty: it is particularly difficult for a declared Roman Catholic to change religion.

The prisoner's declared religion is recorded on the cell card outside the cell-plain white for Church of England, white with an overprinted thick stripe for Non-conformist, red for Roman Catholic and blue for Jewish—for quicker identification by the passing Chaplain.

Every prison and borstal has set aside in it a place for religious worship, and a very large number of them have specially built chapels—some indeed are elaborately consturcted miniatures of the great Victorian Churches. Whether specially built as a chapel or not, is in constant use as a cinema or concert hall or lecture hall. Church services apart, very special duties are laid down for chaplains and 'Prison Ministers' in the prison rules. They have to interview every prisoner of their own denomination before release. It is a special duty of the Church of England Chaplain to visit daily all prisoners of his denomination. There is a belief, sometimes justified, that the chapel is a retreat for homosexuals.

Branches of the Church of England Men's Society and of the Roman Catholic Society of St. Vincent de Paul are formed in many prisons. There are full-time Church of England Chaplains in 24 prisons and borstals (four have two chaplains each) and a part-time chaplains in the remainder.[4]

During 16th and 17th centuries, the conditions of the prisoners were deplorable in the extreme. Prisons were dark fever-breeding filthy dens, in which men, women and children were crowded together without ventilation and with virtually no food except what friends supplied or the jailors furnished for pay. Scarcely less wretched was the lot of those who were deported to distant colonies and forced to labour on plantations.[5]

During the seventeenth century the two types of institutions continued, but the conditions reached such a shocking state that the government was forced to it. On 17 February 1729, the government "ordered that a committee be appointed to enquire into the state of gaols of this kingdom and report the same with their option there upon to the House".[6] The official record and shocking was the scene of cruelty, barbartity, and extortion which they disclosed".[7] Yet, it was not till John Howard, on his appointment as High Sheriff of Bedfordshire, began his exposure of the state of prisons that public criticism at once influence and effective was directed towards these conditions.

(ii) Early English Prisons

Till the end of 18th century prison in England of those days came to be described as places from which the prisoners came out 'to become pests in society, if they did not die earlier'. Towards the end of the eighteenth century the humanitarian movement penetrated the prison. Howard undertook the investigation of English and Continental jails. He contrasted the wreteched jails of England with the more advanced and humane prisons of the Continent. Goaded on by the further exposures of jail conditions by Jeremy Bentham and Elizabeth Fry, Parliament passed a series of laws which finally culminated in the General Act of 1791. That was the beginning of the penitentiary system in England. Due to the sincere efforts of John Howard, the British Parliament laid down in 1824, the first essentials of a decent prison administration. Since then the work of prison imprisonment has steadily forged ahead in the UK and to a greater or less extent in most countries of Europe and in the United States.[8]

2 (i) First Great English Prison Reformer

John Howard (1726-90) was the first great Englishman to make prison reform his life's work. His interest in the subject was aroused when in 1773, as High Sheriff of Bedford, he paid visits to Bedford jail. Terrible abuses were rampant there, as in practically every other prison in Britain. The chief jailor and his assistants were paid no salaries, being dependent on fees received from prisoners, who were kept in confinement until the payment of the same. The result was that many perfectly innocent persons, and many whose guilt had not been proved, were unjustly detained. Moreover, the conditions under which they were forced to exist—they cannot, without exaggeration, be said to have lived—were horrible beyond words.

Howard was galvanized into action by the honors which a tour of country jails revealed to him, and in 1774 he gave an account of his investigations to a sympathetic House of Commons. Very soon afterwards Acts were passed providing for the payment of jailors, the liberation of prisoners against whom no cases could be made out, and the improvement of the sanitary and medical conditions of the prisons.

In 1775-76, Howard visited many prisons in France, Germany, the Low Countries and Switzerland. He discovered that those of Holland were far in advance of all others. Those of Germany, on the other hand, were very bad.

After the publication, in 1777, of his State of the Prisons in England and...Wales and an Account of some foreign prisons, a Bill was drawn up providing for the establishment of prisons, one object of which was to turn the criminal into a useful member of society. This Act may be regarded as the foundation on which the English prison system was built. Its aims were enunciated in these words: "by sobriety, cleanliness and medical assistance, by a series of labour, by solitary confinement during the intervals of work and by due religious instruction to preserve and amend the health of the unhappy offenders, to ensure them to habits of industry; to guard them from pernicious company, to accustom them to serious reflection and to teach them both the principle and practice of every Christian and moral duty."

Needless to say, these lofty sentiments were regarded more as indicating ideals to be aimed at in the distant future than as a practical rule of conduct for dealing with immediate needs. The horrors of the system introduced by the Act of 1778 were very great, but a beginning had at least been made.

From the time of the passing of the Bill until his death from camp fever, contracted while inspecting a Russian hospital, Howard worked ceaselessly for the amelioration of the prisoner's lot. He travelled widely on the Continent, wrote books and articles, drew up plans for prisons, and did research work on the means of preventing contagious distempers. Howard brought light, humaneness and knowledge into an age of darkness, brutality and ignorance, and he will always be remembered with great affection by those who are straggling to lessen the sum total of man's inhumanity to man.[9]

Broadly speaking Howard found three main evils within the prisons of England—"First, the retention in custody of those who, although unconvicted and declared discharged were unable to pay discharge fees; Second, the ravages of gaols fever, and third, the corruption of the morals of prisoners by means of enforced idleness and unrestrained and uncontrolled bad company".[10] Howard's proposals for the overcoming of these evils have been given exhaustively in his great book, *State of Prison*. Some of the reforms suggested by him were concerning the situation, construction and furnishing of prison building, the classification of criminals according to their offences, the provision of baths and ventilators for better sanitation and health, the employment of prisoners in various kinds of useful labour, the appointment of honest, active and humane jailors, the abolition of taps and proper selection of Chaplains".[11] On the question of separation Howard stated, "I wish to have so many small rooms or cabins that each criminal may sleep alone. Women should be quite separate from the men and the young criminals from old and hardened offenders".[12]

The credit for rousing the public conscience to the barbarism of such conditions belongs chiefly to the Englishman John Howard, whose horrifying pictures of prison life forced a change in the treatment of prisoners.[13]

The immediate effect of Howard's work was a series of statutes from 1774 to 1791 directed to "securing a decent level of cleanliness and sanitation, with a view to preventing gaol fever; to the provision of work for prisoners to assist them in their maintenance; to the separation of the sexes; and to the effective supervision of the gaols by the Justice".[14] These statutes, though historically interesting as indicating the movement of instructed opinion, had not much immediate effect, as those were permissive, not mandatory, and as there was no machinery to ensure that they enforced, or even to see whether they were being enforced or not.[15]

It may be noted here that though Howard drew the public attention to the evils of jails. Yet he made no suggestion that they should be used as places of imprisonment. It was the cessation of transportation to America that forced the leaders of prison reform to consider the building of national prisons. In the meantime, however to take care of the prisoners who had been formerly transported to America, England resorted to the use of 'hulks'[16] or floating prisons.[17] It was also decided to transport prisoners to Australia.

(ii) Jeremy Bentham's Ideas

In 1791 Jeremy Bentham (1748-1832) was given the contract for the building of a large prison on the plan outlined in his book called the *Panoctican*. This institution was to be built in a circular form with the cells on the circumference. There was to be an inspection station in the centre, so arranged that every part of every cell should be visible from the centre. This scheme got no further than the purchase of a site at Millbank. However, it left a marked impression on the advocates of prison reform and served as a useful guide to the prison administrators and for the future legislation on the subject, is regarding necessity of preventing crime by discovering and combating causes, Bentham was the founder of the Modem School of Prevention.[18]

In 1813, the task of prison reform was taken up by some members of the Society of Friends. In 1817 was formed the Society for the Improvement of Prison Discipline which had several 'friends' among its leading members. Its report records that in 1818 there were 518 prisons in United Kingdom to which more than 1,00,000 prisoners were committed in the year and that only twenty-three of these had been sub-divided as required by law. The Society reported that 59 prisons had no divisions. In 45 prisons no employment of any kind was provided. The overcrowding was excessive in 100 jails; in the space for 8,545 there had been crowded 13,057.[19]

(iii) Work of Beccaria, Voltaire and Mirabeau

It was not only in England that crime and punishment were attracting the attention of great men. Italy produced Cesare Beccaria (1738-94), mathematician, economist and social reformer. His book on *Crimes and Punishment*, published in 1764, was translated into more than a score of European languages. Howard's Italian counterpart believed in the abolition, not only of torture, but of capital punishment. He felt that more energy should be devoted to the prevention of crime and less to its savage punishment; and what were punishment was deemed to be necessary it should follow the crime as quickly as possible. The French edition of *Beccaria's* book had a preface by Voltaire, who was in almost complete agreement with ideas expressed in it, and who played a noteworthy part in inducting a more humane attitude towards criminals.

In 1791, the leaders of the Revolution in France decreed that reformatory imprisonment should be substituted for the less humane punishments in the penal code. The man chiefly responsible for this notable advance in the treatment of criminals was the Comte de Mirabeau (1749-91), one of the great intellectual leaders of the Revolution.[20]

(iv) Transported for Life

The first British Prisons Act, was introduced in 1777. It was the year following that in which the American Colonies achieved their independence. Before the Colonies won their freedom they were a dumping-ground for undesirable natives of Britain. The power to transport convicts across the seas was given to justices in the reign of Elizabeth. In that of James I "dissolute persons" were sent to Virginia. But, when in 1776, the Colonies broke away from the mother country, transportation to them ceased and English justices were forced to look around for other means of dealing with convicts.

This explains why John Howard's efforts to reform the English jails were so sympathetically considered by the Government. For a short time a good deal of attention was devoted to the new prison system, but soon a substitute for New England presented itself to the anxious gaze of the transportationists. In 1770, Captain James Cook had sighted Botony Bay, Australia. Seventeen years later the first Australian convict fleet left England. It consisted of nine transport vessels and two men-of-war.

Transportation on a scale America had never known was inflicted on Australia. For more than half a centuary convicts—many of whom were guilty of no serious crime, and others who were of the scum of Britain-continued to pour into the newly refound Continent.

The system was bad for the convicts, bad for England, and bad for Australia. It was abandoned because of growing discontent in Australia three years after Queen Victoria's accession (1840).

But for the rediscovery of Australia and its use as an easy way out of the convict problem, the British penal system might have been the envy of the civilized world by the end of the 18th century. As it was, it lagged far behind France, Holland and the United States, and in the words of Lecky, the historian, was "shamefully below the average of the Continent". So bad was it that in 1817, Sir Samuel Romilly (1757-1818), the law reformer was able truthfully to say: "the laws of England are written in blood".[21]

(v) Greatest Happiness of the Greatest Number

Sir Samuel Romilly was a disciple of Jeremy Bentham, who fought determinedly against the evils of the penal system. One of his earliest works was the Rationale of Rewards and Punishments, which although written in 1775 (when John Howard was beginning his inquiries) was not published until 1811.

In "Introduction To Principles Of Morals And Legislation", 1789, Bentham put forward the then novel suggestion that all punishment is of itself evil and ought therefore only to be allowed insofar as it "promises to exclude some greater evil". He saw the proper aim of Government and law as "the greatest happiness of the greatest number".

For about twenty-five years he laboured on the working out of a plan for a model prison system. Although the Government did not accept Bentham's Scheme, it was largely as the result of his agitation that a convict prison was built at Millbank, London, on the site now occupied by the National Gallery Of Modem Art (the Tate Gallery). The prison cost, so it is said, £5,00,000 and took ten years to build (1813-23). Covering an area of sixteen acres, it had accommodation for 1,120 prisoners. It was shut down in 1890 and demolished in 1903.[22]

(vi) Saint Visits the Prisons

In the year that saw the laying of the foundation stone of Millbank Penitentiary a young Quakeress named Elizabeth Fry (1780-1845) paid her first visit to Newgate Prison, in the city of London.

New gate was so terrible a place that, even the Governor was afraid to venture into its cells. Elizabeth Fry was there confronted by a "swarm of drunken, mad, half-naked, starving women, living more like beasts than humans". Such an experience should, one would think, have been enough to cure a gently nurtured, well-off woman of any desire to pursue her investigations further, but it only increased Mrs. Fry's compassion and strengthened her determination to spend herself and her fortune in doing away with such cases.

Nothing about this wonderful woman was more remarkable than the almost magical power she was able to exercise over the most hardened and depraved members of society. A word in her quiet voice, or a glance from her gentle eyes could make the toughest convict her devoted slave. By the sheer force of her goodness she accomplished what all the rigours of an unspeakably barbarous penal system were powerless to effect. "To see", said Sidney Smith, "that holy woman in the midst of the wretched prisoners clinging to the hem of her garment, and worshiping her as the only being who has ever loved them, or taught them, or noticed them, or spoken to them of God! This is the sight which breaks down the pageant of life".

Gathering round her a group of devoted helpers, she threw herself into the struggle and achieved miracles of reform. She was wealthy when she began her crusade, but even when, seventeen year's before her death, her husband went bankrupt, she still continued to spend herself—a gift more precious than gold—for humanity. It is further noteworthy that in her herculean prison labours she did not neglect her own large family.

Her reforming zeal knew no national frontiers: like her forerunner, John Howard, she travelled extensively—in France, Switzerland and Germany, in Belgium, Holland and Denmark, everywhere she went she was eagerly received, nor were the lessons she taught quickly forgotten. All over Europe unhappy prisoners who never knew her name were indebted to this woman whose Christianity belonged to every day of the week and every minute of the day.[23]

During the same years Mrs. Fry began her work among female prisoners. Her own account of her first visit endorses the horrors of Newgate Prison conditions. The filth, the closeness of the room, the ferocious manners and expressions of the women towards each other and the weakness which everything bespoke, were some of the undesirable elements of the prison. She characterised it as "Hell above ground".[24] "By her untiring zeal she tamed, instructed and humanised the female inmates there, got them to work, induced them to adopt rules and effected so many extraordinary changes as to render a visit to the female department of Newgate one of the fashionable sensations of the day". [25]

In 1821 was completed the penitentiary at Millbank, the site of Bentham's abandoned Panoptican. It was the first national prison in England constructed to lodge the prisoners sentenced to transportation till they could be removed to Australia. In Australia they were kept for a time either in Government employment in the penal treatment or on assignment to private employers, and then, it well conducted, released on 'ticket of leave', to be at large in the colony, though under police supervision, until the sentence had expired or a pardon was granted. [26]

The year 1824 brings us to a great landmark in the history of British prisons. In that year Peel introduced a measure which "consolidated as many as twenty-three pre-existing statutes on the subject of gaols and the House of Correction, took the first step towards assimilating these institutions and for the first time made it peremptorily the duty of justices to organise their prisons on a prescribed plan and furnish quarterly reports to the Home Secretary".[27] They were expressly required to adopt, as the basis, Howards four principles of the adoption of sufficient, secure and sanitary accommodation for all prisoners, the transformation of the gaoler or master from an independent profile-maker into the salaried servant of the local authority, the subjection of regiment of all criminals to a reformatory regiment; and the systematic inspection of every part of the prison by visiting justices.[28] The Discipline Society kept the subject constantly in view and little the local authorities too aroused themselves to the necessity for adopting the improvements enjoined by the Act. Nevertheless the rules and practices in the prisons varied excessively and the spirit of the Act was neglected.

The year 1835 marks the end of unrestricted local enterprise and the beginning of a period of partial government control. For it was in this year that an "Act for effecting greater uniformity to provide formity of practice in the government of the several prisons and for appointing Inspectors and a uniform system in all the prisons in Great Britain became law".[29] Thus the period of uncontrolled local government was now gone, and there began a period of supervision by Inspectors appointed by Westminster. A uniform code of rules and a uniform diet were drawn up by a committee of Inspectors under the Under Secretary of State and circulated by the authority of Sir James Graham.[30]

3 (i) Prison Reform Movement in the United States

In the United States of America the prison reform movement was pioneered by the Quakers of Pennsylvania, under William Pen's leadership. They had brought with them to their new home "a mixed heritage of experiences and ideas. In England they had been persecuted for their heterodoxy and in the exile in Holland they learned about the workhouses of that country. Their charitable religion made them humane towards their enying and suffering fellowmen and the work of their co-religionist. John Howard, made them conscious of their own crime problem and opened their eyes to the evils of their own congregate jails".[31]

(ii) Early American Prisons

Across the Atlantic several colonies had erected workhouses. Among them were Massachusetts, Connecticut and Pennsylvania. In 1682 William Pen, that great exponent of Quaker Humanitarianism, established a penal code of exceptional mildness which provided for houses of correction. After his death in 1718 his code was abolished, and the sanginuary laws were restored and continued in force until after the Revolution.

A similar work was done in the United States by a group of Philadelphia Quakers. They were agitating for prison reform immediately at the close of the Revolutionary War and in 1787 founded the Parent prison reform society. Their efforts bore fruit before those of the English reformers, so that the United States became the first country to set an example to the world of really humane treatment of criminals.[32]

(iii) Beginning of the Penitentiary System in the United States

Through the Philadelphia Society for Alleviating the Miseries of Public Prisons, the citizens of Philadelphia in 1790 obtained the passage of a law which marked the beginning of the penitentiary system in the United States. The act established the principle of solitary confinement of felons with productive work and strict discipline. The Walnut Street Jail in Philadelphia was remodelled and became the first American experiment with segregation of the more dangerous criminals in solitary cells, the grouping of misdemeanants, debtors and witnesses in larger rooms while engaged in productive indoor and outdoor work at equitable wages and with reasonable hours of work.

Pennsylvania or Separate System

By 1820, the Walnut Street Jail and its imitators fell into dispute. The Philadelphia Society crystallized its theories in the Pennsylvania or Separate System.[33] The Quakers of Pennsylvania became the leaders of prison reforms in the New World and distinguished Pennsylvania a pioneer in penal reforms after the Revolutionary War. Imprisonment was substituted for corporal punishment and the death penalty was restricted only to murder. To reduce the evils of congregation the so-called Pennsylvania system was experimented upon in the Walnut Street Jail at Philadelphia. This system was established with the purpose of obtaining reformation by introspection, mediation and penitence.[34] It stood for solitary confinement, both by day and night. The prisoner-aided by visits from the officers of the institution and from reading from religious tracts, was expected to reach a full realization of the enormity of his offence against God and society and finally arrive at peace with his maker and leave the institution a better man. There was no companion of the prisoner and penitence his sole occupation. He was completely separated from others and could contact neither his relatives nor any other person except the prison officials.

This was the first cellular confinement in America which the humanitarians of the day felt would put the prisoner on the path of reformation. Here we have the beginning of the prison system in America. The significance of Walnut Street Jail lay in the fact that it became the model in the United States for the next forty years. The institution was looked upon in these early days as an important discovery in the reformation of prisoners. However after a few years the Walnut Street prison steadily deteriorated and became a failure. The discipline relaxed and the whole prison became a hot-bed of disorder. "The chief cause", according to Lewis, "of the ultimate demoralization of the Walnut Street prison lay in the increasingly crowded condition of the institution."[35] The excess of privacy, the monotony of silence, the isolation from the community life and the deprivation of visit from relations and other amenities led to the physical and mental deterioration of the prisoners. Consequently, the system was replaced by the Auburn system.

Auburn or Silent System

The Auburn system gave much latitude to the prisoners. It employed solitary confinement only for short periods and allowed the prisoners to work in association during the day-time under a rule of silence. The prisoners were separately confined at night. Silence was strictly observed at every place and at every time. The prisoners could whisper nor make any gesture. In the night, they were locked in the-separate cells with the Bible as night companion to think over their past and reform for the future.

These two systems of prisons; the Auburn or the silent system and the Pennsylvania or the separate system were not so radically different as the controversy that raged over them for so long would seem to apply. From the beginning the two systems were more alike than different. Both prevented the prisoners from communicating with one another. Both locked the prisoners in separate cells at night. Both believed in the efficiency of labour. The basic difference between the two systems was that under the Pennsylvania system the convicts were separate from each other every moment of their stay in the prison. When they get out no prisoner could be recognised by another because he had never seen him. On the other hand, Auburn prisoners knew each other, although they could not communicate with each other except upon the pain of punishment.[36]

After a controversy between the two systems the Auburn system won the day. The chief argument in favour of the Auburn system was its economy of increased production due to the association of workers. Most American states today follow this system with such changes as time, knowledge and a changing penal philosophy have brought about. The American prison system, now in almost universal use, embodies two main principles: The separation of prisoners by individual cells, and their employment at some form of labour.[37] Till recently a tread-wheel or crank-box was regarded as exemplary punishment. Early in the nineteenth century, the inmates of the Bavaria camps in the United States of America, were deployed on public road construction. So was the case with their counterparts in India. However, work by convicts in both the countries came under criticism for two specific reasons: At the operational level the convicts were required to work under conditions far from satisfactory. Secondly, and most importantly, several administrators, jurists and intellectuals viewed the work by the inmates as causing dissipation of punitive objectives. Nevertheless, in the second-half of the last century work by convicts started gaining importance. In contemporary times, in most of the correctional institutions work by convicts has become almost routine. What however, differentiates the work by the inmates of modem correctional institutions from that of ancient and medieval times is the approach and the basic philosophy behind the work.[38]

4. (i) Reformation of the Prison Administration in British India

The jail system in Western countries is commonly traced to the Poor houses in England during the regime of Queen Elizabeth I. They housed not only the offenders but also paupers. The inmates were provided food and clothing and were also required to work. Within a short period of their existence, these institutions, however, greatly deteriorated and were severely criticised for their sub-human conditions. Eventually, separate institutions were organised for under-trials and convicts. The officials of the East India Company brought the system to the subcontinent.[39]

When the prison reformation commenced in England, then, it was an imperial country. In case of India, it was a colony of the British Empire. Hence, the condition of Britain and India are quite different at the time of prison reformation. England, being a sovereign, independent nation, voluntarily introduced prison reformation. But, in case of India, it was imposed by the Britishers on the Indians to continue their rule.

In sixteenth century during the regime of East India Company the prison condition in India were terrible and inhuman. This was due to the fact that, deterrence was the only aim of the prison system. With the advent of the British the administrative structure in the country began to assume a new form. At first little alteration was made in the existing legal system. In 1773 was passed the Regulating Act which established the Supreme Court at Calcutta to exercise all civil, criminal, admiralty and ecclesiastical jurisdiction. It indicated the intention of the British Government to introduce English rules of law and English superintendence of law and justice. The imprisonment as a form of punishment (or the modern prison system) was first applied in India in 1773.[40]

In 1784, British Parliament empowered the East India Company to rule India and since then some attempts were made to introduce reforms in the administration of justice. At that time, there were 143 civil jails, 75 criminal jails and 68 mixed jails. Infact, these jails were an extension of Mughal rule which were being managed by the personnel of the East India Company in their efforts to maintain peace and establish their trade. The prison institutions were run by District Magistrates who were known for their indifference and reluctance to this aspect of administration, and hence conditions therein were extremely bad. No effort was being made to ameliorate the conditions of prisoners. They were just slave-labourers. The directors of the East India Company were reluctant to spend money on jails and improve the state of affairs therein. There were 75,000 prisoners out of which 65,700 were engaged in the construction of roads and were given exemption from other works inside the prison. There are some references according to which it is known that only in two jails carpets were being manufactured.[41]

Reforms in prison administration came to occupy public attention when the British Parliament passed an enactment in 1824 in regard to the essentials of prison administration.

In 1833, the attention of the British Parliament was drawn to the anomalous and sometimes conflicting judicatures by which laws were hither to being administered. Accordingly, in that year an Act was passed which effected many changes in the constitutional set up of the country. An Indian Law Commission was appointed to prepare an uniform code of legal rules.

In India the first experiment in prison reforms began in the year 1835. In this year there were 43 civil, 75 criminal and 68 mixed jails.[42] These institutions were run by District Magistrates who were known for their indifference and reluctance to this aspect of administration, and hence conditions therein were extremely bad. There was inadequate food, ill clothing and improper medical attention for the prisoners. The directors of the East India Company were reluctant to spend money on jails and improve the state of affairs therein.

(ii) Modern Prison Administration in India Lord Macaulay's Committee

Administrative structure for modern prison system originated from the Minute by T.B. Macaulay.[43] Macaulay drew attention of the Government of India to the terrible conditions in the Indian Jails and on his suggestion a committee was appointed on 2nd of January 1836, to look into the conditions and report thereon.

The history of prison reforms starts from the appointment of 'Lord Macaulay' Committee in 1836. It was a major step taken in this direction by the Company. "Macaulay Committee" was the 'First Famous Committee" on prison reforms in India. After two years of continued sittings, it submitted its report in 1838 criticizing severely "The corruption of the subordinate establishment, the laxity of discipline and the system of employing the prisoners in extra-mural labour on public roads".[44] The far-reaching recommendations of the Committee were:

(a) That Central Jails should be built to accommodate not more than 1,000 prisoners each.
(b) That Inspector-General of Prisons should be appointed in all privinces.
(c) That sufficient building should be provided in all jails to accommodate prisoners comfortably.[45]

In pursuance of the recommendations of the Committee a Central Prison was constructed at Agra in 1846. This was the first Central Prison in India and was followed by construction of Central

Prisons at Bareilly and Allahabad in 1848, at Lahore in 1852, at Madras in 1857, at Bombay in 1864, at Alipore in 1864, at Banaras and Fatehgarh in 1864 and at Lucknow in 1867. In 1844, the first Inspector-General of Prisons was appointed in the North-Western Province (present Uttar Pradesh). His appointment was made on an experimental basis for two years and was extended for another four years. In 1850, the Government of India made it a permanent post and suggested that each province should have an Inspector-General of Prisons. Punjab appointed the Inspector-General in 1852, Bengal in 1854, Bombay in 1854, Madras in 1854, and Central Provinces in 1862.

Upto 1860, the management of the District Jails had devolved on the Magistrate. But, it was found that, in the process of administration, these officials had been overwhelmed with multifarious business of all departments. Another agency was therefore, required and this was most suitably found in the civil surgeon. Henceforth, in 1862 the North-Western Province employed civil surgeons as superintendents of district jails. The experiment proved so successful that the Government of India issued orders in 1864 that all provinces should employ civil surgeons as superintendents of district jails.[46] Finally, civil surgeons had been appointed in every one of the 25 jails. The same course was introduced all over Bengal Presidency and also in Madras and Bombay.

The subject of prison reform was thus placed on a higher plane than might otherwise have been attained and credit for it belongs to Macaulay Committee. Great improvements, however, could not have been expected at once. However, the recommendations of the "Macaulay Committee" could not be implemented because, among other things, the East India Company rule was, in 1858, replaced by the British Crown rule. The English criminal law came to be applied to Indians. The Indian Penal Code and the Criminal Procedure Code which had long been in preparation were enacted in 1859 and 1860 respectively. The Indian Penal Code defined each and every offence and prescribed punishment for it, while the Criminal Procedure Code laid the procedure for procuring the criminals.

The imprisonment as a form of punishment (or the modern prison system) which was first applied in India in 1773 came to be applied on uniform basis throughout India in 1860.[47] The institution of jail as understood these days, is of British origin and was introduced in India as a part of British Administration. Before the institution of jail, the system of punishment did not require any financial burden on the part of the Government. The Directors of the East India Company were reluctant to spend money on jails and although jails were modelled on British lines, there was not enough accommodation and there was inadequate food, clothing and medical attention for the prisoners. Thus, the conditions of jails were extremely bad.[48]

(iii) Second Committee on Prison Reformation

The Second Committee on Prison Reforms was appointed in 1864 to consider questions of jail management, because of high death rate in prisons and by other allied considerations. The Second Committee fixed a minimum space for each prisoner in jail, i.e. 54 superficial feet and 640 cubic feet per prisoner, recommended for improvements in diet, clothing and bedding and insisted upon regular medical inspection of prisoners. They also recommended that every central prison should have cellular accommodation for fifteen per cent of its population and that juveniles be kept separate from other prisoners and that they should be given education.

In 1864 there was, it appears, a great controversy whether jails should have cellular accommodation or association barracks. In United States both Pennsylvania and Auburn systems were based on solitary confinement In England the Lords Committee of 1863 had recommended the separate system to which the Prison Act, 1865 gave approval.[49] In other countries too the cellular system found favour with the prison reformers of the day. In India also cellular accommodation was considered most suitable for prison life, but it could not be adopted on account of huge cost involved. A noteworthy feature of administrative structure of prison system in India, is participation of warders and night watchmen (promotees from prisoners) in the executives duties. This system was introduced by the British in 1864, in order to minimise expenditure on establishment, giving incentives to prisoners, and to implement the policy of ruling prisoners through prisoners only.[50]

In 1870, the Government of India passed the Prisons Act to amend the law relating to prisoners in the country. It laid down that there should be a superintendent, a medical officer, a jailor and such subordinate officers as the local government thinks necessary. The superintendent was authorised to appoint, with the approval of the Inspector-General of Prisons, Jailors and Deputy Jailors.[51] The Act came into force on the first day of December 1876.

5. (i) Prison Reformation Movement from National to International level

Prison reformation movement was spreading to the whole world, though India was still a colony of the British Empire. A remarkable movement commenced to internationalise certain principles or standards for the treatment and punishment of crime by holding the International Prison Congress at London in 1872. Here on wards, the prison reformation in any country required international standards. This further boosted the morale of the prison reformists to continue their efforts in that direction vigorously. The basic detect of this international prison reformation was, the decisions of the International Prison Congress were voluntary and advisory. Yet, it is a milestone in the reformation process. It is noteworthy to mention that, within a century of the national reformation period, the international reformation movement commenced. Its special feature is neither national nor international war was fought for the commencement of the National or International prison reformation. It commenced and continued through peaceful methods only. Here onwards, the Indian Government had to implement the international standard reformation in India. But, it failed. Yet, it continued the reformation movement in India.

(ii) Third All India Jail Committee

The Third All India Jail Committee was appointed in 1877. The Committee was composed entirely of officials actually engaged in prison work. It reviewed the jail management generally and mostly concerned itself more with the matters of detail in prison work than with the general aims and principles of administration.

(iii) Fourth All India Jail Committee

In 1889 was appointed the Fourth Jail Committee on an all India basis. On this occasion the purview of the enquiry was expressly directed towards the routine working of the jails. The report was therefore, a business like report covering nearly the whole field of internal management of jails and laying down elaborate rules for prison management. The Committee recommended the separation of undertrial prisoners and the classification of prisoners into casuals and habituals. Most of the recommendations of the Committee were incorporated in the Jail Manuals of various provinces. The executive staff was divided into two classes. The higher class consisted of Jailors and Deputy and Assistant Jailors who formed a single provincial service with promotion from one grade to another. The lower class, consisting of wardens for supervision of prisoners, also formed a graded local service.

(iv) Fifth All India Committee on Prison Administration

The work of the Committee was supplemented by the next All India Committee of 1892. This was the Fifth All India Committee on Prison Administration. It resurveyed the whole prison administration in India and drew up proposals on the subject of prison offences and punishment.

The Report of the Committee was accepted by the Government of India which passed the Prisons Act of 1894. This Act provided that the convicted criminal prisoners may be confined either in association or individually in cells or partly in one way or partly in the other. The Act fixed nine hours labour a day for a criminal prisoner sentenced to labour or employed on labour at his own desire. It further defined what constitutes prison offences and laid down punishments varying from a formal warming to separate confinement for any period not exceeding six months. Any two of the punishment could be awarded for any offence subject to certain exceptions.

This Act was largely based on deterrent principles and reflected the contemporary English public opinion on the subject. The Legislators took little pains to look into the other side of the problem. They were concerned more with prison working than with prison treatment and gave more consideration to prison offences and punishments than to its effects.

(v) Transportation to Andamans

The British occupied the Andaman Islands. The first settlement was established in North Andamans in the year 1789. Attempts at colonisation were ultimately given up but the penal settlement survied. Then came the Revolt of 1857 in India. The British found that they had on their hands a large number of rebel convicts whom the Indian prisons of those days would hardly contain. The Andamans offered a readymade solution. It is estimated that between 1858 and 1860 some 2000-4000 sepoy mutineers were sent to the Andamans. Many of them died. In 1882 the practice of sending prisoners to Andamans was stopped and they were kept in Central Prison, Bangalore.[52] The construction of Cellular Jail was taken up in 1896. The construction itself carried out by convicts.[53]

(vi) Reformatory Schools Act

The year 1897 made a landmark in the history of prison reforms in India. In that year, was passed the Reformatory Schools Act and according to this Act courts were directed to send youthful offenders below 15 years to reformative schools instead of prisons. Then the prisoners Act 1900 was passed.

Even though different commissions were appointed the Indian prison system lagged behind on the reformative side of the prison work. It failed to regard the prisoner as an individual and conceived of him rather as a unit in jail administrative machinery. It lost sight of the effort which humanising and civilizing influences had on the mind of the individual prisoner and failed to focus attention on his material well-being and problems of diet, health and labour. Thus, it was mainly the idea of deterrence which influenced prison policy till the year 1919.[54]

England was ushering in a new path in prison reforms and a similar spirit could be seen here also. The century was drawing to its close and the old ideas about prison administration were being discorded under the influence of new ones.[55]

6. (i) First World War

The First International War brought many changes in the world. It created internationalism, international organisation like League of

Nations. But, it failed to make any revolutionary change in the prison administration in the whole world. This most destructive war, neither abolished the prison reformation nor prison itself. Simply it continued the reformation of the prison further in the whole world and especially in India. Yet, this war, further boosted the morale of the prison reformists to continue their efforts at the international level.

(ii) Sixth Indian Jails Committee

In order to bring about an overall change in Indian Jails, the Indian Jails Committee was set up in 1919 in which Sir Alexander G. Gadrew was the Chairman. This was the Sixth All India Committee on Prisons. The committee made an extensive tour of England, Scotland, USA, Japan, Philippines and Hong Kong studied the prison system there and submitted a comprehensive report in 1920 suggesting far reaching changes in the various aspects of prison administration. The committee for the first time suggested two conceptual pivots—"prevention" and "reformation" for a more effective base for prison administration in India.[56] "The aim of prison administration is the prevention of further crime and the restoration of the criminal to society as a reformed character"[57] stated the committee. The report contained a number of recommendations dealing among others with such subjects as prison staff, separation and classification of prisoners, prison labour and manufactures, discipline and punishment, reformatory influences in prison, prison hygiene, medical administration, aid to the prisoners, on release, probation and borstal treatment.

Upto 1919, the prison department was under the countrol of Central Government.[58] Soon after the introduction of the Montegu Chelmsford Reforms, jails and other alike services became state subjects. The provincial governments showed great enthusiasm for jail reform and started appointing a series of Jail Reform Committees with a view to improving prisoner's lot in the jails under their jurisdiction. The committees appointed in different States were Punjab Jail Reforms Committee (1919 and 1948), Uttar Pradesh (1929, 1938 and 1946), Bombay (1939 and 1946), Mysore (1941), Bihar (1948), Madras (1950), Orissa (1952), and Travancore Cochin (now Kerala) (1953).[59]

(iii) Government of India Act, 1935

In 1935 was passed the Government of India Act. Dyarchy was abolished in the provinces and the reserved subjects were transferred to the Minister's control. The Congress contested the elections and assumed power in seven out of eleven provinces. The penal reform movement again received an impetus and attention was focused on the hither to neglected prison reforms. During the brief stay of two and a quarter years in the office the Congress Ministry appointed three Committees in succession to look into the prison conditions and put three Acts on the statute book. The first was an expert committee, the second consisted of some of the members of the provincial legislature and the third and the most important of all was the Departmental Jail Committee (DJC) of 1939. The DJC was required to examine the recommendations of the previously appointed Jail Committees with a view to giving effect to them. The Committee endorsed recommendations regarding prison establishment, medical subordinates, officer's training, borstal institutions, prison hygiene and aid on discharge. Besides endorsing these, the Committee also made some new recommendations of its own.

(iv) Closed Prison to Open Prison

Their Origin and Aims

The prison reformation continued further. Closed prison has led to the 'Open Prison'. The open prison, the so-called 'prison without bars' has been a very late development within the prison. This inspite of nearly two hundred years of penological speculation and reform dating back to Beccaria and John Howard. Historically prisons have always been places in which criminals could be securely confined and this 'containment' function has continued to predominate inspite of the gradual emergence of other aims for imprisonment, such as deterrence or rehabilitation. Containment here means not only that prisoners must be kept out of circulation, but also that their deviations, even within the prison, must not be on such a scale as to disturb the peace of mind of the man-in-the-street. The open prison thus begins to appear like a contradiction in terms; a denial of the essential nature of the institution of which it purports to be merely a variant.

The first open prison was almost certainly Witzwil, established in Switzerland in 1891. However, Witzwil was not a thorough going minimum security establishment; it had closed sections. Nor did other countries follow the lead given by the Swiss. Witzwil was the result of the vision of a particular individual, Otto Kellerhals. Other countries were more cautious, gradually developing the minimum security plea pragmatically. Thus in 1916 the Lorton Reformatory, in the District of Columbia, USA, was built without a containing wall, and other similar institutions followed. However, these were not open prisons in the sense in which we understand the word, consisting as they usually did of secure blocks arranged so as to fully enclose a central quadrangle. Another modification of the maximum security regime, and one which has aroused interest in Britain in recent years was the experiment by Howard Gill at Norfolk Massachusetts. The Norfolk Penal Institution was based on the idea of a maximum security parameter, making possible a high degree of free movement within that parameter.

The real breakthrough came in the 1930's in Britain and the 1940's in the USA. In the United Kingdom, Sir Alexander Paterson (a member of the Prison Commission from 1922 to 1947) began to place his liberalising stamp upon penal system. In his dictium 'A man is sent to prison as a punishment and not for punishment'. He tried to set limits to the role of retribution in prisons and make room for what he called 'training'. His second famous aphorism: 'you cannot train a man for freedom under conditions of captivity'; which led to the opening in 1933 of the first British open prison, New Hall Camp, as a satellite of wake field prison. Here there were no walls, and indeed not even a boundary fence—the men sleeping in wooden huts and the bounds designated if at all, by whitewash marks on the trees. But the aim of containment persisted. Sir Lionel Fox, a former chairman of the Prison Commission, in writing about New Hall Camp, saw as the achievement most worth mentioning that in the first fifteen years in its half only seven prisoners had absconded. Other open institutions followed: Leyhill prison in Gloucester shire about ten years later, and Aldington, near Maidstone, in 1947. There were in 1975, thirteen open prisons of various kinds in Britain, with, as we have seen, a total population of 3,230.

The Americans also moved forward, beginning at about the same time as Britain, will open farm camps associated with neighbouring closed prisons. Among the most famous American open prisons are the Californian Institution for Men at Chino in Southern California, and Seagoville, an open federal prison in Texas.

The basic justificatition of this purpose remains that put forward by Alexander Paterson. 'You cannot train a man for freedom under conditions of captivity'. The implication of this is that social behaviour is learned by social experience, and that the restricted life of the closed prison teaches the wrong lessons. The effect thus produced on the individual inmate was called 'prisonisation' by D. Clernmer.The best protection for the public is an effectively rehabilitative prison system.[60]

(v) Progress in International Prison Congress

The prison reformation movement was spreading to the whole world. This made several nations to think over the matter at the international level. There had been spasmodic movements in many countries of Europe for the reform of prisons and prisoners, prison system, so for as they can be said to have existed at all, were devised mainly with a view to repression or deterrence; and what has since become the leading principle in dealing with crime, viz., the individualisation of punishment, i.e., the adaptation of punishment to the different degrees of moral guilt and the infinite variety of mental and physical attributes, affecting responsibility, found only a very limited expression in the penal law and prison management of different countries.

A remarkable movement has been in progress to internationalise certain principles or standards for the treatment and punishment of crime. The movement began in 1872 by the holding of an International Prison Congress in London. For this credit goes to America for having organized in Britain a movement which was the precedent and example which has developed into a well-established movement of all civilized states for discussing and if possible, improving a world-system of punishment. An international commission was created, which by means of quinquennial congresses, held in the different capitals of Europe, furnished the occasion for periodical discussion and exchange of views on all matters affecting both the regime of prisons and the reform of criminal law.

Great Britain and the USA did not adhere to this movement, until the Paris Congress, 1895. At the Congress of Washington, 1910, Sir E. Ruggles Brise was elected president and this led to an invitation of the British Government to hold the next Congress in London, in 1915. Due to the outbreak of the First World War, it was postponed. Accordingly, the International Prison Congress was held in London in 1925.

The leading note was struck by the resolution of the London Congress, 1872, viz., that "moral regeneration should be the primary aim of prison discipline and that hope should always be a more powerful agent than fear."

Twenty-four countries in 1928 annually represented on the International Prison Commission, viz., Great Britain, France, Germany, Italy, Spain, Belgium, Holland, Switzerland, Greece, Sweden, Norway, Denmark, Austria, Hungary, Poland, Bulgaria and Luxemberg, Yugaslavia and outside Europe, the USA, Union of South Africa, British India and New Zealand and Japan. The frequent opportunity for intercourse and exchange of views, afforded by periodical meetings of the commission at their central bureau, Berne, Switzerland has been now for many years slowly creating a solidarity among nations, resulting in a general agreement not only as to the fundamental conditions of imprisonment, but also as to those preventive measures which obviate the necessity for imprisonment at all.

The modern school of hygiene preventive to which succeeding Prison Congresses give increasing voice and impetus, holds the field today. It advocates prevention which will operate by the elimination of the social causes which create unhealthy environment and by the encouragement of scientific treatment of the weak in mind or in body, so that, if possible the germs of anti-social conduct may be diagnosed, before it is too late, and if possible destroyed by appropriate handling and treatment, these are counsels of perfection, which the future may see developed into actualities.

After 2,000 years we are coming back to the old Roman definition of prison viz., *ad contindos, non ad puniendos*. Prison will be primarily for safe custody and there will be no penal infliction beyond deprivation of liberty, which is, after all, the only and the greatest punishment. Subject to this, every possible effort will be made by industrial training, by education, by lectures and debates, by well-recognized visitation to create a sense of dignity and self-respect and of duty to all fellow creatures.[61]

7. (i) Second World War

In September 1939 war broke out on the continent of Europe and the conflagration soon enveloped the entire world. The popular government went out of office on the issue of war thus bringing an era of active penal reforms to an abrupt close. During the war no major legal changes were introduced in the prison system. The rulers were wholly pre occupied with war problems and had no time to devote to prison affairs. In 1942, they were faced with bitterest Satyagraha movement launched by the Congress. Thousands of Congressmen were locked in jails which were filled beyond their capacity. Due to over-crowding proper treatment could not be given to these Satyagrahis and the lot of the ordinary prisoners was even worse. This extraordinary situation continued till the popular government upon resumption of power set itself upon the task left unfinished by it in 1939.[62]

Comparing to the First International War, the Second International War was most destructive war in the world history. The Second World War, produced the most destructive weapons i.e. nuclear weapons, unknown in human history. It replaced the defunct League of Nations by the United Nations Organization. Yet, it failed to create any new ideology to serve the world better. Simply, it continued the Internationalism, which was a product of the First World War. This war failed to create any new idea concerning prison and prisoners. Simply, it continued the prison reformation further throughout the world including British India.

Prior to the arrival of the British, the modern prison system was not in existence in India. The emergence and changes in the Modern prison system are the result of recommendations made by different commissions from time to time.[63]

(ii) Reformation of the Prisoners of War

Modern thought on the treatment of Prisoners of War was succinctly stated by Montesquieu in Del'esprit des lois and by J.J.

Rousseau in his Social Contract. Both held that the right of the captor over the prisoner was limited to preventing him from taking up arms again and ceased altogether with the end of hostilities. Their view was elaborated by Emerich de VATTEL. Although no general international convention was reached before 1899 regarding Prisoners of War, the humane view found wide acceptance, though it was not always practiced. During the American Civil War Francis Lieber drew up General Order No. 100, which was the basis for subsequent conventions. The First International Convention on Prisoners of War was signed at the Hague Peace Conference of 1899.[64] It was widened by Hague Convention of 1907. The existing law on the subject is based on Convention IV of the Hague Conference of 1907, which conference adopted, with certain changes, the rules made by the Hague Conference of 1899, and the articles relating to PoW contained in the Geneva Convention of 1906. After the First World War, in which the Hague rules proved insufficient, the International Red Cross proposed a more complete code. At the invitation of the Swedish government, 47 governments meeting at Geneva in 1929 signed the Geneva Convention Relating to the Treatment of Prisoners of War. Chief among the nations that did not adhere to the Geneva Convention of 1929 were Japan and the USSR. Japan however, gave a qualified promise (1942) to abide by the Geneva rules and the USSR announced (1941) that it would observe the terms of the Hague Convention of 1907, which did not provide (as does the Geneva Convention) for neutral inspection of prison camps, for the exchange of prisoner's names, and for correspondence with prisoners. According to the Geneva Convention no Prisoner of War could be forced to disclose to his captor any information other than his identity (i.e., his name and rank, but not his military unit, home town, or address of relatives). Every Prisoner of War was entitled to adequate food and medical care and had the right to exchange correspondence and receive parcels. He was required to observe ordinary military discipline and courtesy, but he could attempt to escape at his own risk. Once recaptured he was not to be punished for his attempt. Officers were to receive pay either according to the pay scale of their own country or to that of their captor whichever was less; they could not be required to work. Enlisted men might be required to work for pay, but the nature and location of their work was not to expose them to danger and in no case could they be required to perform work directly related to military operations. Camps, were to be open to inspection by authorized representatives of a neutral power. In the Second World War, Switzerland and Sweden acted as protecting powers. The International Red Cross at Geneva acted as clearing house for the exchange of all information regarding Prisoners of War and had charge of transmitting correspondence and parcels. It accomplished its true gigantic task with remarkable efficiency. With minor and inevitable exceptions on the lower levels, the United States and Great Britain fully honoured the Geneva Convention throughout the conflict. Japan at first committed such attrocities as the "Death March of Bataan", but began to abide by the rules after a sufficient number of Japanese prisoners had fallen into Allied hands to make reprisals possible. Germany did not treat all its prisoners alike. Americans and British subjects received the best treatment, Polish prisoners the worst. The changed methods of the Second World War, the maltreatment of Prisoners of War which constituted an important part of the war crimes indictments, and the retention of a great number of German Prisoners of War by the USSR for several years after the war, showed that the 1929 Convention required revision on many points. In 1945 the Nobel Peace Prize was awarded to the International Red Cross Committee for its work done on behalf of Prisoners of War of all nationalities during the Second World War. In 1946,1947 several meetings were held at Geneva, organised by the International Red Cross, to consider revision of the Clauses of the 1929 Convention which affected Prisoners of War.[65] A new convention, reaffirming and supplementing the 1929 Convention, was signed at Geneva in 1949 and subsequently ratified by almost all nations. It broadened the categories of persons entitled to the Prisoner of War status, clearly redefined the conditions of captivity, and reaffirmed the principle of immediate release and repatriation at the end of hostilities. The Korean War raised new problems, however. Although the North Koreans promised to respect the Geneva Convention, they refused to recognize the impartial status of the Red Cross and denied it access to the territory they controlled. The unprecedented refusal of prisoners to be repatriated, moreover, established, a new principle of political asylum for Prisoners of War.

References

1. Amrendra Mohanty and Narayan Hazary: *op. cit*, p. 18.
2. Datir (R.N.): *op. cit.*, pp. 1-2.
3. Wolff (Michael): *op. cit.*, p. 251.
4. *Ibid.*, pp. 251-54.
5. Compton's Pictured Encyclopaedia and Fact—Index, *op. cit.*, p. 415.
6. Vidya Bhushan: *op. cit.*, p. 5.
7. *Ibid.* p.5.
8. Amrendra Mohanty and Narayan Hazary: *op. cit.*, p. 19.
9. International Encyclopaedia of Facts ed. by Harold Wheeler: *op. cit.*, pp. 593-94.
10. Vidya Bhushan: *op. cit.*, p. 5.
11. *Ibid.* p. 5.
12. *Ibid.*
13. Compton's Pictured Encyclopaedia and Fact—Index, *op. cit.*, pp. 415-16.
14. Vidya Bhushan: *op. cit.*, p. 6.
15. *Ibid.*
16. *Ibid.*
17. Encyclopaedia Britannica., Vol. 18, p. 515.
18. Vidya Bhushan: *op. cit.*, p. 6.
19. Encyclopaedia Britannica: Vol. 18, p. 515.
20. Vidya Bhushan: *op. cit.*, p. 7.
21. International Encyclopaedia of Facts, *op. cit.*, pp. 594-95.
22. *Ibid.*, p. 595.
23. *Ibid.*, p. 596.
24. *Ibid.* pp. 596-97.
25. Vidya Bhushan: *op. cit.*, p.7.
26. *Ibid.*
27. *Ibid.* pp. 7-8.
28. *Ibid.*
29. *Ibid.*
30. *Ibid.*
31. *Ibid.*
32. *Ibid.* p. 262.

33. Compton's Pictured Encyclopaedia and Fact—Index, *op. cit.*, pp. 415-16.
34. Encyclopaedia Britannica, Vol.14, 1977, p. 1103.
35. Vidya Bhushan: *op. cit.*, p. 262.
36. *Ibid.* p. 263.
37. *Ibid*, p. 264.
38. Compton's Pictured Encyclopaedia and Fact—Index, *op. cit.*, pp. 415-16.
39. Dr. Trivedi (B.V): *op. cit.*, p. 1.
40. *Ibid.* pp. 24-25.
41. Madan G.R.: *Indian Social Problems*, Vol. 1, Allied, New Delhi, 1997, p. 126.
42. Indra J. Singh: *op. cit.*, p. 23.
43. Vidya Bhushan: *op. cit.*, pp. 17, 104
44. Nagla B.K.: Prison Administration in India. Indian Journal of Public Administration, XXXV, October-December, 1989, p.116.
45. Vidya Bkushan: *op. cit.*, p.17.
46. Madan G.R.: *op. cit.*, p. 127.
47. Vidya Bhushan: *op. cit.*, p. 18
48. Madan G.R.: *op. cit.*, p. 126.
49. *Ibid.* p. 127.
50. Vidya Bhushan: *op. cit.*, p. 18.
51. Nagla B.K.: *op. cit*, p. 1017.
52. *Ibid.*
53. Karnataka State Gazetteer, Part II, 1983, pp. 438-40.
54. Manorama Year Book, 1994, pp. 695-99.
55. Amrendra Mohanty and Narayan Hazary: *op. cit.*, p. 26.
56. Vidya Bhushan: *op. cit*, p. 22.
57. Kum Kum Chadha: *op. cit*, p. 151.
58. Armendra Mohanty and Narayan Hazary: *op. cit*, p. 26.
59. Nagla B.K.: *op. cit.*, p. 1017.
60. Planning Commission. Plans and Prospects of Social Welfare in India, 1951-61, Government of India, New Delhi, 1963, p. 143.
61. Howard Jones and Paul Comes: *Open Prisons*, Routledge and Kegan Paul, London, 1977, pp. 1-13.
62. Encyclopaedia Britannica, 14th ed., Vol, 18, p. 518.
63. Vidya Bhushan: *op. cit*, p. 31.

64. Nagla B.K.: *op. cit*, pp. 1017-18.
65. Columbia Encyclopaedia, Columbia University Press, New York, 1968, p. 1724.

4
Prison Administration in Independent India

1. Post-Second World War System

The whole world was divided into Capitalist camp and Communist camp. Both the camps, i.e., Capitalist and Communist, were ever-ready to fight the Third International War to establish supremacy of one over another. In this Cold War nationalism was still spreading along with internationalism. In such an international dangerous environment, the Imperial Britain granted national independence to India on 15th August 1947. Independent India, did not align to any camp. Yet, it adopted the Capitalistic system. India joined the UNO before it secured independence and continued its membership after independence. Already India was a member of the International Prison Congress. Consequently, India was expected to follow the international standard in prison administration.

2. Prison Administration in Independent India

Towards the reformation of the prison administration in independent India, the Government of India took some interest in the matters of changes in the prison system. The Government of India passed the Exchange of Prisoners Act, 1948.[1] In 1950, the Transfer of Prisoners Act, was passed by the Government of India. This Act made provision for the removal of prisoners from one State to another.[2]

The leaders of the movement of the Indian independence and internationalism specially UNO repeatedly suffered incarceration at the hands of imperial rulers. Prison under foreign rulers was "The Gaol a place of dread". It was, therefore, legitimately assumed that the leaders of movement of Indian independence and upholders of internationalism and the UNO who became rulers of independent India would accord highest priority to prison reforms by converting them from institution of horror to modern reclamation and correctional centres.

In the Constitution of India prison administration has been included in the State List.[3] As prison rules and regulations vary from one State to another, the much-needed co-ordination was lacking. However, it was realized soon after independence that the Jail Manuals of the States of the Union Territories based on the antediluvian Prisons Act of 1894, could not cope with the changing times. It was felt very strongly that some broad guidelines should be given from the Centre with a view to co-ordinating the prison reform programmes of the different State Governments.

The decade 1951-60 in India was a decade of enthusiasm for prison reforms. Local committees were appointed by some State Governments (viz., Madras, Orissa, Uttar Pradesh and Maharashtra) to suggest prison reforms.

3. UN Assistance

To follow international standard in prison administration, India had requested the UNO in 1951 to send an expert in prison reformation under its Technical Assistance Programme, for imparting a training course to the selected jail officers and to suggest progressive programmes for the scientific care and treatment of offenders. Accordingly, Dr. W.C. Wreckless came to India and in his report suggested many valuable changes, most of which were not, in essence, radically different from the recommendations of the Indian Jails Committee of 1919. Dr. Wreckless made a number of recommendations.[4] The chief among which were regarding the setting up of a Central Bureau of Correctional Services at Delhi and revising the Jail Manuals. He specifically wanted the development of whole time probation and after care services, the establishment of new jails to perform specialised functions, legal substitutes for short sentences of imprisonment, reduction in the number of under trial prisoners, separation of juvenile delinquents from the adults and the revision of jail manuals.[5] Dr. Wreckless's services were also utilised in training a batch of 47 senior jail officers drawn from different states in modem methods of jail administration. In 1952, the Uttar Pradesh Government started a new experiment in open prison under the name of Sampurnanand Camp. In some other States also open prisons were set up. Prison welfare officers were appointed in a number of States in later years. A few new ideas of prison reforms were introduced in the country during this decade. The prisoners could now avail of furlough and parole. They were granted wages, albeit nominal, for the work done by them. In 1952, the Government of Bombay introduced the system of prison panchayats in the prisons.[6] Prior to this, the Uttar Pradesh Jail Reforms Committee endorsed the observation and recommendations made by previous committees concerning introduction of 'panchayat' system, etc. The introduction of panchayat system led to some improvement in the living conditions of prisoners. Jail Training Schools were set up in some States.

4. All India Conference of Inspectors-General of Prisons

The year 1952 further witnessed a breakthrough in national coordination on correctional work. An All India Conference of Inspectors-General of Prisons was held in Bombay in 1952 which also recommended the setting up of a committee to draft a skeleton Model Jail Manual. The Central Government passed Prisoners (Attendance in Courts) Act, 1955.[7] Whipping was abolished in 1955 and the Probation of Offenders Act was enacted in 1958.[8]

5. UNO Standard Minimum Rules for the Treatment of Prisoners

The UNO held its First Congress on the Prevention of Crime and Treatment of Offenders at Geneva in 1955. The Congress approved the UNO Standard Minimum Rules for the Treatment of Prisoners and urged the Member Nations to modify their national practices accordingly. This further strengthened the international standard of prison administration. India was expected to follow the UNO Standard Minimum Rules for the Treatment of Prisoners.

6. All India Jail Manual Committee

In pursuance of the recommendations of Dr. Wreckless and All India Conference of Inspectors-General, the Government of India appointed an All India Jail Manual Committee in 1957 to (i) prepare an All India Skeleton Jail Manual, (ii) examine the Prisons Act and other relevant Central Laws, and suggesting any necessary Central legislation, and (iii) make proposals for prison reforms to be adopted uniformly throughout the country. In order that the problems peculiar to different parts of the country and the need of coordination by the Centre might be given due emphasis, the All India Jail Manual Committee was constituted, among others, with the then Inspectors-General of Prisons of Bombay, Madras, West Bengal, Uttar Pradesh, Punjab and Kerala.

This Committee of 1957-59 studied the problems of crime and delinquency from a very progressive angle and poignantly observed that the solutions to these problems do not only in prisons but in the larger socio-economic fields as well. It felt, that these problems "can be solved neither by making punishment more deterrent nor by making the system of punishment too weak and diluted". The Committee wanted prisons to be transformed into correctional institutions. In consonance with its radical approach to the problems of crime and delinquency and to the prime objective of correctional administration, this Committee furnished a detailed report containing necessary principles of modernization of prisons together with a Model Prison Manual in 1960 on a broad guide line for the States to revise their outdated Prison Manuals.

Among the various recommendations of the Committee, the following are the important ones: (i) The Correctional Services, i.e. the prisons, probation, after-care and institutional services for children should be integrated under a Director or Commissioner of Correctional Administration and be under the control of the Home Department, (ii) An O&M Division should be established to devote exclusive attention to the orderly growth and dynamic development of the organization, (iii) The Deputy Inspectors-General should be incharge of various divisions and there should be a separate Deputy Inspector-General for health services in prisons, (iv) The probation system should be used on a more extensive scale than at present in order to reduce the pressure on prisons, (v) There should be a well arranged network of diversified institutions, (vi) A Central Bureau of Correctional Services should be organized at the Union level, (vii) A Central Advisory Board should be set up by the Government of India and there should be a Research and Planning unit in each state, (viii) An All India Correctional Services should be set up, (ix) There should be a separation of executive and clerical functions and of executive and accounts functions, (x) There should be a State After Care Organization in each state, (xi) The Jail Manual should be revised periodically, (xii) Classification of prisoners should be dynamic.

7. Central Bureau of Correctional Services

Another major post-Independence development in the Indian prison administration took place, i.e., in pursuance of the recommendations of the All India Jail Manual Committee, the Government of India set up a Central Bureau of Correctional Services in 1961 as a central technical advisory body. Its main functions are to coordinate and develop uniform policy, to standardise the collection of statistics on a national basis, to exchange information with foreign government and the UN agencies and to promote research, training and studies and surveys in the field of prevention of crime and treatment of offences. The Bureau functioned under the Government of India's Ministiy of Home Affairs until 1964, when it was transferred to the newly created Department of Social Security, now known as the Ministry of Social Welfare. It was reconstituted in 1975 as the National Institute of Social Defence. Its functions were enlarged to include preventive, correctional and rehabilitative aspects of social defence, viz., welfare of prisoners, prison reforms, prison administration, juvenile vagrancy, probation, beggary, social and moral hygiene, alcoholism, gambling, drug addiction etc. The Institute continues to work under the Ministry of Social Welfare and has been playing "a useful role" in its enlarged field of social defence.[9] The Bureau convened an All India Seminar on Correctional Services at New Delhi in 1969. The seminar reported that excepting in very few States the recommendations of the All India Jail Manual Committee were not implemented.

During the decade 1951-60 the Central and State Governments took the task of prison reforms with spirit and enthusiasm. But, this did not last long. The valuable recommendations of these committees were not implemented effectively. Official apathy and bureaucratic bungling continued. Even after the end of another decade (1961-70) the general state of prison administration in the country was described by an official committee as "depressing".

Our jails were terribly overcrowded. In 1961, there were 1,176 prison institutions in the country and these included 52 central jails, 180 district jails, 919 sub-jails, 2 juvenile jails, 9 Borstals, 3 women's jails and 5 open jails. By 1970 the total number of institutions had come down to 1,170 and yet admissions to jails in 1970 were 13,78,657 as compared to 11,05,896 in 1961. During this period the number of undertrials also rose: in 1960 there were 5,93,398 undertrials as against 4,12,498 convicts. In 1970 there were 9,38,598 undertrials as against 4,40,059 convicts.Thus while the convict admission rose by 7 per cent only, the admission of undertrials rose by 58 per cent. As the total accommodation remained the same it had led to more and more undertrials living with convicts, contrary to the requirement of Section 27 of the Prison Act, 1894. The huddling together of a large number of undertrials with convicted prisoners and the mixing together of old and hardened ciiminals with young first offenders tend to promote in the minds of all inmates feelings of criminality instead of remorse and regret for their previous conduct and a desire to reform.

Apart from the overcrowding in jails, the general manner in which the rituals of the daily life inside the jails were rigidly administered and enforced tends to dehumanise the prisoner who is cowed down by oppressive atmosphere around with all its brutalities, stench, degradation and insult. Instead of functioning as a reformatory house to rehabilitate the criminal to reform him and made him see the error of his ways and return a better and nobler man, the ethos inside our jails was tragically set in the opposite direction, making it practically difficult for any reformatory process to operate meaningfully.[10]

8. Working Group on Prisons

In 1972, the Government of India's Ministry of Home Affairs appointed a Working Group on prisons for (i) examining the physical and administrative conditions of the jails in the country and suggesting ways and means of their improvement, (ii) laying down standards in respect of different services and facilities in the jails, (iii) laying down an order of priorities for the prison development schemes, and (iv) considering their allied matters concerning prisons and prisoners. This Committee submitted its report in 1973. The Working Group on Prisons made a number of recommendations and the State Governments were asked by the Central Government to implement such recommendations. This Committee recommended for (i) the establishment of a Research Unit at the headquarters of the Inspector-General of prisons in each State, (ii) the setting up of a training institute in each State as well as of Regional Training Institute, (iii) diversification of the institutions, accommodation and other connected matters, etc. The most remarkable recommendation of this Working Group was that it recommended the inclusion of prisons in the Five-Year Plan and a provision of Rs. 100 crore. It thought that a prison administration could not be streamlined unless the Government of India and the State Governments made available more resources for developing every aspect of the existing system. As a follow up of this report, the Ministry of Home Affairs initiated efforts for the improvement and modernization of jail administration by making a grant of Rs. 2 crore in the budget for 1977-78 and of Rs. 4 crore in the budget of 1978-79. The Working Group on Prisons emphasized the need for a National Policy on Prison and Correctional Administration, it discarded the traditional prison-based policy. The report of the Group identified the main elements of proposed National Policy.[11] The more important of them being as follows:

1. A suitable system should be established for coordination among the three organs of the criminal justice system i.e. the police, the judiciary and the prison and correctional administration, for the effective prevention of crime and treatment of offenders.
2. The supreme aim of punishment was to be the protection of society through the rehabilitation of offender. The principal goals of the criminal justice system was the reassimilation of the offender in society and the prevention of crime. Accordingly, the aim of the prison administration was to be the employment of all resources, human and material, to provide scientific

treatment to every offender according to his peculiar needs and circumstances.

3. The deprivation of liberty and segregation from society was to be limited mostly to the habitual, the incorrigible and the dangerous criminals and the Government should make fullest possible use of various alternatives to imprisonment as a measure of sentencing policy. Non-institutional and semi-institutional forms of treatment should be resorted to as far as possible.
4. There was to be close coordination between the prison and the probation and other correctional services.
5. Free legal aid to all indigent prisoners.
6. Undertrial prisoners were to be kept in separate institutions as far as possible. Facilities were to be provided to them for work on a voluntary basis.
7. The Union and State Governments declare that there was to be no bar or restriction on the employment of ex-convicts of specified categories in the public services.
8. The prison administration should systematically involve enlightened individual citizens, associations, societies and other community agencies on the treatment, after-care and rehabilitation of offenders.[12]

To bring desired changes in the prison administration as a whole, the Group recommended that the top priority was to be given to the adoption of the National Policy on Prisons as suggested by them along with the inclusion of certain aspects of the prison administration in the Five-Year Plan, to include the subject of prisons and allied institutions in the Concurrent List, the enactment of suitable legislation by the Centre as well as by the States, and the revision of the State Prison Manuals.

To help the State Governments in their efforts to undertake jail reforms, the Central Government formulated a scheme in 1977 to give financial assistance for prison reforms. Accordingly, the Seventh Finance Commission had recommended allocation of Rs. 48.31 crores to 11 states in the form of grants-in-aid for five years (1979-84) for upgradation of standards of jail administration including upkeep of prisoners. Priority was accorded by the Commission to ensure adequate direct expenditure on food, clothing and medicines for prisoners, to improve basic amenities like water supply, sanitary facilities, electrification, etc. and to develop additional jail capacity in States.[13]

9. Conference of Chief Secretaries

In 1979, a Confèrence of Chief Secretaries made a number of recommendations to reduce the overcrowding in jails. This included the establishment of an effective system of regular review of cases of undertrials, appointment of part-time or whole-time law officers in jails to enable the undertrials to contest their cases in courts, setting up of new courts and amendment of the law relating to the transfer of prisoners. The other recommendations made by this conference were: creation of separate facilities for the care, treatment and rehabilitation of women offenders, segregation of juveniles, improving the system of inspection and supervision in jails, strengthening of training facilities for jail staff, work programme for all able bodied persons, setting up of state and national boards of visitors and revision of state Jail Manuals on the lines of the Model Prison Manual.

In response to a national demand in 1979, the former Prime Minister Morarji Desai dedicated the cellular jail of Andaman and Nicobar Islands as a National Memorial.[14] The planning and monitoring of the schemes recommended by the Seventh Finance Commission were assigned to the National Institute of Social Defence through the Ministry of Home Affairs.

10. All India Committee on Jail Reforms

Several reports and articles appeared in the press about the conditions of jails, particularly in Tihar Jail, Delhi, and most of the jails in Uttar Pradesh and Bihar where a number of undertrial prisoners were confined without trial for over 10 years.The Supreme Court of India in various judgements had brought out the shortcomings in the prison administration in the country and pointed out the inadequacy of prisons to function as centres of reformation. The Government of India, therefore appointed a committee, viz., the All India Committee on Jail Reforms headed by Justice A.N. Mulla (retired) in April 1980 for making a comprehensive review of prison administration in the country and suggesting suitable measures for its improvement. This committee submitted its final report in 1983.

There was overcrowding in the prisons and the buildings were dilapidated. All types of prisoners including undertrials, convicts, casuals, habituals juvenile and young adult offenders, female offenders, mentally sick and physically handicapped were generally lodged in the same institution. It left little scope for their specialised treatment and training. According to the All India Committee on Jail Reforms, 1980-83, there were 16 Central Prisons, 250 district prisons, 822 sub-jails, 27 open jails and 20 special jails in 1980. The total capacity of all these institutions was 79,544, 63,654, 26,057, 6,640 arid 4,626 respectively. There were also 6 institutions for women offenders, 8 juvenile jails and 11 Borstal schools with an inmate capacity of 975, 1,827, and 2,102 respectively. Out of a total of 1,59,692 prisoners, 92,276 were undertrials.[15] Thus more than half of the total prison population were undertrials. While commenting on the problem of overcrowding, the Committee observed, "Overcrowded prisons tend to be unmanageable on correctional lines. In some of the States, prison barracks are so overcrowded that inmates have to sleep in shifts. Under such conditions custody of inmates becomes the primary and probably the only, concern of the staff and even the care and welfare of inmates is neglected. The frequent influx of large number of agitators further worsens the situation and aggravates the problem of prison management". It noted with profound regret that the United Nations Standard Minimum Rules for the Treatment of Prisoners were not being generally observed in several States and Union Territories in India and that the conditions of prisons in the country had been deteriorating and had reached a point of crisis. One of the main reasons for this general deterioration, according to the Committee, was the lack of national commitment arising out of a national consensus on the goals and objectives of prison administration and modalities of achieving them. The Committee had, therfore, formulated the draft of a National Policy on Prisons and recommended for its adoption by the Government of India in consultation with the State Government and Union Territory Administrations. The goals and objectives of prisons in India, according to the proposed National Policy on Prisons, were to protect society and to reform and reassimilate offenders in the social milieu by giving them appropriate correctional treatment. The Committee, however, felt that crime being a social problem cannot be tackled merely through legislation or pronouncement of laudable objectives.

It therefore recommended that a regular plan aiming at creating a favourable rehabilitation culture in the society should be drawn up and implemented by prison administration. Among the important suggestions made by the Committee were:

(a) Directive Principle of National Policy on Prisons had to be formulated and embodied in Part 4 of the Indian Constitution.

(b) The subject of Prisons and allied institutions were to be included in the Concurrent List of Seventh Schedule of the Constitution of India.

(c) Provision of an uniform framework for correctional administration by a consolidated, new and uniform comprehensive legislation to be enacted by the Parliament for the entire country.

(d) Revision of Jail Manuals should be given top priority.

(e) Suitable amendment of Indian Penal Code.[16]

The follow up action on the report had been initiated by the Ministry of Home Affairs in consultation with concerned ministries and department of the Central and State Governments.

11. Committee on Women Prisoners

The Government of India further constituted a Committee on Women Prisoners in May 1986 with retired justice of Supreme Court V.K. Krishna Ayer as the chairman. The Committee submitted its report in 1987. The major recommendations of this committee were:

(a) Provision of a national policy relating to the women prisoners in India.

(b) Formation of new rules and regulations relating to their punishment and conduct.

(c) Maintenance of proper coordination among the Police, Law and Prison for providing due justice to women prisoners.

(d) Provision of legal-aid for them.

(e) Construction of separate prisons for women prisoners.

(f) Proper care of the baby born in jail to a woman prisoner and provision of nutritious diet for the mother and the child.[17]

12. Juvenile Justice Act

With a view to providing a uniform pattern of justice to juveniles throughout the country, the Juvenile Justice Act, 1986 was enacted by Parliament in December 1986 replacing children's Acts in various states and union territories, and it came into force in 1987 throughout the country. It provides for care, protection, treatment, development and rehabilitation of neglected or delinquent juveniles and adjudication of certain matters relating to, and dispose of, delinquents. It laid down a uniform legal framework so as to ensure that no child under any circumstances is lodged in jail or police lock-up. Juvenile welfare boards and juvenile courts have been established to provide for a specialised approach towards neglected and delinquent juveniles respectively. During the pendency of any enquiry regarding the juvenile, be sent to an observation home or a place of safety. After the completion of enquiry neglected and delinquent juveniles be lodged in juvenile homes and special homes respectively. The Act represents a blueprint for fair, equitable and just treatment of juveniles with due emphasis on the rights of child.[18]

In order to effectively implement this Act, Union Ministry of Welfare implemented a centrally-sponsored scheme for prevention and control of juvenile maladjustment since 1986-87. Under this scheme, assistance is provided for setting up/upgradation of observation homes, juvenile homes, special homes and after-care facilities as well as training of functionaries. Expenditure is shared between Central and State Governments equally.

There is a dearth of after-care organisation for the rehabilitation of juveniles who have no one to back upon after their release from the correctional institutions. As Professor K.S. Shukla points out, "After-care schemes were started in the last decade of the last century, but they have not shown signs of growth numerically or structurally. Although they have an unenviable role in the rehabilitative process and are important for a released juvenile, yet, except in Maharashtra, Tamil Nadu, U.P., West Bengal and Delhi, they have not been able to assume systematised and concrete shape. Both official and non-official agencies may have to share the blame for inadequate attention to this scheme".[19] Thus special efforts will have to be made to make up this deficiency in States which lack these facilities.

Fact Sheet

Total number of prisons, prisoners etc. in 1994	
Total number of prisons	584
Population (appx.)	2,00,000
Category of Inmates	
Undertrials	77%
Detainees	0.02%
Convicts	22.96%
Jail Term	
6-12 Months	46%
Life imprisonment	13.1%
Capital punishment	0.1%
Type of Offenders	
First-time offenders	87.29%
Repeaters	12.47%
Habituals	0.29%

Source: National Prison Statistics, 1994.

13. 1.5 Lakh Undertrials to be Freed

Union Minister of State for Home Ram Lal Rahi said in 1996 that, there was a proposal to release over 1,55,000 undertrials languishing in 1,215 jails across the country on probation, leave and work release permits. This would not only decongest the jails, but also improve maintenance and management of the overcrowded jails. The State Governments would be directed to set up review committees to "expedite disposal of undertrial cases". These committees would make wider use of alternative to imprisonment including probation, open institution and work release permits.

Mr. Rahi, after reviewing the problems of jails at the National Conference of Inspectors-General of Prisons, said there was need for a one-time review of all cases. He said there were 2,26,580 prisoners in the country and the ratio of undertrials was around 70 per cent. Most of them were without trial for a long period of time and it was necessary to provide them justice by reviewing their cases.[21]

The conditions of Indian prisons are highly deplorable. These are the walled houses of cruelty, torture and defiled dignity. The jail manuals are antiquated, the architecture is primitive and the attitude of the jail authorities towards crime and criminals is not only indifferent, but unpardonably dehumanising. Sub-human living conditions, prison riots, jail breaks and frequent escape of detenus are other disturbing aspects.

As per our judicial philosophy, all the jails are expected to serve the four major objectives: retribution, incapacitation, deterrence and rehabilitation. Crimes against society have to be punished and, therefore, criminals have to pay to society by loosing part of their freedom. The law-breakers have to be segregated.

The ground realities are no jail in the country has the sources for keeping prisoners in healthy surroundings. No prison has an imaginative reformatory system governed by officers and men who want to bring about a change of heart, or of attitude towards self and society, in a criminal. In fact, casual wrong-doers become hardened criminals during their period of stay in jails. Poor sanitation and overcrowding plague almost all the jails. About the plight of women inmates and young persons less said the better. The funds made available for jail inmates are often misappropriated.

The Government has still to evolve guidelines for prison management on modem lines. Although the subject has been examined in depth by four committees that have probed it since 1919-20 and in four landmark judgments of the apex court in 1978, 1980 and 1981, the fact remains that prison authorities pay scant regard to the guidelines evolved. They do not adhere even to the UNO Standard Minimum Rules for Treatment of Prisoners 1955. Worse still, their decisions are dictated by a piece of legislation—the Prisons Act—which was enacted in 1894 by a colonial government that saw jails as places to break the back of the nationalist movement. No wonder our prisons continue to uphold archaic rules like allowing "convict officers", mostly hardened criminals, to manage the affairs of their fellow inmates. This is because there is no all-India cadre of officers to manage the overcrowded prisons.

The NHRC asked for a radical change in the entire prison system. It wants all the States and the Union Territories to come up with a consensus for bringing about a standard jail manual applicable uniformly throughout the country. It can initiate meaningful changes which can ultimately find a concrete form in a "Model Prison Act". It is necessary to have such conditions in the prisons as have non-discriminatory treatment, proper medical facilities and a modium of human dignity reflected through the behaviour of those who look after the inmates. A multi-disciplinary approach of this kind is needed to tackle the various problems. The Ministry of Law, the Institute of Criminology and Forensic Science and voluntary organisations committed to the protection of human rights can play a meaningful role in this regard.

A visible prison policy should focus primarily on the reductionist methods adopted by several countries, including Japan, England, America and Holland by which they are to reduce the prison population and the infrastructure as well. In order to do this, a multi-pronged strategy was formulated. The judiciary was asked to exercise restraint as regards incarceration for minor offenders. Undertrials were let out on parole, probation and bail. Also in the late seventies, Holland, England and Japan introduced heavy fines and confiscation of property as viable alternative to imprisonment. In India this concept is yet to be implemented seriously.

Similarly remand homes in India meant for juveniles need urgent reforms. The infrastructure is not even in keeping with the Juvenile Justice Rules. Political patronage and destructive trade unionism have adversely affected the welfare of juvenile in most such homes. Legal experts and social welfare organisations should have a major say in jail reforms in india and should make self-determination, not determinism.[22]

The Central Government has been adopting some outdated methods in the name of reformation of prisoners. The Central Government told the States in January 1996 to play cassettes containing excerpts from religious scriptures and sermons of spiritual leaders in all prisons and spiritual leaders be invited once or twice a week to personally address the jail inmates to inculcate the ideals of tolerance and compassion, among the prisoners.[23]

Mr. H. D. Devegowda's Central Government announced the United Front's Common Minimum Programme in 1996. In this programme the following were there: (i) Backlog of all court cases to be cleared within three years, (ii) United Nations Convention on Torture to be adopted, (iii) Penal laws to be reviewed and amended with human rights protected.[24]

The National Commission of Women in 1996 visited several jails and talked to women undertrials and prisoners who were languishing in various jails as undertrials for over five years which meant they had already spent more years in prison than they could had if they had been convicted. As a ray of hope, by the end of 1996 the Commission hoped to get 5,000 women released.[25]

14. Role of National Human Rights Commission in Prison Administration

According to the protection of Human Rights Act, 1993, the National Human Rights Commission (NHRC) has been established. Since its inception, the NHRC has been playing an important role in prison administration. It has made the following major recommendations.

The NHRC in its annual report of 1994-95, had recommended that the Indian Prisons Act of 1894 revised to reform the prison system and a new all-India jail manual be prepared to serve as a model. It concluded that the prison system is "seriously in need of reform, nationwide. It is mired in attitudes and practices that are antiquated at best, but that often border on the intolerable."

'"Reliance on the century-old Act of 1894 is symptomatic of the lack of vision or progress in this area", the Commission Chaired by Justice Ranganath Mishra, felt. The report said that many such as Tihar Jail in Delhi were overcrowded. Yet, others like the open jail in Hyderabad, were underutilised. In some jails, it said, "callousness prevailed, prisoners were seen in shackles, mentally disturbed inmates-regardless of whether they were criminal or otherwise were incarcerated with others, with no real effort being made to rise above the very minimum required for the meanest survival". Where prisoners worked, their remuneration was often a pittance, offering scant hope of savings being generated for future rehabilitation in society. The Commission during its visits saw many jails which are squalid, such as the newly constructed central jail in Patna. In yet others, it said the diet was inferior, and the management was denounced by the inmates as brutal and corrupt, often within a single state, conditions varied from one jail to another.

The Commission which had in the past expressed deep concern over overcrowding, lack of sanitation, poor medical facilities and inadequate diet in prisons, the core of the problem is the apathy and lack of priority accorded to prison conditions. What lies at the root of the difficulties was the apathy towards the rights of prisoners and undertrials, said the Commission, which has already expressed dismay at reports of the delay in the disposal of cases and mismanagement in the administration of prisons.

In its endeavour to remedy the inadequacies in the prisons, the Commission under took a study of certain key reports to examine the best ways in which their recommendations can, wherever necessary, be reactivated. These include the report of the all-India Jail Manual Committee of 1957-59, the report of the All-India Committee on Jail Reforms 1980-83, report of the National Expert Committee on Women Prisoners of 1987 and the Report of the Group of Officers on Prison Administration. In addition, The Commission remains most mindful of the need for the country to abide by the UN Standard Minimum Rules for the Treatment of Prisoners, 1955, the annual report said.

Proceeding in a number of ways, the Commission was updating its data on a nationwide basis and called a meeting of all home secretaries and inspectors general of prisons to look into all aspects of prison reform. The meeting was to focus on the nature and reasons for overcrowding in jails and the steps needed to remedy the situation, besides the question of remission which varies from state to state, the issue for wages for different categories of work and the question of admission and classification of prisoners. In addition, issues like separate facilities for women and juveniles, custodial arrangements for delinquent children, dietary and medical facilities and improvement of management was also to be discussed.

The Commission raised the matter of sub-jails with state governments and intended to press for minimum standards of decency and responsibility. It said the state legal aid and advice boards and non governmental organisations had a critical role to play. Indeed, the report said, both the creation of public awareness and specific acts that are required to rectify wrongs, call for the continued efforts of all who believe that human dignity must not be left behind when a person enters the gates of a prison.[26]

The report of the NHRC on the state of jails in the country may not add much to the information on the matter but it selves as yet another reminder of the urgent need to improve the country's prison system and the conditions in the prisons. Most of the ills and problems in the jails have been well documented in the past and suggestions for improvement had also not been lacking. However, the situation has only progressively deteriorated and every ill of the jail system had in the past only became worse or grew bigger in spread and magnitude. The Human Rights Commission's report also detailed them and proposed changes in laws and altitudes, adoption of measures by the Government and creation of public awareness to rectify the situation. What was needed was the willingness and wherewithal to translate the proposals and decisions that emerge out of such meeting into concrete measures. The conditions in our jails help only to perpetuate criminal conduct and to make inmate a life-long outlaw. The situation will not change as long as jails continue to be centres for punishment as opposed to these for reforming errant individuals.[27]

The NHRC had recommended systematic reforms of police and prisons and far reaching measures for protection of civil liberties in areas hit by terrorism and insurgency. In its annual report for 1994-95, the Commission recommended to the Government that in States where security forces were called to assist the civil authorities, local magistrates or police officers should be associated, particularly with cordon-and-search operations. Further a suggestion was made to celebrate December 10 as Human Rights Day in all schools, colleges and universities. [28]

Section 12(c) of the Protection of Human Rights Act, 1993, provides that the "Commission shall visit, under intimation to the State Government, any jail or institution under the control of State Government where persons are detained or lodged for purpose of treatment, reformation or protection to study the living conditions of the inmates and make recommendation there on." Accordingly, the NHRC in a letter to chief secretaries of all States and administration of Union Territories, in 1997 urged them to help NHRC investigating teams to undertake visits to police lock-ups in the country to eliminate incidents of custodial violence.[29]

Chairman of the NHRC Ranganathan Mishra said in February 1996 that the Prison Act, 1894 was to be replaced soon alongwith a new jail manual for its countrywide implementation. He said the new Prison Act of 1996 had been finalised and further action on its implementation was to be taken soon. The NHRC also pressed the State Governments to set up State Human Rights Commissions and Human Rights Courts at the district level.[30]

The NHRC rapped the Delhi Government in 1995 for making a mockery of the parole system, as practiced in Tihar Jail. The parole system, originally introduced to give undertrials an opportunity to go out of the jail in cases of medical or any similar emergency. It is supposed to be granted when their near and dear ones are either seriously ill or have died, with the detenu needed to perform the last rites. The Delhi Government which screens and grants parole requests, however, usually takeover two months to grant the permission. Though permission was given in most cases, the purpose of parole was thus defeated. In the light of growing criticism, it was proposed to authorise the jail officials to grant parole as soon as a request comes in.[31]

It was unfortunate that India explored privatisation of jails in 1996 to improve the conditions of prisoners. Two members of the NHRC visited Britain to study privatisation of jails. The visit followed earlier discussions in Britain between Mrs. Kiran Bedi, then Inspector-General of Tihar Jail, and British prison managers. This visit demonstrated willingness to consider privatised jails in India, an option unthinkable until recently.

Private prisons were still relatively new in Britain. In Britain privatisation of prisons commenced only in 1992. The first of the private prisons called "The Wolds" in Northumbersiade in North England was opened in April 1992. In February 1996, there were only four privately run prisons, with more planned, compared to 133 prisons run by the government. There were 2,090 prisoners in privately run jails. The inmates of private prisons were all male. In privatised jails the government pays the jail a fixed sum per prisoner and leaves the rest to the prison managers within given rules. Indian officials say more privately run jails could be a way out of overcrowding in Indian jails.[32] But privatisation of jails is not a remedy neither to jail problems nor jail itself.

Concerned over reports that several non-criminal lunatics have been languishing in normal jails and are being treated on par with criminals, the NHRC has asked the State Governments and Union Territories to transfer mentally ill people from prisons to mental asylum before 31 October 1996. Because, Mental Health Act, which came into force on 1 April,1993, does not permit the mentally ill people to be put into prison.[33] But, this NHRC order directing that all mentally unfit prisoners in Bihar jails should be transferred to mental hospitals, has come as an unexpected boon for the State's prisoners. As many as 113 of them, facing severe charges of murder, loot, arson and dacoity, have got themselves admitted to the *Ranchi Mansik Arogyashala* alone since the order came in October 1996. But, at least 50 per cent of them are sane and mentally sound. Not only does it help them escape life in prison but also strengthens their cases in courts, and it is easy for these hospitalised prisoners to escape from there.[34]

Chairman of the NHRC, Mr. M.N. Venkatachaliah said in an interview in December 1996 that our prisons are a reflection of the state of our society. We have prepared a Prison Bill, to improve prison conditions and to prepare prisoners for a useful life after they are free. The law itself was 102 years old and required updating. Now every custodial death is to be reported to the Commission with a videotape of the post-mortem. Custodial deaths include deaths in jail and police custody.[35]

Alarmed by the rise in the number of custodial deaths and killings during the police encounters, the NHRC has demanded formation of an independent machinery at the State Government level to probe into every single instance of death at the hands of police. This decision was arrived at after consultations with the Solicitor General of India.[36]

To prevent fraud and manipulation in post-mortem examinations in custodial deaths, the NHRC in 1997 had recommended to all the States a model autopsy form and appropriate procedure for conducting inquests.[37]

The NHRC Chairman M.N. Venkatachaliah in 1997 had stressed the need for setting up Human Rights Commissions in states saying it could lighten the workload of the NHRC.[38]

Deaths in police and jail custody are constant reminders of the imperfections that mark civil society. Such human rights abuses are less likely to occur in countries where the role of civil authorities under the law is duly recognised. The NHRC acknowledged this and in August 1995 a letter to chief ministers recommending that videotape of all post-mortem examinations of deaths in police or jail custody, together with the postmortem reports themselves should be sent to the Commission. Because, medical personnel conducting such post-mortems were being pressurised by the police into hiding the full facts of the case and writing slanted, in accurate or even plainly false reports. Earlier in 1997, the Department of Home Affairs and Justice, along with the NHRC, sent another letter reiterating this and insisted that custodial deaths and rapes be reported within a day of their occurrence to the Secretary General, NHRC.

While most of the State Governments fell in line, with the Punjab Government even directing all district magistrates in the state to ensure the adoption of the UN model autopsy protocol, four states felt constrained to demur. As it happens, these four states—Maharashtra, Uttar Pradesh, Rajasthan and Delhi also had some of the worst records of such abuse.

The issue assumes importance in the context of the sharp rise in cases of such abuse. According to NHRC figures, 888 cases of custodial deaths were reported in 1996-97. A state like Maharashtra, now tops the list with 201 instances of deaths in police and jail custody. In its 113th report, the Indian Law Commission had recommended the insertion of Section 114(B) in the 1872 Indian Evidence Act, to the effect that injuries sustained by a person in police custody may be presumed to have been caused by a police officer and the onus of proving that this was not so rested with the police. Such a measure will go some way in demonstrating that the country is committed to fighting human rights abuse, both in letter and spirit.[39]

Probably for the first time in the history of the Central Bureau of Investigation (CBI) in a significant move, the NHRC has asked the country's premier investigating agency, the CBI to pay a compensation of Rs. one lakh for a custodial death in 1996.[40]

The NHRC in December 1997 ruled that an undertrial cannot be put to hard work. It asked the Uttar Pradesh Government to pay an interim compensation of Rs. one lakh to the parents of Ashoka Kumar, an undertrial in Roorkee sub-jail who succumbed to injuries on 28 August, 1996, while carrying a load at the behest of the Roorkee sub-jail authorities. It further said that the State was under obligation to provide adequate medical facilities to every prisoner. The Commission further recommended that this sum be paid within a month.[41]

Concerned over large number of custodial deaths in the country, the NHRC constituted a high level committee of experts to examine the medical facilities in jails in February 1998. Though the prison manuals make medical examination of a person being jailed mandatory, "this in many of the prisons has remained a more procedural formality" presumably because of lack of adequate medical staff and the relative unimportance of the procedure in the scheme of things, NHRC said.[42]

The NHRC, in March 1999, has reiterated that the State Human Rights Commission (SHRC) should be set up in States as expeditiously as possible. The reiteration comes in the wake of the delay on part of the States in setting up the commissions. Only eight States in the country, have set up SHRCs, while Kerala, Gujarat, Rajasthan, Andhra Pradesh, Karnataka and Sikkim are yet to take action, despite expressing their intention to set up the Commission. However, Bihar, Haryana and Delhi have taken the stand that it is not necessary to set up State commissions. In Uttar Pradesh, from where maximum number of cases of custodial deaths are reported, the State Government has rescinded on its decision to set up the SHRC and in a recent notification, said that constituting the UPHRC is not necessary. [43]

The NHRC headed by M.N. Venkatachaliah condemned in a report on increasing criminality among the police. Referring to the NHRC's experience since its inception four years ago, it said, "there can be no substantial improvement in the human rights situation in this country unless those whose duty is to protect such rights, cease to be predators themselves". He said 60 per cent of all the arrests made by the police were "unnecessary and unjustifiable". At least 43 per cent of the prison's total expenditure was incurred on accommodating the innocent persons arrested, without evidence.

There has been unabated cases of heinous crimes including murders and rapes and daylight assaults on children and women. The rate of acquittals, particularly in heinous crimes, is also at increase. It is almost 80 per cent and the delays in trials have now become proverbial.

Realising that the victims of crime are invariably treated as criminals by the police, Supreme Court Chief Justice A.S. Anand has suggested setting up a board for awarding compensation to them for they are forgotten in the existing criminal justice delivery system. Such a fund exists in various countries such as Canada, Australia, New Zealand, the United Kingdom. The fund must be kept under the control of the proposed board which will award compensation.[44]

The NHRC further claimed that of all the arms of the state, it is the police in which the average citizen has the least confidence. Indian criminal justice system suffers from substantive and procedural deficiencies, once a citizen is arrested, even if on a relatively minor charge, he could be held in custody for years before his case comes up for trail. Often, prisoners serve more time in jail waiting for their day in court than they would if convicted for the crimes they have been accused of. The result: convicted offenders are vastly out numbered by undertrials. In the Capital's Tihar Jail, only 10 to 15 per cent of prisoners are convicts. The NHRC chairman, Justice M.N. Venkatachaliah has drawn attention to the very low rate of convictions secured by the police for heinous crimes. Nearly 80 per cent of such cases end in acquittals, it is clear that the police are not doing their job properly. Either the wrong persons are acquitted or incomplete and ham-handed investigations are conducted, which ensures that the offenders get off scot-free.

From time to time the Supreme Court addresses itself to the plight of undertrials and has issued directives to lower courts for the speedy disposition of cases against those accused of minor charges and yet, these cases drag on. In its annual report, the NHRC has made specific recommendations for the reorganisation of the criminal justice system. Apart from advocating the system of honorary judicial magistrates, the Commission has called for 'decriminalisation' of various offences so that much of what is today categorised as 'crime' would be treated as civil violations. The lack of an effective system of legal aid is also a cause for concern. Most states do not even spend the amount budgeted under this head, and what little they do spend is not properly accounted for. The entire bail system process too needs to be overhauled and streamlined. Often, poor plaintiffs are asked to provide sureties which are beyond the means of their families; as a consequence, they are forced to rot in jail for no social purpose what so ever. Courts should grant bail as a matter of course, especially given the long delays involved in cases coming to trial.

Wherever a court feels it is unable to release an alleged offender on bail, care must be taken to expedite the actual trial. For a massive backlog of cases throughout the nation, the reason is also the failure of successive governments to expand the judicial system—either in terms of manpower or physical facilities—so that it can cope with the growing population. Those who are affluent are still able to negotiate their way around the numerous obstacles that lie on the road to justice. But for the ordinary citizen, an encounter with the law is very much the stuff of night mares.[45]

Today, our prisons are governed by the antediluvian Prisons Act of 1894. Article 21 of the Constitution forbids deprivation of personal liberty except according to the procedure prescribed by law. This law has to be fair, just and reasonable. The executive fiat called Prison Act of 1894 prescribes that law is not just, fair and reasonable. The statute of 1894 would reflect the mores of the day where words just, fair and reasonable; the concepts of world war, internationalism, World Government, League of Nations, UNO, Universal Declaration of Human Rights etc. were not in practice.

References

1. Encyclopaedia of India and Her States, Vol.11, ed. by Verinder Grover & Ranjana Arora, Deep & Deep Publications, New Delhi, 1996, p. 447.
2. Law Publishers Bare Act., Law publishers, Allahabad, p. 17.
3. Item No. 4 in List II (State List) in the Seventh Schedule of the Constitution.
4. *Vidya Bhushan*: *op. cit.*, p. 34.
5. Amrendra Mohanty & Narayan Hazary: *op. cit*, p. 27.
6. Nagla B.K.: *op. cit.*, p. 1019.
7. Encyclopaedia of India and Her States, *op. cit.*, 461.
8. Vide Report of the Working Group on Prisons in the country, 1972-73 and Report of the All India Comimittee on Jail Reforms, 1980-83.
9. Roy, J.G.: Prisons and Society—A Study of the Indian Jail System, Gyan Publishing House, New Delhi 1989, p. 18.
10. Encyclopaedia of Police in India, Vol. III, ed. by S.K. Ghosh, Ashish Publishing House, New Delhi, 1997, p. 2217.

11. Amrendra Mohanty and Narayan Hazary: *op. cit.*, p. 28.
12. Govt. of India: Ministry of Home Affairs,Report of the Working Group on Prisons in the country, 1972-73, pp. 20-24.
13. India 1983: Ministry of Information and Broadcasting, Government of India, New Delhi, 1983, p. 450.
14. Manorama Year Book, 1994, pp. 695-99.
15. Report of the All India Committee on Jail Reforms, 1980-83, Vol.1, New Delhi, Ministry of Home Affairs, Government of India, 1983, Vol. 1, p. 19.
16. Report of the All India Committee on Jail Reforms, 1980-83. Vol. II, Government of India Press, New Delhi, p. 365.
17. Amarendra Mohanty and Narayan Hazary: *op. cit.*, p. 30.
18. India: A Reference Annual, 1990, pp. 229-30.
19. Encyclopaedia of Social Work, Juvenile Delinquency, Vol. II, ed. by K.S. Shukla, Ministry of Welfare, Government of India, 1887, p. 141.
20. *Indian Express*, 9th August 1998, Bangalore.
21. *Ibid.*, 2nd February 1996, Bangalore, p.1.
22. *Ibid.*, 21st May 1996, Bangalore,
23. *Ibid.*, 17th January 1996, Bangalore,
24. *Ibid.*, 6th June 1996, Bangalore, p. 11.
25. *Ibid.*, 4th March 1996, Bangalore, p. 9.
26. *Deccan Herald*, 28th August 1995, Bangalore.
27. *Ibid.*, 29th August 1995, Bangalore.
28. *Ibid.*, 27th August 1995, Bangalore.
29. *Indian Express*, 13th August 1997, Bangalore.
30. *Ibid.*, 9th February 1996, Bangalore.
31. *Ibid.*, 4th November 1995, Banglore.
32 *Ibid.*, 1st March 1996, Bangalore, p. 13.
33. *Ibid.*, 23rd September 1996, Bangalore.
34. *Ibid.*, 21st December 1996, Bangalore.
35. *Ibid.*, 15th December 1996, Bangalore.
36. *Ibid.*, 6th May 1997, Bangalore, p. 7.
37. *Ibid.*, 5th May 1997, Bangalore.
38. *Ibid.*, 2nd September 1997, Bangalore.
39. *Ibid.*, 10th October 1997, Bangalore.
40. *Ibid.*, 8th July1996, Bangalore.

41. *Ibid.*, 17th December 1997, Bangalore.
42. *Ibid.*, 19th Febraury 1998, Bangalore.
43. *The Hindu*, 6th March 1999, Bangalore, p. 5.
44. *The Times of India*,15th March 1999, Bangalore, p. 9.
45. *Ibid.*, 15th March 1999, Bangalore, p. 12.

5
Prison Management in Karnataka

Imprisonment is the common punishment for offences. The problem of housing hundreds of criminals in one institution requires a code of rules and regulations for safety for efficiency for running the establishment. The prison establishment requires special restrictions, which grow out of the necessity of keeping prisoners within the prison and preventing conflicts, riots or escapes and to rationalise prison reformation.

1. Admission in Prison

(i) Admission of Prisoners

Under Section 3 of the Karnataka Prisoners Act, the officer-in-charge of a prison receives and detains all persons duly committed to his custody. The officer in charge of prison after the execution of such warrant or order, returns such writ to the Court. A prisoner on admission is searched and all weapons and prohibited articles are taken from him. A female prisoner is searched by matron or woman warder. Every prisoner on admission as soon as possible is examined by the medical officer and records it.

All money and other articles belonging to the prisoner is placed in the custody of the jailor and the signature of the prisoner taken. Separate warrant is issued for every prisoner even though two or more prisoners are jointly charged and convicted. Before admitting a prisoner the jailor examines the warrant and by questioning the prisoner as to his name and other particulars satisfies himself that he is the person referred to in the warrant.

Prisoners are admitted at any time after the opening of the prison and before it is locked-up. Prisoners who have gone to appear before the Sessions Court or those who come from long distance from other prisons are admitted at any time. On admission of a prisoner the jailor furnishes the officer-in-charge of the police escort with a receipt. Civil debtors are admitted to the jail at any hour. Prisoners received in a prison after it has been locked-up are confined in a separate cell or yard for the night, barracks are not opened at night for this purpose. After the admission of a prisoner, his warrant is examined by the superintendent.

On admission to jail, every prisoner washes his person and his clothing thoroughly. If prisoner comes from an epidemic disease background, his clothing is also disinfected by soaking in a solution of corresive sublimate or by being boiled. In such cases special care is taken to cleanse the prisoners person especially his hair.

Every article whether clothing, bedding, jewellery, documents or otherwise are taken away from prisoners sentenced to rigorous imprisonment or imprisonment for life to whom jail clothing and bedding in accordance with rules are provided.

From prisoners sentenced to simple imprisonment every article is taken away except personal clothing; from undertrial prisoners money and property other than clothes, bedding, personal ornaments, paper and letters are taken; from civil prisoners only dangerous weapons articles calculated to facilitate escape and such prohibited articles like spirits, drugs and immoral books are taken. The caste thread of Brahmins, or other thread wearing castes and the *tali* or wedding ring from a woman are not removed.

All articles removed from a prisoner are dealt with under the rules regarding prisoners property. A Sikh prisoner is allowed to wear iron bangle and *Kirpan*. Further, newly admitted prisoner is subjected to such period of quarantine as the superintendent on the advice of the medical officer, directs which is at least ten days.

During the period of quarantine, prisoner is strictly separated by day and by night from all prisoners not undergoing quarantine. If any epidemic disease appears in the quarantine ward no resident of the ward is taken into the jail until the expiry of fourteen days from the date of disappearance of the last case of disease. Elementary orientation is given to the prisoners during the quarantine period.

The jail staff including medical officer explains to the prisoners, simple rules of jail discipline of personal and communal hygiene, or their behaviour towards jail officials and towards other prisoners, the new outlook in regard to the treatment of prisoners, the concession and liabilities of prisoners, the necessity of utilising the period of his jail life in preparing himself for rehabilitation after his release.

After admission every prisoner is brought before the chief jailor for entering his details including his property in the admission register. Every convict is provided a history ticket in which all occurrences of importance in his jail life are recorded. He is also given a medical sheet in which all important events of his health are recorded. A weighment chart is also given in which all fortnightly weighments are noted. Within a week after a prisoner's admission, he is brought before the medical officer for making necessary entries in the convict register and then for verification by the superintendent of the other entries already made in that register.

The descriptive entries on the head of the ticket is made by the remission clerk from the convict register, also relating to appeals and petitions as they occur. Remission is entered and the progressive totals noted monthly or periodically as the case may be against each award.

Other entries such as receipt of intimation of payment of fine, judicial solitary confinement undergone, diet on which placed, fact of verification under Sub-rule 2, promotions in the class, grade, issue of clothing, nature of labour, ordinary changes there in extra mural appointment, suspension of sentence, letter writing and interviews, attendance in court, service of civil court process, imposition and removal of letters, escapes and recaptures, transfer, death, release or other mode of disposals, parole, leave etc., are made by the remission clerk and the superintendent's initials obtained.

History ticket is in the custody of remission clerk. Medical sheet and weighment charts are in the custody of the hospital and are issued to prisoners for fortnightly weighment parade, inspections, attendance at hospitals etc. The names of convicted prisoners are entered in convict register and the names of the undertrial prisoners are registered in the undertrial registers. The names of civil prisoners are entered in the register of civil prisoners.

In the case of convicts the date on which the sentence expires will be in the convict register. If the convict is under sentence of less than three months, an entry of his name and number is made in the register of prisoners to be released under that date, and if the sentence is three months and over, the probable date is calculated by deducting one-third sentence and his name and number entered on page of that date in release diary and on that date his date of release calculated with reference to remission rules and his name and number reposted in the release diary and also the date of expiry is entered on his remission sheet.

At the same time the prisoner's register number, name, sentence, death sentence and date of release will be on his warrant and signed by the chief jailor and the superintendent. In case where imprisonment is awarded in default of payment of fine, the alternative dates of release will both be included in the endorsement on the warrant, in the convict register and in the register of prisoners to be released and remission ticket.

The prisoner is produced before the superintendent. He compares the entries in the register and history ticket with those in the warrant and initial the convict register in token of its correctness regarding undertrials and civil prisoners a similar procedure is followed as regards the warrants and admission registers.

The superintendent sees that necessary alterations are made in the registers and documents when a prisoner's sentence is enhanced or reduced on appeal or realisation of fine. The superintendent and the chief jailor will initial these alterations.

Prisoners warrants are arranged according to dates of release and kept in monthly bundles, the warrant of prisoners to be released in a particular month being placed in one bundle and each bundle being docketed outside with the month and year. Copies of judgements, orders of appellate courts and order of Government disposing of prisoners petitions together with correspondence relating to payment of fine, classification, etc., are in a separate file for each prisoner and kept serially according to their register numbers. Every convicted prisoner is given a thick paper ticket noting his number, name, date of sentence and date of release.

Ankle ring is imposed on any male convict for purpose of security. The prisoners' going on extra mural gang wears ankle rings invariably. Female prisoners are not imposed ankle rings.

Every male convict sentenced to rigorous imprisonment for a larger term than one month or to imprisonment for life, have the hair of his head cut or trimmed only to such an extent and at such times as may be necessary for the purpose of health and cleanliness, unless he desires that it should be cut shorter.

Prisoners who are Sikhs except on medical grounds are allowed to retain hair, Hindus are allowed to retain the *kudumi* or *jutu* or top knot and Muslims on religious grounds are allowed to have their beard and mustaches trimmed to length of an inch. Long mustaches are not allowed. A prisoner who is exempted under Rule 212 of the Karnataka Prison Manual have the hair of his head or face cut or shaved.

The hair of a female prisoner is cut with her consent except when the medical officer deems it necessary on the ground of health and cleanliness. They are supplied with a comb each and seven grams of coconut oil daily for dressing the hair. They are allowed to use a looking glass. One or two such glasses are provided for the purpose in each ward or dormitory.

The superintendent fixes on the wall of each barrack a copy of the rules relating to appeals, offences and punishments, remission of sentence and rules under which early or premature release of prisoners is allowed in the regional language. The officer incharge of the barrack fully explains the rules to every illiterate prisoner.

(ii) Letters of Transfer from One Prison to Another

Every prisoner on transfer from one prison to another is allowed to write special letters to his friends or relatives intimating the change of address before leaving the prison or after arrival in the other prison. The superintendent is empowered to censor letters. A letter is delivered only after superintendent has satisfied himself that its transmission is not objectionable. The subject-matter of letters should be limited to private and domestic matters only and it should not extend to politics. Unnecessary delay is not allowed in the delivery or despatch of letters.[1]

(iii) Interviews and Communications with Prisoners

Every newly admitted prisoner is allowed reasonable facilities for seeing or communication with his relatives, friends, or legal advisers with a view to the preparing of an appeal or revision or procuring bail or payment of fine etc. He is also allowed to have interview with or write letters to relatives, friends or legal advisors once or twice or often if the superintendent considers it necessary to enable him to arrange for the management of his property or other family affairs.

Every prisoner is allowed to communicate by letter and to have interview at reasonable time with relatives or friends for purposes of arranging for payment of fine or for furnishing of security. A prisoner sentenced to death is allowed interview and communications with his relatives, friends, and legal advisors. Every lifer is allowed to have one interview with his friends and relatives before transfer to the prison where the sentence is to be executed.

He is permitted to sign and attest a power of attorney or other statements concerning his properties. Every prisoner is carefully searched before and after an interview. The superintendent may refuse to allow any interview if in his opinion it is inexpedient in public interest not to allow any particular person to interview a prisoner. In every such a case, he records reasons for such refusal in his diary.

Interview between an undertrial prisoner and his legal advisor takes place within the sight but not out of hearing of prison officials. Unconvicted criminal prisoners and civil prisoners get all reasonable facilities. Any bona fide confidential written communication prepared by the convicted criminal prisoner as instructed by his legal advisor may be delivered personally to such legal advisor without being previously examined by the superintendent. Letters in cypher are not allowed. Interviews are not allowed when a prisoner is on hunger strike.[2]

(iv) Letter and Interview Facilities

In addition to the privileges mentioned in the Karnataka Prison Rules, vide Chapter XXIII prisoners are allowed reasonable facilities for letter writing, seeing or communicating with their relatives, friends and legal advisors, with a view to the preparation of an appeal or rivision or to the procuring of bail or for the purpose of payment of fine or furnishing of security if committed to prison in default of the payment of fine or on failure to furnish security. The following letter and interview facilities are allowed:

(a) **A and B Class Prisoners**: To write four letters a month out of which two at Government cost and two at his own cost.

(b) **C Class Prisoners**: To write two letters in a month out of which one at Government cost and the other at his own cost.

(c) **Undertrial Prisoners (Special Class as well as Ordinary Class)**:

- Once on admission
- Four letters in a month out of which two at Government cost and two at his own cost and also letters for legal matters like defence, bail, security etc.

Ordinarily, all letters delivered to prisoners are destroyed after a week from the date of delivery. With prior permission a convict may retain any letter which is delivered to him. All letters written by or for prisoners recorded in the history ticket and posted without delay. A register is maintained for recording the entries of interview. All interviews are entered in the register.

(d) **Interview**:

- **A, B, and C Class Prisoners**: One interview with parents or wife or husband; sons and daughters once a fortnight and with others once a month is allowed.
- **Undertrial Prisoners Special and Ordinary Class**: Once a week including legal interview for filing application; executing powers of attorney and defence of the case etc., is permitted.

The superintendent is given discretion to grant interviews or allow the despatch or receipt of letters at shorter intervals on special grounds. Place and time of the interview is decided by the superintendent. The time for interview is maximum forty-five minutes. The conversation at the interview is limited to private and domestic matters. The number of persons present in the interview is between four to six. Any interview may be terminated at any time. Every interview with a prisoner takes place in the presence of an officer of the jail. Matron or female warder is present at interview with female prisoners. No interview is allowed on any Sunday and Prison holiday except in case of emergency.

After admission a prisoner is brought before the superintendent. The superintendent enquires as to whether the prisoner desires to appeal, against his conviction and sentence. If the prisoner desires to appeal, he is allowed to do so. The result of an appeal is entered in the convict register as well as in the prisoner's history ticket.

Every petition from a convict is submitted through the superintendent. All money and other articles which are brought into prison by any prisoner or sent to prison for his use is placed in the custody of the jailor (chief jailor) and the prisoner is informed and his signature is obtained in the prescribed register. Cash of prisoners is taken to cash book. On the transfer of a prisoner all his property is sent along with him.

A prisoner is allowed to make any representation to the superintendent. The chief jailor and other officers visit all prisoners and gives them an opportunity of making representation on any urgent matters like appeals, ill-treatment etc. Any prisoner wishes to make any complaint or to appeal is brought by the officer before the superintendent.[3]

(v) Prisoners Panchayat

Rule 296 of the Karnataka Prison Manual, 1978 says that with a view to create a sense of responsibility and self-reliance among the prisoners, Prisoner's Panchayat Board is constituted for each jail. The following rules govern the selection of convicted and undertrial prisoners to the Prisoners Panchayat Board:

In the case of Central Jails, the Panchayat Board consists of convicted prisoners only and in the case of District Jails it consists of convicts and undertrial prisoners also. In a Central Jail one Panch is elected for each barrack and the maximum strength of the Board is limited to ten and in a District Jail the number does not exceed five. No convicted prisoner who has less than six months of his sentence to serve on the date of election is eligible for election to the Panchayat Board and no undertrial prisoner who has not spent one month in the jail on the date of election is eligible.

The following prisoners are not eligible for election to the Panchayat Board:

(a) Prisoners whose conduct in the jail has not been satisfactory;

(b) Prisoners who have previous convictions.

The election is held in such manner at such place and at such time as may be specified by the superintendent and his decision on all matters relating to election is final. The duration of a Panchayat is six months in the case of Central Jails and three months in the case of District Jails. Any vacancy falling due to transfer, death or release of any member or otherwise is filled in for the unexpired period by holding a bye-election.

The powers and functions of the Panchayat are advisory and limited to a discussion and suggestion on matters relating to the welfare of prisoners, i.e. ration, sanitation, recreation, books and newspapers etc. The Panchayat is also empowered to inquire into minor complaints against individual prisoners referred to it by the jail authorities and to suggest to the superintendent suitable punishment permissible under the prison rules. The Panchayat also has the privilege of supervising over the kitchen and offering suggestion for its betterment.

The superintendent is the head of the Panchayat Board and he is empowered to reject any suggestion of the Board which he considers to be not in the bona fide interest of jail administration or beyond the scope of the prison rules.

The Panchayat meets once in a fortnight or earlier if considered necessary by the superintendent. The superintendent conducts the meetings of the Panchayat. In his absence the assistant superintendent in the case of Central Jail and chief jailor in the case of a District Jail duly authorized by the superintendent conducts the meeting.

Any Panch abusing his position will be removed by the superintendent from office after making due enquiries and his decision is final. Such removed person is not eligible for any election unless it is specifically permitted by the superintendent.

2. Classification and Separation of Prisoners

(a) Karnataka Prison's Act's Classification and Separation of Prisoners

Even in the twenty-first century also, all prisons in Karnataka are co-prisons. Section 26 in Chapter V of the Karnataka Prisons Act, 1963 has the following requisitions with respect to the separation of prisoners:

Under Sub-section (1), in a co-prison women prisoners are imprisoned in separate builcings or separate parts of the same building, in such manner as to prevent their seeing or conversing or holding any intercourse with the men prisoners.

Under Sub-section (2), men prisoners under the age of twenty-one years are separated from the other prisoners and separated those who have arrived at the age of puberty from those who have not.

According to Sub-section (3) unconvicted criminal prisoners are kept apart from convicted criminal prisoners; and under Sub-section (4) civil prisoners are kept apart from criminal prisoners.

Under Section 27, subject to the provisions of Section 26, convicted criminal prisoners may be confined either in association or individually in cells, or partly in one way and partly in the other.

According to Section 28, a prisoner is imprisoned in solitary confinement. Under Section 29(2), a prisoner under sentence of death is confined in a cell apart from all other prisoners.[4]

(b) Classification and Separation of Prisoners by Karnataka Prisons Rules

Chapter IV of the Karnataka Prisons Rules, 1974, has dealt, with the classification and separation of prisoners.

(i) **Habitual Prisoners:** According to Rule 12(1), habitual prisoners are kept separate from others at all times. For habitual prisoners a separate barrack or ward is kept. Inspector-General may transfer habitual prisoners to a jail earmarked for the habitual prisoners.

(ii) **Undertrial Prisoners:** Rule 13(1) has kept the confessing undertrial prisoners separate from other undertrial prisoners. According to Sub-rule (2) undertrial prisoners are accommodated in separate cells at night, if separate cells are not available for all, priority is given to young offenders and non-habituals who are kept separate from one another and from ordinary undertrial prisoners, both by day and night.

(iii) **Prisoners Convicted for Rape etc.:** Rule 14 has separated convicted prisoners sentenced to imprisonment for an offence of rape, unnatural offence or kidnapping for the purpose of prostitution from other prisoners and are kept separate. Where structural arrangements permit they are lodged separate from other prisoners at night.

(iv) **Juveniles:** According to Rule 15, juvenile prisoners confined in ordinary prisons are kept entirely separate from other prisoners, both by day and night. Habitual juvenile prisoners are kept separate from casual juvenile prisoners.

(v) **Prisoners Sentenced to Simple Imprisonment:** According to Rule 16(1) prisoners sentenced to simple imprisonment remain during the day-time in that part of the prison which is assigned to them and are not allowed to enter the labour yard or communicate with labouring prisoners unless they elect to work, in which case they remain with the gang to which they are allotted.

Detenus are kept separate from other class of prisoners, on the basis of Sub-rule (2), and are not allowed to mix up or to communicate with other class of prisoners. Civil prisoners always are kept separate from other class of prisoners, according to Sub-rule (3), and are not allowed to mix up or to communicate with other class of prisoners.

(c) Classes of Prisoners

Prisoners are divided into two categories:

(i) Undertrial or unconvicted prisoners, and

(ii) Convicted prisoners.

Rule 17(1) has divided undertrial prisoners into two classes, namely Special Class and Ordinary Class. According to Sub-rule (2) convicted prisoners are divided into three classes namely

1. 'A' Class
2. 'B' Class, and
3. 'C' Class.

(d) Further Classification and Separatioin of Prisoners by Karnataka Prisons Rules

Again Chapter XVI in the Karnataka Prisons Rules, 1974 has dealt regarding classification and separation of prisoners.

(i) **Habitual Prisoners:** According to Rule 125, Sub-rule (1) habitual prisoners are kept separate from others. If possible a separate barrack or ward is set apart for habitual prisoners. Sub-rule (2) has empowered the Inspector-General to transfer to the habitual prisoners section of a prison any prisoner who is not a habitual prisoner, whom he believes to be of vicious character and exercises evil influence on his fellow prisoners.

(ii) **Undertrial Prisoners:** Rule 126(1) has kept separate confessing undertrial prisoners from other undertrial prisoners. According to Sub-rule (2) undertrial prisoners are accommodated in separate cell at night. If sufficient separate cells are not available for all, priority is given to young offenders and non-habituals who are always kept separate from one another and from ordinary undertrial prisoners both by day and night.

(iii) **Prisoners Convicted for Rape etc.:** According to Rule 127, convicts sentenced to imprisonment for offences like rape, unnatural offences or kidnapping for purpose of prostitution, are always kept away from other prisoners and where structural arrangements permit, they are lodged separate from other prisoners at night.

(iv) **Juveniles:** According to Rule 128(1) juvenile prisoners confined in the ordinary prisons are kept entirely separate from other prisoners both by day and night. Habitual juvenile prisoners are kept separate from casual juvenile prisoners. On the basis of Sub-rule (2), if there is only one juvenile or young offender instead of keeping him in solitude the superintendent may with the permission of the Inspector-General will transfer him to a prison where there are other such prisoners.

(v) **Military Prisoners:** According to Rule 129, military prisoners are kept entirely separate from ordinary convicts.

(vi) **Prisoners Sentenced to Simple Imprisonment:** Prisoners sentenced to simple imprisonment, according to Rule 130, remain during the day in that part of the prison which is assigned to them. They are not allowed to enter the labour yard or communicate with the labouring prisoners unless they elect to work in which case they remain with the gang to which they are allotted.

(vii) **Female Prisoners:** Rule 131 in Chapter XVII of the Karnataka Prisons Rules, 1974, has classified and separated the unconvicted female prisoners from the convicted female prisoners, adolescent female prisoners from older female prisoners, habitual female prisoners from non-habitual female prisoners and prostitutes and procuresses from respectable women.

A child up to six years of age is admitted to the prison with its mother if it cannot be placed with relatives or otherwise properly taken care of. Children born in prison remain with their mother up to six years of age;

(viii) **Lunatics:** Rule 137 in Chapter XVIII of the Karnataka Prisons Rules, 1974, has dealt with the classes of lunatics. This Rule says lunatic is a person of unsound mind who may be criminal or non-criminal prisoner. If any convict becomes insane after admission to the prison according to Sub-rule (1), a report of his case will be immediately submitted to the Inspector-General for moving to Government to order his removal to the mental hospital under Sub-section (1) of Section 9 of the Karnataka Prisoners Act, 1963.

Sub-rule (2) of Rule 137 says, on receipt of a warrant issued by the Government under Section 9 of the Karnataka Prisoners Act, 1963, the superintendent forwards the lunatic to the mental hospital specified in the warrant together with the following documents:

1. Nominal Roll
2. Copy of the Warrant
3. Medical Officer's Certificate in the Prescribed Form
4. Medical History Sheet
5. Medical Officer's Fitness Certificate for Travel.

(ix) **Lepers:** Under Rule 143 in Chapter XIX of the Karnataka Prisons Rules, 1974, an undertrial or convict prisoner suffering from leprosy until he is transferred to leper asylum is segregated from all other prisoners. Further Section 144 says, medical officer is the ex-officio superintendent of the leper asylum, who exercises all rules, as far as possible under the Prisons Act as the criminal leper ward is deemed to have been constituted as a place for the confinement under Section 417 of Criminal Procedure Code and Prisons Act applies thereto.

Under Rule 143, Sub rule (3), until a T.B. convict in a prison is transferred to a T.B. hospital, he is segregated from all other convicts in a cell or ward or temporary shed set apart for the purpose.[5]

(e) Karnataka Prisons Manual

Classification and Separation of Prisoners

Rule 173 of the Karnataka Prison Manual says under Section 26 of the Karnataka Prisons Act, 1963, the following separation of prisoners is required viz.

1. Prisoners are classified on the ground of sex into male and female. Female prisoners are separated from male prisoners.
2. Male prisoners are classified on the basis of age. Male prisoners under twenty-one years of age are separated from male prisoners above that age.
3. Among male prisoners under twenty-one years of age, those who have reached the age of puberty are separated from those who have not attained puberty.
4. Convicts are kept apart from unconvicted prisoners. Under Section 27 convicted criminal prisoners may be confined either in association or individually in cells or partly in one way and partly in the other.

(i) Classes of Prisoners

Under Rule 175 of the Karnataka Prison Manual, a prisoner may be:

1. A criminal prisoner, which term includes:
    (a) a convicted prisoner, including a prisoner committed to or detained in a prison under Section 123 of the Code of Criminal Procedure on his failure to give security when ordered to do so under Section 117 of the said Code.
    (b) an unconvicted or undertrial prisoner.
2. A detenu or a prisoner to be detained in prison without trail under any law relating to preventive detention; and
3. A civil prisoner.

Lunatics may also be temporarily detained in jails under the order of the magistrate.

(ii) Short Termers

Under Rule 177 of the Karnataka Prison Manual for the purpose of treatment in jails; prisoners are grouped as short termers (having sentence of less than three months) and long termers (having sentence of three months and above).

(iii) Classification of Habitual Prisoners

Rule 178 of the Karnataka Prison Manual says that the classification of a convicted person as "Habitual" is ordinarily made by the convicting court, but if the convicting court omits to do so, such classification may be made by the District Magistrate or in the absence of an order by the convicting court of District Magistrate and pending the result of a reference to the District Magistrate, by the officer-in-charge of the jail where such convicted person is confined.

Convicting Courts or District Magistrates as the case may be, may revise the classification made by them, and the District Magistrate may alter any classification of a convict including a person committed to or detained in prison for failure to furnish security, made by a convicting court provided that the alteration is made on the basis of facts, which were not before such court at the time when such classification was made.

Under Rule 180 of the Karnataka Prison Manual, habitual convicts are separated from others. If it is impossible to separate the class entirely during work, superintendents are authorised to locate habitual convicts in a definite part of the several work sheds or otherwise. The Inspector-General may transfer to the habitual section of an ordinary jail any prisoner not being a habitual criminal whom he believes to be of so vicious character. A prisoner so transferred is not subject to the special rules affecting habitual convicts.

(iv) Military Prisons

Rule 181 of the Karnataka Prison Manual, held the opinion that military prisoners are usually not real criminals and those of them who have been sentenced for purely military offences are kept apart as far as possible entirely from ordinary convicts. In the case of military prisoners application for higher classification may be made to the concerned Court Martial which sentenced the prisoner. Ex-military prisoner belonging to Karnataka State convicted by Court Martial and admitted to jail may be transferred to the following jails:

1. **Central Prison, Bangalore**: Long and short-term ex-military prisoners belonging to Hassan, Chickmagalur, Bangalore, Mysore, Tumkur, Mercara, Mangalore, Mandya, Chitradurga and Kolar Districts.
2. **Central Prison, Belgaum**: Long and short-term military prisoners belonging to Belgaum, Karwar, Dharwar and Bijapur Districts.
3. **Central Prison, Gulbarga**: Long and short-term ex-military prisoners belonging to Raichur, Bidar and Gulbarga Districts.
4. Prisoners belonging to Bellary District are kept in Bellary Central Prison. Short-term ex-military prisoners are also confined in Bijapur and Mysore District prisons. There is provision for the transfer of ex-military prisoners confined in jails of other states on reciprocal basis.

(v) Classes of Convicted Prisoners

According to Rule 459 of the Karnataka Prison Manual, convicted criminal prisoners are divided into two divisions or classes.

Class I and Class II:

A. Prisoners will be eligible for Class I if

- (i) They are non-habitual prisoners of good character.
- (ii) They by social status, education and habit of life; have been accustomed to a superior mode of living, and
- (iii) They have not been convicted of:
  - (a) Offences; involving elements of cruelty; moral degradation or personal greed;
  - (b) Serious premeditated violence;
  - (c) Serious offences against women and children;
  - (d) Serious offences against property;
  - (e) Offences relating to the possession of explosive fire arms and dangerous weapons with the object of committing an offence or of enabling an offence to be committed;
  - (f) An offence under the Suppression of Immoral Traffic in Women and Girls Act;
  - (g) Abetment or incitement of offences falling within these sub-clauses.

B. Class II consists of prisoners who are not classified as Class I. Notwithstanding anything contained in A above any person convicted of an offence involving gross indecency or exhibiting gross depravity of character may not be placed in Class I.

The State Government is competent at any time to alter division of a convicted criminal prisoner for such reasons as it considers sufficient. According to Rule 464 of the Karnataka Prison Manual, Class I prisoners are kept separately from Class II prisoners.

The military prisoners convicted by military courts who require classification the superintendent informs the District Magistrate who in turn recommends to the State Government, by whom the recommendation would be confirmed or reviewed.

Rule 476 of the Karnataka Prison Manual says under Section 26 of the Karnataka Prisons Act, in a co-prison women prisoners are confined in a separate building or separate part of the same building to prevent their seeing or conversing or having any connection with men prisoners. Under Section 26(3) of the Act unconvicted criminal women prisoners are kept apart from convicted criminal women prisoners. The locks of the enclosure and compartments where females are confined are different from those in use in other parts of the jail, so that keys of the latter may not open the former.

(vi) Classes of Lunatics

Rule 495 of the Karnataka Prison Manual says, "Lunatic" means an idiot or person of unsound mind. Lunatics in a jail may be non-criminal or criminal. Non-criminal lunatics are those who have committed no crime but are sent to jail for medical observation under the provisions of the Indian Lunacy Act, 1912, i.e. Section 16(i).

Criminal lunatics are those who are accused of having committed or have committed a crime for whose detention in or removal to an asylum, jail or other place of safe custody an order has been made in accordance with the provisions of Section 330 or Section 335 of the Code of Criminal Procedure or Section 9 of the Karnataka Prisons Act, 1963. Criminal lunatics are broadly classified into the following categories:

(a) Prisoners who have become insane after their conviction and admission into prison.

(b) Prisoners incapable of making their defence owing to unsoundness of mind and detained under Section 330 of the

Code of Criminal Procedure pending transfer to a mental hospital.

(c) Prisoners who have been tried for a criminal offence and found to have committed the act alleged but who have been acquitted on the ground of being insane when the act was committed and who are detained under Section 335 of the Code of Criminal Procedure either permanently or pending transfer to a mental hospital.

(d) Recovered lunatic remanded from a mental hospital to a prison with a view to ultimate release.

Under Rule 496 of the Karnataka Prison Manual, every mental patient whether detained or confined in a jail, is kept separate from other prisoners. A dangerous lunatic prisoner is confined in a cell. A leper or T.B. convict is segregated from all other prisoners and kept in a temporary cell or ward set apart for this purpose.

(vii) Youthful Prisoners

Under Section 26(2) of the Karnataka Prisons Act, male prisoners under the age of 21 are separated altogether from other prisoners and separated those who have arrived at the age of the puberty from those who have not.

Rule 688 of the Karnataka Prison Manual says, youthful prisoner is one who has attained the age of twenty-one years. A child offender is one who when convicted was under the age of sixteen years.

If there is only one such prisoner in the jail and it is considered inadvisable to keep him in solitude, the superintendent may transfer the prisoner to Borstal School, Dharwar where prisoners of the same class are confined and obtain sanction from the Inspector-General. Habituals are kept separate from casual youthful prisoners.

According to Rule 689 of the Karnataka Prison Manual, an adolescent offender means a male offender who has attained the age of sixteen years and consequently attained the age of puberty.

In jails, where there are no adequate means of separating youthful prisoners who have attained puberty from those who have not, they are kept under the eye of a prison officer during the day who does not allow neither familiarity nor communication between the two classes. At night, they are locked-up separately. When in transit from one prison to another youthful offenders are kept separate from all other prisoners and if possible, are despatched in separate gangs.

All youthful offenders sentenced to imprisonment for six months and above are transferred to Dharwar for confinement in the special institution attached to Borstal School for youth offenders. Male prisoners under the age of twenty-one years are kept separate from any prisoner of another class. Wherever possible, youthful prisoners who have attained the age of puberty are separated from those who have not.

(viii) Undertrial Prisoners

Under Section 26(2) of the Karnataka Prisons Act, unconvicted criminal prisoners are kept apart from convicted criminal prisoners. Regarding treatment of approvers, according to Rule 698 of the Karnataka Prison Manual, undertrial prisoners are of two classes viz., special and ordinary according to the classification made by the court subject to the approval of the District Magistrate. The former class are those who by social status, education and habit of life have been accustomed to a superior mode of living.

Rule 705 of the Karnataka Prison Manual says that undertrial prisoners are strictly segregated from convicted prisoners, where male undertrial prisoners under the age of twenty-one years are confined, arrangements are also made for separating such prisoners from other prisoners, and for separating those who have attained the age of puberty from those who have not. Undertrial prisoners who have previous conviction, are kept separate from those who have no previous conviction.

Under Rule 706 of the Karnataka Prison Manual a notified undertrial prisoner by the trying magistrate or police as an approver or confessing accused is kept separate at all times from others concerned in the same case. Care is taken to see that confessing accused person and approver in the same case are kept separate where there are separate cells or compartments in the undertrial yard.

(ix) Prisoners Sentenced to Death and Infectious Disease

Prisoners sentenced to death are removed to one of the condemned cells. Prisoners of infectious disease are immediately segregated and the strictest isolation is maintained until the medical officer considers it safe to discontinue the precaution.

Identification of Prisoners

For the purpose of identification of prisoners of certain special categories small patches of coloured cloth may be sewn on the front upper left side of the shirt or saree. The patch may be of the size and shape of rupee coin. The colour of thin piece of cloth may be of:

(i) Black colour in the case of habituals
(ii) Green in the case of life imprisonment prisoners or those sentenced to more than twenty-one years in the aggregate.
(iii) Red in the case of escapees.[6]

3. Borstal Schools

"Borstal School" means a place in which young offenders, whilst detained in pursuance of the Mysore Borstal Schools Act, 1963, are given such industrial training, other instructions and are subject to such other disciplinary and moral influences as will conduce to their reformation and the prevention of crime.[7]

Subject to the general control and superintendence of the Inspector-General and subject to the rules made under the Karnataka Borstal Schools Act, 1963 the control and management of every Borstal School is vested in a superintendent appointed by the State Government.

(i) Visiting Committee

Constitution, Powers and Duties

Every Visiting Committee appointed under Sub-section (2) of Section 3 consists of the Sessions Judge, the District Magistrate, the District Education Officer within whose respective jurisdictions the Borstal School is situated, and four non-official members appointed by the State Government. The non-official members hold office for a period of two years, and are eligible for reappointment on the expiry of such period. Its duties are:

(a) To visit the Borstal School on prescribed occasions.

(b) To make such suggestions for the improvement of the training therein and to report to the State Government or to the Inspector-General.

(c) To interview the inmates immediately after their arrival and to make suggestions regarding special training which each should receive.

(d) To consider cases of release on license.

(e) To consider regarding inmates whose control and detention is almost to expire.

Every member of the Visiting Committee is entitled to call for information, from the superintendent, to examine the records of the Borstal School and to take such action as he deems necessary for due discharge of his duties.

(ii) Classification of Inmates

The inmates of a Borstal School are divided by the superintendent according to their industry and good conduct into four grades namely—

(a) Penal Grade

(b) Ordinary Grade

(c) Star Grade

(d) Special Star Grade.

The privileges of each grade are higher than those of the grade preceding, if any. Every inmate, on reception in a Borstal School will be placed in the Ordinary Grade. Subject to the general instruction of the Visiting Committee, the superintendent may promote or reduce any inmate from one grade to another in accordance with the provision of Sub-section (5), and the rules, if any made under this Act.

Promotions and reductions are regulated by a close personal observation of the inmates and depend specially on their general behaviour, amenability to discipline and attention, to instruction, both literary and industrial.[8]

4. Juvenile Prisons

According to Karnataka Prison Rules, 1974, "Juvenile Offender" means a child found guilty of an offence.[9]

(i) Classification of Juvenile

A juvenile is classified on the basis of his age, physical and mental health, length of stay period, degree of delinquency and his character. Besides, factors like sequence of the juvenile's delinquent behaviour, his social processing, type of delinquency, possibilities of functioning as a contamination risk requirements of custody, his educational and vocational training needs, his total background, possibilities of his social adjustment, his prospects after release and his rehabilitation needs will be taken into consideration. There is a Classification Committee to classify the juvenile in each juvenile or special home.

(ii) Classification Committee

The Classification Committee in each juvenile or special home consists of the following personnel:

(a) Superintendent: Chairman
(b) Dy. Superintendent: Vice-Chairman
(c) Case Worker/Psychologist: Member
(d) Medical Officer: Member
(e) Workshop Supervisor: Member
(f) Instructor in Vocation: Member
(g) Teacher: Member
(h) Head of Care-Taking Staff: Member
(i) Officer in-charge of the Reception Unit: Member-Secretary.

The Classification Committee meets periodically to review:

(a) Custodial care, housing, place of work, area of activity and type of supervision required.
(b) Individual problems of juveniles, family welfare, family contacts and adjustment, economic problems and institutional adjustment, etc.
(c) Vocational training and opportunities for employment.
(d) Social, academic, vocational and moral education regarding health.
(e) Social adjustment, recreation, group work activities, guidance and counselling.
(f) Special instructions, collecting moral information and special precautions to be taken etc.

(g) Adjusting the institutional programmes to the needs of the inmates.
(h) Planning post-release rehabilitation programmes in collaboration with after care services.
(i) Pre-release preparation.
(j) Release, and
(k) Any other matters which the superintendent may like to bring up.

The procedure for classification and review and follow up of the decision taken by the Classification Committee as laid down by the Chief Instructor will be followed in each institution.

(iii) Visits to and Communication with Juveniles

1. The parents and near relatives of the inmates are allowed to visit an inmate once a month or in special cases more frequently at the discretion of the superintendent. The visiting hours are laid down by the superintendent.
2. The receipt of letter by the inmates of the institution is not restricted. They have freedom to write as many letters as they like at all reasonable times. However, the institution ensures that where parents, guardians or relatives are known, at least one letter is written by the inmate every week for which the postage is provided.
3. The superintendent may refuse any letter written by or to an inmate, and may, having regard to the inmate's health, or well-being if he considers it necessary to refuse to deliver or issue the letter, destroy the same after recording his reasons in a book maintained for the purpose.

(iv) Transfer of Juveniles

The superintendent sends proposal for transfer of a juvenile to the State Government stating the reasons for such transfer. The transfer may be proposed only if it is in the interest of the juvenile, namely—

(a) For further education or special training which is not available in the institution.
(b) For change of environment or change of climate on health grounds, for taking treatment which is not available in the institution.

(c) To bring the juvenile near his family and would help him in his rehabilitation, or

(d) Any other reason for which the transfer would be in the interest or welfare of the juvenile.

Ordinarily, transfer would not be proposed on the ground that the juvenile created problems or was difficult to manage in the institution. On receipt of transfer order from the State Government, the superintendent arranges to escort the juvenile to the new institution. The juvenile would be properly dressed and proper arrangements for his food would be made till he reaches the new institution. The juvenile's case file containing the record of the juvenile would be sent along with the juvenile. The parents or guardian would be informed about the juvenile's transfer and reasons.

(v) Maintenance of Case File and Other Matters

The case file of each inmate would be maintained in a juvenile home or special home, containing the following information, namely—

(a) Admission papers, court documents and other relevant papers
(b) Probation officer's report
(c) Information from previous institution
(d) Initial interview materials, information from family members, relatives, friends and miscellaneous information
(e) Sources of further information
(f) Observation reports from staff members in-charge of admission programmes
(g) Reports from medical officer, I.Q. testing, aptitude testing, educational tests
(h) Social history
(i) Summary and analysis by officer-in-charge of the reception unit
(j) Initial Classification Sheet
(k) Instruction regarding training and treatment programme and about special precaution to be taken
(l) Leave and other privileges granted
(m) Violation of rules, regulations
(n) Special achievements
(o) Quarterly Progress Reports from various sections.

(p) Review sheet
(q) M.C. report (in case of girls)
(r) Pro-release on license
(s) Final Progress Report
(t) Release Programme
(u) Final Discharge
(v) Follow-up Reports
(w) Central Index Numbers, and
(x) Remarks.

Without the permission of the Chief Inspector or the Superintendent, strangers are not admitted to the premises of a juvenile prison. On admission to an institution established under the Act, every juvenile is photographed and three copies of the photograph are obtained. One photograph is kept in the case file of the inmate. One is fixed with the index card and the third one is kept in an album serially. The negative is kept in another album.

While dealing with juveniles under the provisions of the Act or those rules at the time of arrest the police officer wears plain clothes and not the police uniform. Juveniles are not handcuffed or fettered.

A visitor's book is maintained in which the persons authorised to visit the institution records the dates or their visits with any remarks or suggestions, which they may think proper. The superintendent forwards a copy of every such entry to the Chief Inspector with his remarks or otherwise and thereon the Chief Inspector issues such orders as he may deem necessary. The superintendent maintains in his office such registers and forms as may be required by the Chief Inspector from time to time.

(vi) Chief Inspector and Other Staff

The State Government appoints a Chief Inspector for the supervision, control and development of services under the Act. There is an Inspector for each district to assist the Chief Inspector and such number of Assistant Inspectors to assist the Inspector.

The Headquarters' Organisation has a separate wing for the development of education, vocational training and rehabilitation services as well as for the placement of juveniles released from institutions. This wing also has a unit for women with a specific function of securing for the girls, opportunities for their reintegration into the community through marriage, employment, vocational placement, etc. One of the main objectives of the headquarters organisation is the development of infrastructure in voluntary sector for providing services under the juvenile justice system.

The functions of the Headquarters Organisation are as follows:

(a) Planning, directing, co-ordinating, controlling, supervising and guiding the activities in the field of juvenile justice
(b) Advising the State Government on the formulation of progressive policies and implementation of juvenile services
(c) Implementing Government policies regarding juvenile justice development
(d) Preparing plan and non-plan schemes for the development of juvenile justice programme
(e) Formulating annual budget and exercising financial control
(f) Releasing grant-in-aid for juvenile justice programme
(g) Inspection of juvenile justice programme
(h) Departmental audit of juvenile justice institutions and activities
(i) Training of both Governmental and voluntary functionaries engaged in juvenile justice activities
(j) Preparation of annual reports and compilation of statistics and
(k) Research and evaluation.

The Chief Inspector is responsible for the inspection of institutions set up or recognised under the Act. His inspection report contains comments and suggestions on the following items pertaining to the working of the institutions, namely—

(a) Physical setting in terms of building's space requirements, living quarters for juveniles, classrooms, sick rooms, water supply and sanitary arrangements, playgrounds, quarters on the premises for essential staff, general cleanliness, etc.
(b) Quality and quantity of food to the juveniles
(c) Clothing and bedding
(d) Facilities for medical treatment including arrangements for curative services
(e) Arrangements for education and vocational training
(f) Maintenance of case files of juveniles in institutions
(g) Arrangements made for recreation, games, physical training library etc.

(h) Provision of staff of various categories
(i) Maintenance of registers and accounts
(j) Difficulties and grievances of personnel and juveniles, and
(k) Review of the impact of the institutional programmes.

(a) Inspection of Institution

Every Chief Inspector, Inspector and Assistant Inspector during his inspection to an institution gives every inmate in such institution an opportunity to make any complaint or application to him.

The Chief Inspector, Inspector or Assistant Inspector at the conclusion of his inspection notes in the inspection book of the institution. Every Inspector and Assistant Inspector submits to the Chief Inspector a detailed report of his inspection. The Chief Inspector, either on his own inspection or on the inspection report of other inspecting staff, communicates to the superintendent of the institution so inspected such suggestions or directions as he may deem fit and necessary.

Any place of safe custody in which a juvenile is kept open to inspection by the District Magistrate, any Magistrate deputed by the District Magistrate, any member of the Board, Magistrate of a Juvenile Court. The Chief Inspector and his inspecting staff or any other officer of the State Government empowered in this behalf.

The in-charge of such a place of safe custody gives every facility to the probation officer who visits the juvenile for the purpose of making inquiries into his case. Any registered medical practitioner empowered by the State Government may visit any institution in order to report to the Chief Inspector on the health of the inmates and the sanitary condition of the institution.

(b) Duties of Superintendent

The general duties, functions and responsibilities of the superintendent are as under:

- Providing homely atmosphere of love, affection, care and welfare of juveniles
- Planning, implementing and co-ordinating all institutional activities, programmes and operations
- Maintaining minimum standard at the institution

- Classification of juveniles, training and treatment programmes and correctional activities
- Supervision over juvenile discipline and morale
- Allocation of duties to personnel
- Attending to personnel welfare and staff discipline
- Preparation of budget and control over financial matters
- Supervision over office administration
- Monthly office inspection
- Daily inspection of institution
- Inspecting and testing food prepared for juveniles
- Weekly inspection of institutions during night time
- Proper maintenance of statistics, sending periodical reports to the concerned authorities etc.

(c) Duties of Probation Officer

On receipt of information from the officer-in-charge of a police station under Clause (b) of Section 19 or an order from the Board under Rule 26, the Probation Officer enquires into the antecedents and family history of the juvenile, and such other material circumstances as may be necessary and submits a preliminary report in Form IX to the competent authority.

Every Probation Officer performs the following duties:

- Makes inquiries regarding the home and school conditions, conduct and character and health of juveniles under his supervision
- Attends regularly to the competent authority and submits reports
- Maintains diary, case files and necessary registers
- Visits regularly juveniles placed under his supervision and also places of employment or school attended by such juveniles and submits regularly fortnightly in Form IX
- Takes juveniles wherever possible from the competent authority to observation home, to juvenile home, special home or fit person institution
- Brings before the competent authority immediately juveniles who have not been of good behaviour during the period of supervision
- Follow up of juveniles after their release from the institutions and extends help and guidance to them

- Establishes linkages with voluntary workers and organisations to facilitate rehabilitation and social reintegration of juveniles and ensures the necessary follow up.

A Probation Officer is prohibited to employ a juvenile under his supervision for his own private purposes or take any private services from him.

(d) Duties of Case Workers

The general duties, functions and responsibilities of the case workers are as under:

- Makes social study of the juvenile through personal interview and from the family, social agencies and other sources
- Classifies problems of the juvenile and deals with his difficulties in institutional life
- Participates in the orientation, classification and reclassification programme
- Establishes co-operation and understanding between the juvenile and the administration
- Assists the juvenile to develop contacts with his family and also provides assistance to his family members, and
- Participates in the pre-release programmes and helps the juvenile to establish contacts which provides emotional and social support to juveniles after their release.

(e) Duties of Care-takers

The general duties, functions and responsibilities of care-takers are as follows:

- Handles juveniles with love and affection
- Takes proper care of welfare of juveniles
- Maintains discipline in institution
- Sanitation and hygiene
- Implements daily routine in an effective manner
- Looks after the security and safety arrangements of the institution, and
- Escorts juveniles whenever they go out of the institution.

A job chart for care-takers is worked out by the Chief Inspector to follow it strictly in all institutions.

(f) Institutional Management

The State Government as far as possible sets up separate observation homes for neglected and delinquent juveniles. Separate homes may be established for juvenile below and above the age of twelve years. In any case boys above twelve years would be lodged in a separate home.

Each institution has a reception unit under the charge of a case worker for the admission of new arrivals. Newly admitted juveniles may in suitable cases be kept in the reception unit for ten days initially. Where necessary, the superintendent extends this period to facilitate a detailed study of the juvenile. The juveniles suspected to be suffering from contagious diseases, mental ailments, addiction etc., are immediately segregated in specially earmarked dormitories or wards.

The following procedure is followed in respect of the newly admitted juveniles:

- Receiving and search in the receiving unit
- Hair-cut (Unless prohibited be religion), issue of soap and disinfectant lotion
- Disinfection and storing of juvenile's personal clothing and other personal effects
- Bath
- Issue of disinfected clothes, bedding and other outfit and equipment
- Housing
- Medical examination and treatment where necessary
- Attending to immediate and urgent needs of the juveniles like letters, interviews, family matters, personal problems etc., and
- Verification of the order of the competent authority, identification marks, cash property entries in the registers etc. by the officer in-charge of the juvenile.

Each institution follows a schedule of orientation talk for newly admitted juveniles covering the following aspects:

- Interpretation of rules and regulations
- Health, sanitation and hygiene
- Institutional discipline and standards of behaviour, respect for elders, teachers, etc.

- Self improvement opportunities, and
- Responsibilities and obligations.

An overall study of the juveniles admitted to an institution is undertaken on the basis of their social history, behavioural pattern and attitudes towards others. Information regarding their socio-cultural and economic background is collected. The educational level and occasional aptitude is assessed on the basis of tests and interviews conducted by the teacher, the workshop supervisor and other technical staff.

All the inmates in the reception unit are given work like

- Self-help in maintaining their own establishment
- Cleaning of open spaces, gardening etc., and
- Preliminary operations for crafts.

All staff in the homes of girls will be ladies as far as possible.[10]

5. Open Prisons

"Open Prison" means any place so used permanently or temporarily under any order of the State Government for the detention of prisoners under Section 5 of the Karnataka Prisons Act, 1963.

(i) Selection Committee

For the purpose of selecting prisoners for confinement in any Open Prison, there is a Selection Committee consisting of the following members:

(a) Deputy Inspector General of Prisons is the Chairman.
(b) Superintendent of the prison from which the prisoners are to be selected for confinement in an open prison.
(c) Medical Officer of the prison from which the prisoners are to be selected.
(d) Factory Manager or the Technical Assistant to Superintendent.
(e) Psychiatrists if available at the Headquarters. The Selection Committee prepares a list of prisoners and submits the same to the Inspector General for his orders.

The following categories of prisoners may be selected for confinement in open prison. Convicted criminal prisoners who:

(a) Have good behaviour and are physically and mentally fit.
(b) Willing to do hard work and abide by the rules and regulations of the open prison, and

(c) Sentenced to a term of imprisonment of five years or more and have undergone one-fourth of their sentence excluding remission or

(d) Are sentenced to imprisonment for life and who have undergone five years of sentence excluding remission.

(ii) Procedure for Selection

The superintendents of prisons prepares separate lists of prisoners falling under Sub-rules (1) and (2) of Rule 988 of the Karnataka Prison Manual and who are willing to be confined in an open prison and then forwards such lists together with case histories including the medical report certifying his fitness for work at open prison to the Selection Committee. The Committee examines such lists along with case histories and files of the prisoners at the respective prisons and also by personal interview.

The case of each prisoner is screened, regard being had to the following factors:

(a) Physical and mental health to with stand confinement in open prison.

(b) Behaviour and conduct in prison and sense of responsibility displayed.

(c) Progress in work, vocational training, education and in other like matters.

(d) Group adjustability.

(e) Character and self-discipline.

(f) Extent of institutional impacts (whether he has reached peak points of training and treatment).

(g) Whether he is fit for being trusted for confinement in an open prison.

Selection Committee selects such prisoners and submits a list of selected prisoners for the approval of the I.G. of Prisons. After the approval of the list, selected prisoners are transferred to the open air prison. For Fast and Festival Days in prisons[11] see Annexure V.

"In the twenty-first century also, the prison management is a Lock-in and Lock-out and Neglected Management in Karnataka".

References

1. Karnataka Prison Manual 1978, Vols. I and III, pp. 68, 77-84, 193, 232-34.
2. Datar, H.B.: *Karnataka Prisons Rules, 1974*, Lawyer's Law Book, Bangalore, 1993, pp. 87-89.
3. Karnataka Prison Manual 1978, pp. 234-45, 308, 312.
4. Sathpal Puliani: *The Guide to Police Laws in Karnataka—Karnataka Prisons Act, 1963*, Karnataka Law Journal Publications, Bangalore, 1999, pp. 306-07.
5. *Ibid.*, Karnataka Prisons Rules, 1974, pp. 344-45, 385-88.
6. Karnataka Prison Manual, 1978, pp. 61-68, 186-88, 192, 197-98, 210, 270-77, 328-29.
7. The Mysore Borstal School Act 1963, and The Mysore Borstal School Rules, 1969, Government of Karnataka, Government Press, Bangalore, p. 1.
8. Patil Shivraj: *The Karnataka Acts and Rules*, Vol. 2: *The Karnataka Borstal Schools Act, 1963*, Lawyers Law Book, Bangalore, 1998, pp. 624-25.
9. Datar, H.B.: *The Karnataka Acts and Rules*, Vol.17, Karnataka Prisoners Rules 1974, *op. cit.*; 1993, p. 12.
10. Patil Shivraj: *The Karnataka Acts and Rules*, Vol. 9, The Juvenile Justice (Karnataka) Rules 1987, *op. cit.*, 1989, pp. 657-59, 663, 665-66, 670-76, 652-54.
11. Karnataka Prison Manual, 1978, pp. 157-58, 369-73.

6
International Contemporary Scene

1. International Efforts Towards Prison Reformation

Growing problem of crime control in contemporary world, has proved that no country can deal with its crime problem effectively without participation, of the whole world. It also requires broader public participation in programmes and activities of social defence aiming at prevention of crime and treatment, reclamation and rehabilitation of criminals.[1]

Since its inception, the UNO has been playing an important role in prison reformation. Under its Technical Assistance Programme, the UNO helped the Member Nations in suggesting progressive programmes for the scientific care and treatment of offenders, for example, India.

It was keenly interested in establishing minimum international standard in prison administration throughout the world. The UNO held its First Congress on the Prevention of Crime and Treatment of Offenders at Geneva in 1955. The Congress approved the UN Standard Minimum Rules for the Treatment of Prisoners and urged the Member Nations to modify their national practices accordingly. This helped all the nations to join the international mainstream in prison administration. But, implementation of these rules being voluntary and left to the individual Member Nations, most of the members on one or the other ground failed to implement.

The Universal Declaration of Human Rights, 1948, is a milestone towards international prison reformation. The Sixth United Nations

Congress on Prevention of Crime and Treatment of Offenders, held at Caracas, Venezuela in 1980 declared "the success of criminal justice systems and strategies for crime prevention, especially in the light of the growth of new and sophisticated forms of crime and the difficulties encountered in the administration of criminal justice, depends above all on the progress achieved throughout the world in improving social conditions and enhancing the quality of life". The Congress, therefore, called upon all Member-States of the United Nations to take every measure in their power to eliminate the conditions of life which detract from human dignity and lead to crime, including unemployment, poverty, illiteracy, racial and national discrimination and various forms of social inequality.[2]

As at 31 December 1994, 86 States had become parties to the 1984 UN Convention against Torture and Other Cruel, Inhuman or Degrading Treatment or Punishment.[3] India has not yet adopted this Convention like some other States. This shows some of the States are not willing to join the international mainstream against torture, though it is an outdated form of punishment.

The Universal Declaration of Human Rights and other specific international instruments of the United Nations, advocate the abolition of capital punishment. More than half of the world has put an end to this form of punishment-including Britain, South Africa and some States in the USA The death sentence was officially abolished in Nepal on 1st May 1999 and replaced by a maximum 25 year jail term and confiscation of property. "We have taken a more courageous step than the United States or other advanced democratic countries by abolishing the death sentence", the Secretary for Law and Justice, Tirtha Man Shakya, said.[4]

The Commission on Crime Prevention and Criminal Justice, has been established by the Economic and Social Council in 1992. In many countries, the prison authorities do not adhere even to the UN Standard Minimum Rules for Treatment of Prisoners, 1955.

Conference on Torture in the Middle East and North Africa held at Athens in 1996, said that torturers are becoming more sophisticated, inventing methods that leave no scars. The language and the methods of torture are fairly universal, the same in Africa, the Middle East and Lathin America. Many Middle East States have signed a UN Convention against Torture, but have failed to make laws against it, giving torturers a virtual free hand. The Conference agreed to form a network to exchange information, to intensify efforts to prevent torture by educating people, such as medical and prison staff and to continue to treat tortured people.

Torture always involves both physical and psychological pain. It is a very efficient power instrument. The public becomes more aware of the problem of torture, especially against government sanctioned torture. About 100 centres in about 50 countries treating victims are giving human right workers the ammunition to fight torture by recognising its marks.[5]

Medical experts specialising in care for torture victims called for an amendment to the Indian Prisons Act to accommodate a clause on ethics of State-employed police doctors. In a function to observe UN International Day in support of victims of torture at Calcutta in June 1998, torture specialists felt the need to fix accountability of police doctors to specify their stand in cases of organised State sponsored custodial torture.

The organised State torture evolved from whipping to sophisticated medical torture, has assumed alarming proportions and needed to be contained in keeping with the new definitions of human rights laid down by the United Nations.[6]

The NHRC in December 1994 urged the Prime Minister that India should accede to the UN Convention against Torture and Other Forms of Cruel, Inhuman and Degrading Treatment or Punishment. Because of the growing number of complaints of custodial deaths, rapes and torture received by the Commission. It was placed before Parliament, but Parliament neglected it.[7] India has not yet, acceded to the Convention.

The United Nations has fired the first shot in a global war against bribery and corruption in international trade and commerce. The UN's Economic and Social Council has approved a declaration to criminalise all acts of bribery in international transactions. The European Union felt that the criminalisation of corruption particularly in its international aspects, had serious political, economic, social and legal implications. The declaration will be formally ratified by the General Assembly in 1996.[8]

United Nations along with the World Bank and the International Monetary Fund, is getting ready to unleash a global attack on bribery and corruption. All three institutions, along with the Organisation for Economic Cooperation and Development and the Inter-American Development Bank, will participate in an Anti-corruption Conference in Peru in September 1997. The conference will argue that corruption hinders economic development. The Lima Conference also has attracted delegates from the UN Development Programme, UNESCO and several NGOs, including transparency international, the 1997 "corruption perception index", published by the Berlin-based transparency international in August identified Nigeria, Bolivia, Colombia, Russia, Pakistan, Mexico, Indonesia, India, Venezuela and Vietnam as the world's 10 most corrupt nations.[9]

The World Court has intervened for the first time in a death penalty case, demanding that the United States spare the life of a Paraguayan facing execution in Virginia in April 1998. But it appeared unlikely that the legal life line thrown to Angle Francisco Beard on death row for the 1992 murder and attempted rape of Ruth Dickie of Arlington, Virginia, would reach across the Atlantic ocean. The World Court has no enforcement powers and relies on countries to comply voluntarily with its decisions.[10]

Amnesty International in March 1997, called for worldwide suspension of electric shock equipment used in more than 50 countries as instruments of torture.[11] Amnesty International has demanded that Afghanistan's Taliban Government release upto 2,000 men whom they claim were taken from their homes and are being held in prison in July 1997. It had received information that the fundamentalist Islamic Government had arrested the men from the tajik and hazara minorities over the past few days.[12]

The father of Italian prison reform, Mario Gozzini, died in January 1999, Gozzini was the author of a 1986 Prison Reform Bill that is controversial to this day. Under Gozzini's reforms, prisoners are allowed partial freedom, including long furloughs.[13] Police officer Kiran Bedi received the 25,000 Marks Joseph Beuys Prize in Frankfurt in October 1997. President of the German Bundestag Rita Suessmuth praised Kiran Bedi's reform work in New Delhi's central Tihar Jail.[14]

Prison is not only a source of income, now it is a guest house for general public. The authorities of the London Jail, which has the highest security net in that country called upon the general public in

September 1998 to spend one night in its high security cell. These cells which are similar to London's common hotel room charges Rs. 3,650 for one night. Daily such 200 guest thieves are allowed to reside. After entry in jail in evening at 6 O'clock they are supplied the same food which is supplied to prisoners. Night at 10 O'clock they are locked in a cell. They will be waked up at 6-30 in morning, after supplying breakfast, these guest thieves at 7-30 will be released from jail. In India thieves living in jails is difficult but in England guests are invitied to reside.[15]

A captivating prison for families was built in Spain. The Aranjuez prison represents a new and more 'humane' approach to incarceration policy. With a swimming pool, tennis courts, a gym and a hair dressing saloon does not sound exactly like our typical jail. In addition to luxuries normally not associated with the punishment of criminals, the prison near Madrid is the first in Spain partly designed to families, where incarcerated couples with small children can live in apartment—type cells almost as comfortably as in real homes. The first inmates—among them 30 couples were due to arrive in October 1998. Until now, the family life of prison inmates had been limited to short conversations through bars or hasty marital embraces once a month. But in the new prison, 72 couples with children under three years of age had "family cells" 25 square metres in size at their disposal. The cells had a double bed, a sofa which is convertible into a child's bed, a bathroom and a minimal amount of furniture. There was a nursery and a Kindergarten, Couples will comprise upto 144 of a total of 1,008 inmates in the new prison.

The other inmates were allowed of family life. Inmates were able to spend three to four hours with their families every three months in special rooms reserved for the purpose. Leisure rooms had toys for children and families were allowed to have, meals together and take walks within prison grounds. The prison, which cost more than 48 million dollars to build, also included craft workshops, a supermarket and computer facilities. The "family cells" were expected to encourage inmates to develop a better sense of social responsibility and to spare their children their usual fate, the break-up of their families, experts say.

The new facility i.e. five-star treatment for white-collar criminals in Dubai's centrally air-conditioned new prison, a brain child of Crown Prince Sheik Mohammed Bin Rashid Al-Maktoum, will be adjacent to the existing prison, operates on Islamic principles when it opens in 2000. Only those convicted of white-collar crimes and jailed for more than one year will get the luxury treatment. Prison officials call these criminals "guests". All legitimate activities are allowed.These criminals in Dubai's new prison will have everything they need to conduct business behind bars—including a hotel style conference centre complete with access to the Internet. Along with fax machines, computers and telephones, prisoners will have access to the Internet. Unlike many prisons in the West Asia, this one will have central air-conditioning, a gym and a theatre. Construction of this prison began in September 1998 for 2000 "guests". Brig. Abbas Ali, Chief of prisons for this affluent emirate said "instead of destroying them, we will help them get back on their feet. This inturn will help their families and subsequently, the economy. Many of the convicts have legitimate business, a state-of-the-art business centre is planned with everything seen in an international company".

This region is known for harsh treatment of convicts, even the old prison is no dive upto six inmates shares a cell about 10 feet by 13 feet, sleeping on comfortable mattresses and eating meals of rice, meat, chicken, soup and vegetables.[17]

Well-behaved long-term inmates of prisons in the Indonesian province of North Sumatra will be allowed 'biological home leaves" to visit their wives under a plan in November 1996. "It is humane to let the prisoners go on home leave during which they can meet their biological needs with their wives".[18]

Angry survivors of World War II prison camps threatened protests during May 1998's State visit by Emperor Akihito of Japan after he was awarded England's highest award of chivalry. In a letter to Queen Elizabeth II, Japanese Labour Camps Survivors Association, London, recalled "the atrocious behaviour of the imperial Japanese forces" and called the award "a direct insult" to those who served in the far East during the war.[19]

In USA, electronic courts are established for speedy disposal of cases. Till the disposal of the case prisoner remains in jail. But his case is disposed off within a week. Prisoner from a special room in jail though TV curtain and audio system speaks to the judge and his lawyer to get his case settled. If acquitted, immediately he will be released from jail.[20]

2. Below International Minimum Prison Standard in Different Nations

It is unfortunate that, even today, prison administration in most of the nations is below international minimum prison standard. The following are some of the examples.

Authorities in the South Western Chinese city of Chongging have executed 26 people convicted of first-degree murder, robbery and rape, in September 1997. The executions followed a mass sentencing rally yesterday attended by 1,000 ordinary citizens. The strike hard campaign has greatly accelerated use of the death penalty, since its launch in April 1996. According to Amnesty, China handed down 6,100 death sentences last year.[21]

Thirty three people found guilty of genocide will be publicly executed in Rwanda in April 1998. But Jose Louis Herrero, a spokesman for the United Nations High Commission for Human Rights in Rwanda, said in addition to opposing the death penalty in principle, his agency was protesting at the specific executions. About 1,30,000 people are in Rwanda's prisons accused of genocide about a tenth of those who took part in the mass killings, according to the Deputy Justice Minister, Gerald Gahima. No verdicts have yet been handed down by the United Nations international tribunal on Rwanda, sitting in Arusha, Tanzania. The tribunal's maximum sentence is life imprisonment.[22]

Thirty-eight of Pakistan's 2,599 juvenile offenders in prisons across the country are on death row, according to the Child Rights Cell of the legal firm AGHS in March 1999. About 1,600 children are being held in jails across Pakistan's Punjab province alone. They comprise 62 per cent of the total Juvenile prison population in the country is 2,599. At least seven of the convicted children are below 14 years of age. Many others of the same age currently facing trial. The presence of so many child offenders in prisons points to the absence of correctional or reformatory institutes for juvenile prisoners in Punjab. This is in violation of the Convention for the Rights of the Child, of which Pakistan is a signatory. Another grave violation of international standards is the death sentence passed on the 38 children while nearly 50 per cent of convicted children are given life sentences ranging from 14 to 50 years of rigorous imprisonment. In the North West Frontier Province and Baluchistan, the concept of reformatory houses is totally alien. [23]

The number of aborigines dying in Australian prisons has risen dramatically since an official 1989 inquiry ordered sweeping reforms to prevent them from committing suicide, according to a news report released in November 1996. Aborigines number about 3,30,000 in a total population of 18.5 million. The aborigines are 17.3 per cent more likely to be arrested often on minor charges such as drunkeness, than the rest of the population.[24]

Describing as a "flagrant violation of human rights on a mass scale", the cremation of thousands of "dead bodies" during the past one year by the Punjab Police in India on the ground that they had been "unclaimed", the Supreme Court in December 1997 referred the issue to the NHRC for a thorough probe.[25]

A total of 400 Filipinos have been sentenced to death since the country readopted the capital punishment two years ago in a bid to curb crimes. However, none of them has been lethally injected to death due to controversy over who would execute the death sentence. Local media said earlier that the first convict was expected to be executed in June 1997.[26]

In 1997 many of those tortured to death at the police station are petty criminals, or the targets of vendettas which the police have been paid to settle in Zaire. Whippings and electric shocks are routine besides more imaginative agonies, such as slipping the victim through a car tyre and jumping on his spine, a speciality of the civil guard. Then there is "the coat"—police wrap their pray in a wet animal skin and wait for it to contract and squeeze the life out of their victim. People are tortured for many reasons. Even petty thieves are tortured to death in Zaire.[27]

Swaziland cannot afford a full-time hangman so it is looking for someone to do the gruesome job on a part time basis, in November 1998. The last execution in Swaziland was due to take place 15 years ago but the hangman failed to appear. Since then the job has been vacant although there are currently 10 convicted criminals on death row. Some of them have been waiting 10 years for their sentence to be carried out.[28]

Death penalty should be retained, the Indian Law Commission has reported in its report in June 1998 and rejected suggestions and worldwide movement for abolition of capital punishment.[29] But, retaining death penalty is not the panacea for all ills.

Sekula Mandic, 58, Bosnian Serb of Om Miljevina, after serving 121 days in Muslim jails in Sarajevo, said that he had been tortured and humiliated during that period, in November 1996. Mandic and Ceda Vukadin, 62, renowned businessman and former mayor of Srbinje, were kidnapped by Muslim military police last July on the 3 Trrnovo-Sarajevo road as they were on their way to the Sarajevo Serb suburb of Lukavica. The prisoners had spent 99 days blind folded and handcuffed to make shift beds made of wooden boards in a windowless 25 squre meter cell. They were guarded at all times by four military police officers, who brought them some dry food twice a day. The prisoners were never interrogated during three-and-a-half months, "once they beat me up just because they thought I had attempted to remove the blind fold", Mendic said, and added that the prisoners had not had bath or a change of clothes during the entire time. The four men were released after pressures by Serb authorities and international representatives.[30]

A remote controlled electro-shock stun belt is the latest device the American police is using to control prisoners in jail or in vans on way to courts. The Amnesty International has expressed concern in September 1996 over this device saying it is violative of human rights of prisoners. Amnesty International believes that the use of such belts could constitute a violation of international human rights standards which prohibit cruel, inhuman or degrading treatment or punishment. It asked the USA to immediately suspend the use and export of such belts and other electro-shock weapons.[31]

Rebellious inmates freed 17 hostages in April 1996, ending an 8-day mutiny that had spread through the country's prisons in Argentina. The hostages, seized on March 30 when more than 1000 Sierra Chica inmates revolted after guards blocked an escape attempt. At least 10 other hostages, chiefly guards seized at other provincial prisons were also released. At least three inmates had been killed in fighting between rival prisoner groups. Negotiators had accepted a rebel demand that ring leaders of the Sierra Chica rebellion be transferred to other prisons and they would not be punished. Authorities did not immediately say what agreement, if any, had been reached on demands for better living conditions in the chronically overcrowded prisons, improved visiting privileges and a shorter wait for trial. The federal penitentiary service, in a recent report to Congress, said as much as 70 per cent of the 1994-95 federal prison population had not been convicted.[32]

Inmates at the Sao Vicente high security prison outside Brazil's largest city have seized hundreds of hostages in a revolt and demanded talks with authorities in May 1997. The prisoners initially took about 500 people hostage, but after several hours released the women and children. They still held a few hundred men, including five prison warders. The Sao Vicente prison is the largest of its kind in Latin America, with about 6,400 inmates. It was the site of a bloody uprising in 1992 during which 111 prisoners were killed as police crushed the riot.[33]

A riot involving rival gangs at a notorious prison in the Amazon jungle left at least 42 prisoners dead and another 22 injured in Venezuela in August 1997. Because the El Dorado prison is so isolated that it lacks phone service and radio contact was unreliable. National Prisons Director Monica Fernandez said most vicitms had been stabbed. But a doctor at a clinic where 13 wounded were taken said "some had been shot". It was not clear if by inmates or guards. The fighting apparently was between long time prisoners and Guajiro Indians who had been transferred to El Dorado, 730 km South East of Caracas, from Sabaneta prison in Northwest Venezuela. El Dorado is where the worst prisoners are sent, often from Venezuela's other 31 prisons. It was the deadlist occurrence since January 1994, when 109 inmates died in a riot and fire at Sabaneta prison. Human rights officials claimed guards stood and watched the inmates fight it out. Venezuela's prisons are among the most overcrowed, understaffed and violent in the hemisphere, according to the Amnesty International and Human Rights Watch. The 31 institutions hold about 25,000 inmates.[34]

The two British nurses, whose trial for murder resumed on 15 June 1997 and could end in their public beheading, are the first Westerns in Saudi Arabia's 63 year history to face charges of this gravity. But they are also the first to be given the fundamental right of having their defence lawyers in court to represent them and question witnesses. A family of Pakistanis, including children, who are facing death penalty have not been so fortunate. Public beheading, once rare has become routine under Saudi justice, which enforces Sharia (Islamic) law by executing convicted murders, smugglers and rapists. Fifty people have been beheaded in 1997, 21 of them foreigners, including an Afghan man in June. None of them was defended by lawyers. There has only been one partial precedent for legal representation in court—a recent case involving an American who killed an intruder in his house. His lawyer was in court but was not allowed to speak. When the British nurses, Luicille Me Lauchlin and Debroah Parry, are on trial before three judges in a non-descript office block in Al Khobar, then lawyers can put questions through the judges to challenge police evidence. In confessions written in their own hand and authenticated by a panel of judges, the two women admitted the murder. Three months later, they maintained they had confessed after having been stripped and threatened with sexual abuse by Saudi police officers. Few in Saudi Arabia believe the two women will be executed. " They are white, they are women, they are British. They might have murdered and they might have stolen, but nobody around here believes they will be executed", commented a local journalist who has been following the case. "Foreigners who are from Europe or the US are given at bodily example not isolated in suffering the say", Dorothy Thor the inaie officers , Dorotny luoinas, director 01 tin dits Watch, told. The roughly 70,000 women private parts of women's bodies and more serious charges, like threats to force sexual relations said Robert Gangi, executive director of the Correctional Association of New York, which monitors State's prisons. The US Justice Department testified to the United Nations last year that it would seek to improve conditions for women inmates, Ms.Thomas noted. In a report released in December titled 'all too familiar: sexual abuse of women in US state prisons', Human Rights Watch cites an Illinois inmate, 'Zelda', who said she was raped three times in 1993 and 1994. But the Illinois department of corrections declined to investigate because Zelda did not identify her attacker immediately.[36]

Demanding their right to have sexual relations with their partners, 70 women inmates created an uproar at Rafey prison in

Santiago in the Northern Dominican Republic in November 1998. Male prisoners in the Dominican Republic are allowed to have sex with their partners, but judicial authorities had rejected the women's demand, saying it would turn the prison into a maternity home. "Don't they know there are ways to prevent pregnancy?" asked Janet Altagracia Sanchez, a spokesman for the protestors. "The law permits inmates, without sexual distinction, to have sexual relations with their partners", the Dominican Commission for Human Rights President Porfirio Rojas Nina said.[37]

The judiciary acquiesced in the decision to send Rashtriya Janata Dal leader Laloo Prasad Yadav to an air-conditioned guest house in the name of jailing him. Lesser mortals accused of the same crime languish in the overcrowded Patna Central Jail.[38]

More than 300 prisoners lodged in Old Central Jail in Bangalore resorted to rioting and attempted to break jail in August 1997. There were 2,337 prisoners of which, 1,800 were undertrials. The prisoners were unhappy about three things: the food being served to them; the visiting hours for their relatives to meet them in prison and the medical treatment given to them in the event of ill-health. They were also unhappy about the quality and quantity of the rice that was served. The Additional Director General of Police (Prisons) H.T. Sangliana had introduced some changes. "The jail has many loopholes and there is no discipline. It looks like a fish market", Mr. Sangliana said. He also said prisoners who had money power flouted the rules. The life convicts joined the agitating prisoners and demanded release of prisoners who had served six years in jail on the eve of 50 years of independance. While the Tamil Nadu and Andhra Pradesh Governments had decided to release prisoners who had served for six years, the State Government had decided to release prisoners who have served 12 years. The jail is facing severe shortage of staff. Most of the times, one person looks after over 300 prisoners. The barracks in the jail are overcrowded. Over 90 persons are lodged in one barrack, meant for 25 prisoners. The staff often have to plead with the prisoners. The prisoners were not being taken to court due to the shortage of police escort. So their trials prolong due to non-appearances.[40]

As the wheels of justice move ever so slowly, thousands of undertrials rot in overcrowded jails across India for years, in October

1998. While the Supreme Court asked all State Governments and Union Territories to file affidavits detailing the current status of undertrial prisoners, authorities put the blame on number of jails not keeping pace with the growth of population. The list presented by the Asia's biggest jail Tihar authority showed that there were undertrials in the jail for periods ranging from one to 11 years. The confinement of undertrials for indefinite period of time is 'extremely unjust', says eminent human rights activist and jurist V.M.Tarkunde. According to him due to indiscriminate dumping of undertrials, the jails were getting overcrowded and as a result, 'a cell meant to detain two persons huddle 80 persons. It is 'inhuman'.[41]

Even if Mumbai police were to arrest one-tenth of the over 30,000 wanted criminals tomorrow, they would have a tough time lodging the criminals in Mumbai jails, in April 1999. For, all of the city's jails are already burdened with three times then actual accommodation capacity. The Mumbai Central Prison or Arthur Road Jail, Thane Central Prison whose official capacity is 1,105 has 2,422 undertrials in it. At Adharwadi, 505 undertrials are supposed to be kept, but the number has now gone upto 1,527. Except for Adharwadi prison, which was built in 1970, all the other jails came up during the British Raj. Work on construction of a jail at Taloja, Raigar, began a decade ago is still nearing completion. The increase in the number of criminals in jails has also increased problems of jail officials. Problems like hygiene and sanitation are of course persistent, but they are overshadowed by the phenomenon of inter-gang clashes within the jail premises.[42]

Russia's Kharbove is the biggest prison in the whole world.[43] Conditions for inmates in Russian prisons are 'inhuman', Justice Minister Pavel Krasheniouni Kov said in November 1998. More than a million people are held in Russia's jails and each prisoner has on average only one to 1.5 square metres living space, whereas international standard stipulate a minimum of four square metres per person. Moreover, 1,00,000 prisoners were suffering from tuberculosis.[44]

Untouchability as a practice persists both in its traditional and modem forms. An attempt on the part of Dalits to insist upon better treatment is also seen as an act of crime and this sometimes leads to bloody attacks on their community. The fight between the Thevars and the Dalit Pallars in Tamil Nadu and the bloody clashes between the Ranbir Sena and Dalits in Bihar are only two glaring examples. This overt, often open and violent, form of untouchability is witnessed mostly in rural India.[45] There are vast areas where barbers refuse to serve untouchables. They are served in separate plates and glasses which they later have to wash in hotels and restaurants at Anantapur in Andhra Pradesh and at Bellary in Karnataka. What's worse even in the national Capital, Scheduled Caste students of a medical college are segregated in the college hostel. This discrimination is covert in the cities and overt in the villages.[46] The practice of untouchability is a violation of Universal Declaration of Human Rights.The New York based 'Human Rights Watch', a Human Rights Organization has said in April 1999 that the Indian Government has failed in controlling the exploitation of Dalits, Untouchables and asked it to ban private armies and to formulate law to prevent caste based wars. In many States in India Dalits are completely segregated from upper castes, Dalits now also are not allowed to use their wells, no entry in temples and legitimately the lands which have to go to them, have to struggle hard to get them. Untouchability is a bane on human rights, said the international human rights control institution. To remedy this political will is inevitable, it said in its report.[47]

Amnesty International in July 1997, accused Israel and its Lebanese allies of holding more than 150 Lebanese as prisoners without trial, some for more than 12 years. The detainees are being held up as "a bargaining chip" with Islamic groups for the release of missing Israeli servicemen. According to Amnesty, 21 of the Lebanese were abducted and taken to Israel. Some are being held as administrative detainees after prison sentences handed down by Israeli courts expired. At least 130 others are being held at El-Khiam prison in South Lebanon which is run by the South Lebanese army, a military group backed by Israel. Forty of them belong to Hezbollah, the Iranian-backed Shiite militia fighting to oust Israel from the strip it occupies in South Lebanon. Some have been held since 1985. The report further said that the detainees will be released only when missing Israeli airman Ron Arad is returned and information is received about the fate of other missing Israeli servicemen. In a related development, Israel was accused in the same month of abducting a Lebanese journalist from his home in South Lebanon.[48]

Some 1600 prisoners incarcerated in Venezuela's prisons were on hunger strike in July 1997. Inmates of the El Rodeo Jail began their strike to draw attention to the constant abuse by prison guards. Inmates also were protesting against alleged brutality towards their visitors.[49]

Eight people convicted of drug trafficking have escaped death sentences in April 1998 because a fire had destroyed the records of their cases, in Kuala Lumpur. The federal court changed their sentences from death to life in prison after it changed the charge against them to drug possession. The court also ordered all, except one woman, to receive 10 strokes of a cane.[50]

More than 28 prisoners died in a fire at a jail in the Moroccan city of Casablanka in September 1997. The cause of the fire may have been an electrical short circuit. The prison, which is biggest in the city, has a capicty for 4,500 prisoners.[51] At least 37 prisoners were killed when infiltrators attacked a jail near Rwanda in May 1996.[52]

Afghan opposition forces have executed 10 Taliban prisoners held in northern Afghanistan, the private, Afghan Islamic Press reported in July 1997, quoting a Taliban spokesman Wakil Ahmed. The troops grabbed a group of 11 Taliban prisoners from the Central Jail in Mazar-I-Sharif on July 3, drove them to near by Dashte Arseen and shot them. Ten died but one, Mulla Shehazada, survived with injuries and managed to escape back to the Taliban.[53]

The report of the Central Home Ministry said in February 1997 that in India the number of criminals in custodial death has increased 100 per cent comparing to last year. The number of such deaths last year was 444, which has increased to 888 this year. This number is based on recorded cases. Such unreported deaths number is still more. Such deaths are considered a big blow to human rights and the NHRC has expressed its serious concern.[54]

Chief of the rebel Chechen Army General Aslam Maskhadov has issued orders to shoot all Russian Prisoners of War captured during the current battle in Grozny, the capital of Chechnya, reports UNI in August 1996.[55]

Pul-E-Charkhi Prison in Afghanistan in June 1997 has a story of men buried alive, of hideous torture cells, of brothers and fathers taken in the middle of the night and never seen again. When Islamic insurgents threw out Afghanistan's Communists in 1992, they openend the gates and vowed the prison would never be used again. Then the insurgents turned on each other. Last year, they too, were expelled from Kabul by the Taliban religious army. The infamous prison is open again, this time to house war prisoners captured by the Taliban. A look behind the rocket-punched stonewalls found haggard men living amid the stench of stale food, garbage and human waste. The country's former Communist rulers are said to have buried their prisoners alive inside the Pul-E-Charkhi compound. The ground outside is strewn with landmines. So is the dirt yard inside, which is littered with broken tanks and rusted trucks left over from Afghanistan's war. Therefore 1,500 prisoners, all crowded into one cell block. There was no running water though the Red Cross has trucked in water and repaired two of the compound's water pumps. The Taliban, adhering to its strict version of Islamic law, prohibits photography. The Red Cross said that 20 children also had been held in the prison.[56]

Iran freed 450 Iraqi prisoners of war held since their eight-year war, Iraq announced in March 1999. Iraq for its part had handed back 56 Iranians. The last prisoner handover was in mid-December, when 196 Iraqis and 16 non-Iraqis, plus the body of one Iraqi who died in captivity, were sent back across the land border. Since the end of the 1980-88 war, more than 90,000 prisoners have been exchanged, but the issue is one of the main bones of contention between the two sides, which have yet to sign a peace treaty. Tehran says at least 5,000 Iranian soldiers are still held in Iraq. Baghdad says it has freed all Iranian PoWs but holds only 64 "criminals" from Iran.[57]

Three captured US soldiers were released by Yugoslavia into the custody of US civil rights leader Jesse Jackson on 2nd May 1999.[58]

References

1. Roy, J.G.: Role of Voluntary Agencies in Prevention of Crime and Treatment of Offenders, Indian Journal of Public Adminstration 1933 (3), July-September, 1987, p. 654.

2. Report of the Sixth United Nations Congress on the Prevention of Crime and the Treatment of Offenders, pp. 3-4.
3. Year Book of the United Nations, 1994, Vol. 48, Department of Public Information United Nations, New York, p. 1016.
4. *The New Indian Express*, 3rd May 1999, Bangalore, p. 17.
5. *The Indian Express*, 9th July 1996, Bangalore.
6. *Ibid.*, 27th June 1998, Bangalore, p. 11.
7. *Ibid.*, 13th October 1995, Bangalore.
8. *Ibid.*, 30th November 1996, Bangalore.
9. *Ibid.*, 2nd September 1997, Bangalore.
10. *Ibid.*, 11th April 1998, Bangalore.
11. *Ibid.*, 6th March 1997, Bangalore, p. 18.
12. *The Times of India*, 27th July 1997, Bangalore.
13. *The New Indian Express*, 5th January 1999, Bangalore, p. 17.
14. *The Indian Express*, 24th October 1997, Bangalore.
15. *Janavarthe*, Kannada Local Daily, 16th September 1998, Shimoga, Karnataka, p. 1.
16. *The Indian Express*, 11th October 1998, Bangalore, p. 18.
17. *Ibid.*, 1st August 1998, Bangalore, p. 17.
18. *Ibid.*, 6th November 1996, Bangalore.
19. *Ibid.* 12th April 1998, Bangalore.
20. *Janavarthe*, Kannada Local Daily, 13th April 1997, Shimoga, Karnataka, p.1.
21. *The Indian Express*, 7th September 1997, Bangalore, p. 21.
22. *Ibid.*, 24th April 1998, Bangalore.
23. *The New Indian Express*, 31st March 1999, Bangalore, p. 17.
24. *The Indian Express*, 26th November 1996, Bangalore.
25. *Ibid.*, 14th December 1996, Bangalore.
26. *Ibid.*, 3rd June 1997, Bangalore.
27. *Ibid.*, 16th April 1997, Bangalore.
28. *Ibid.*, 4th November 1998, Bangalore, p. 19.
29. *Ibid.*, 11th June 1998, Bangalore, p.9.
30. *Ibid.*, 6th November 1996, Bangalore.
31. *Ibid.*, 10th September 1996, Bangalore.
32. *Ibid.*, 9th April 1996, Bangalore.
33. *Ibid.*, 20th May 1997, Bangalore.
34. *Ibid.*, 30th August 1997, Bangalore.
35. *Ibid.*, 23rd June 1997, Bangalore.

36. *Ibid.*, 13th December 1996, Bangalore.
37. *Ibid.*, 26th November 1998, Bangalore, p. 17.
38. *Ibid.*, 18th September 1998, Bangalore, p. 8.
39. *The Times of India*, 13th August 1997, Bangalore.
40. *The Indian Express*, 14th August 1997, Bangalore p. 5.
41. *Ibid.*, 7th October 1998, Bangalore, p. 5.
42. *The New Indian Express*, 22nd April 1999, Bangalore, p. 5.
43. *Janavarthe*, Kannada Local Daily, 2nd November 1997, Shimoga, Karnataka.
44. *The Indian Express*, 27th November 1998, Bangalore, p. 22.
45. *The Deccan Herald*, 21st March 1991, Bangalore, p. 11.
46. *The New Indian Express*, 31st March 1999, Bangalore, p. 8.
47. *Janavaithe*, Kannada Local Daily, 13th April 1999, Shimoga, Karnataka.
48. *The Indian Express*, 12th July 1997, Bangalore.
49. *Ibid.*, 26th July 1997, Bangalore.
50. *Ibid.*, 29th April 1998, Bangalore.
51. *Ibid.*, 9th September 1997, Bangalore.
52. *Ibid.*, 23rd May 1996, Bangalore.
53. *The Hindustan Times*, 14th July 1997, New Dalhi.
54. Janavarthe, Kannada Local Daily, 17th February 1997, Shimoga, Karnataka, p.1.
55. *The Indian Express*, 10th August 1996, Bangalore.
56. *Ibid.*, 30th June 1997, Bangalore.
57. *The New Indian Express*, 18th March 1999, Bangalore, p. 17.
58. *Ibid.*, 3rd May 1999, Bangalore, p. 17.

7
The Future of Prison

Third and the Last Epoch

Rationalisation of the Prison Administration

Everything that is done in International Affairs must be done from the viewpoint of whether it will advance or hinder the establishment of the World Government

Albert Einstein in 1946 A.D.

Emergence of crime led to the origin of prison. During the first epoch prisons were detention centres. Punishments were met outside the prison. Death by hanging, by hurling over the tarepeian rock, crucifixion, beheading and drowning in the sack, exile, beating with rods, torture and forced labour were the older forms of punishment. Ex-communication, dismissal of workers etc. were other forms of punishments. The first epoch was the formation of the institution of prison throughout the world. This epoch lasted towards the end of the eighteenth century A.D.

With the breakdown of feudalism, the fencing of the pastures and the general social and economic upheaval of the middle age, a new class of petty criminals arose who obviously could not be punished so cruelly. These petty offenders were sentenced to hard labour in workhouses, which later became the houses of correction of the sixteenth century.

The second epoch was the reformation of the prison administration. This epoch was of universal adoption of imprisonment as a substitute for virtually all corporal or capital penalties. It came to be realised that the process of imprisonment, involving detention in isolation from family and community, under not so pleasant conditions, could itself be considered as a convenient mode of punishment to replace the old corporal punishment, most countries readily took it.[1] Imprisonment was also considered as a Christian form of punishment. The Christian religious heads retained the power of ex-communication and other religious punishments. The wealth concentrators supported it because they were continued with the power of punishment of dismissal of workers etc.

It was the cessation of transportation to America that forced the leaders of prison reform to consider the building of national prisons. In the meantime, however to take-care of the prisoners who had been formerly transported to America, England resorted to the use of 'hulks' or floating prisons.[2] During this epoch, prisons became reformation centres. Punishments are meted out inside the prison. The humanitarian movement played an important role in replacing the formation of the prison by the reformation of the prison. During this epoch, National Prison Movement created International Prison Movement, formation of the Prisoners of War to the reformation of the Prisoners of War, Closed Prison to Open Prison, Open Air Camps etc.

When in 1776, the Colonies broke away from the mother country, transportation to them ceased and England was forced to look around for other means of dealing with convicts. This explains why John Howard's efforts to reform English jails were so sympathetically considered by the Government.

During transformation from first epoch to second epoch crime continued. Consequently, the institution of prison continued as a detention centre. During second epoch prison has been renamed as reformation centre. In second epoch also, prison failed to establish a crimeless world. Yet, in both the epochs, prison succeeded in controlling human behaviour. Formation and reformation of the prison have taken place gradually.

1. Emergence of Modern Governments as the Supreme and most Dangerous Powers

Before First World War, governments were necessary and inevitable for maintaning peace internally and externally. They exercised police functions. These governments never threatened the very existence of mankind itself, including the institution of prison.

In the modern state system, power intoxicated national governments to quench their thirst for power fought the First International Power Test, which was the most destructive war in world history. Again the power addicted governments to establish supremacy of one over another fought the Second International Power Test which was the most destructive war than the First International War. In the Second International War nuclear weapons were used by the governments, which were unknown in human history. Soon after this war again the modern powers were ready to fight the Third-cum-Last International War which had the capacity to end the very existence of mankind itself. In the Cold War race for storing modern weapons continued. Nuclear weapons were stored. Invention of mass destructive weapons continued. In the Cuban Missile Crisis, national governments made all arrangements and were ever-ready to fight the Third-cum-Last International Power Test.

Fortunately, it was postponed. Today, all modem governments are armed to the teeth with traditional and modern weapons to fight the Last World War. Prof. Arnold Toynbee rightly said in One World and India: "If we do not abolish war, war is going to abolish us....Abolishing war would involve setting up at least a rudimentary World Government." Even accidental nuclear war or explosion leads to the destruction of the whole world. Today the very existence of mankind is at the mercy of the modern state system. The Third-cum-Last International Power Test will be the most and the last destructive war comparing to previous international wars. After this power test, no war will be faught, because this wipes out the mankind itself including prison and crime.

The present governments are the most dangerous, barbarian,uncultured and uncivilized governments comparing to medieval and ancient govemments. But, by replacing the modem governmental system by a new kind of governmental system is not the end of the mankind. This change is a sign of progress in human behaviour. Miss Joan Baez, a folk singer of America appopriately said in Without Marx or Jesus: "I have contempt for all flags and not only the American Flag. A Flag is the symbol of a piece of territory that is considered to be more important than the men who live in it. We have to rid ourselves of even the concept of nation." All the international wars are fought among governments themselves.

In the history of prison not geven a single local or international war is fought to establish "Prisonless World System." The modern powers have proved that power intoxication is the worst intoxication more than this there is no any worst intoxication.

Historical Development and Future of Weapons

Sl. No.	*Name of Weapon*	*Year of Invention*	*Name of Military*	*Expansion of Battle Field*	*Name of Age*	*Period of Age*
1	Nil	Before 4000 B.C.	Nil	Nil	Primitive	Upto 4000 B.C.
			I. Traditional Weapons			
1.	Stone & Stick	4000 B.C.	Army	Ground	Ancient	4000 B.C.
2.	Bow-Arrow	3500 B.C.	"	"	"	
3.	Sword	1000 B.C.	Army-Navy	Ground-Overseas	"	4423
4.	Gunpower-Canon	1243 A.D.	"	"	Feudal	Years 1100
5.	Bazooka Gun	16th Century	"	"	Modern	Years 1522
6.	Machine Gun	1718	"	"	"	
7.	Submarine	1776	"	"	"	
8.	Revolver	1835	"	"	"	4
9.	Air Ballon	1783	Army-Navy	Ground-Overseas	"	
10.	Aeroplane	1903	Army-Navy-Airforce	Ground-Overseas-Sky	"	
11.	Helicopter	1924	"	"	"	7

Cont....

Sl. No.	Name of Weapon	Year of Invention	Name of Military	Expansion of Battle Field	Name of Age	Period of Age
			II. Nuclear Weapon 1945			
12(i)	Atom (Uranium, Plutonium) Bomb	1945	Army-Navy-Airforce	Ground-Overseas-Sky	Modern	8
13(ii)	Inter-Continental Bomber	1948	Army-Navy-Airforce	Ground-Overseas-Sky	Modern	
14(iii)	First Hydrogen Device	1952	Army-Navy-Airforce	Ground-Overseas-Sky	Modern	
15(iv)	Hydrogen Bomb	1953	Army-Navy-Airforce	Ground-Overseas-Sky	Modern	Yrs
16(v)	Bacterial Bomb	1958	Army-Navy-Airforce	Ground-Overseas-Sky	Modern	Yrs
17(vi)	Chemical Bomb	1960	Army-Navy-Airforce	Ground-Overseas-Sky	Modern	Yrs
18(vii)	Biological Bomb	1964	Army-Navy-Airforce	Ground-Overseas-Sky	Modern	Yrs
19(viii)	Megaton Bomb	1970	Army-Navy-Airforce	Ground-Overseas-Sky	Modern	Yrs
20(ix)	Germs Bomb	1972	Army-Navy-Airforce	Ground-Overseas-Sky	Modern	Yrs
21(x)	Neutron Bomb	1977	Army-Navy-Airforce	Ground-Overseas-Sky	Modern	Yrs
22(xi)	Star Bomb	1983	Army-Navy-Airforce	Ground-Overseas-Sky	Modern	Yrs
23(xii)	Laser Bomb	1988	Army-Navy-Airforce	Ground-Overseas-Sky	Modern	Yrs
24(xiii)	Still inventions are goings on	1999	Army-Navy-Airforce	Ground-Overseas-Sky	Modern	Yrs
III.	Nil	Nil	Nil	Nil	World	2000 AD on wards

In the first epoch and after firm establishment of the second epoch of the prison administration political powers never acquired such a worst, dangerous and destructive capacity. Till the invention of nuclear weapons, their destructive capacity was limited. But, after the invention of nuclear weapons it has become unlimited. It is the national sovereignty of the modern governments which has made them to acquire such a vast destructive capacity. Yet, the modem governments are not criminals. These are actors of the international society. International society is the jungle society, in which might is right is the international law.

Individual criminal is sacrificed at the altar of the state. Because, state is more important than individual and state is a compulsory association. But, states are not sacrificed at the altar of the world though world is more important than the states. Because, modern state is not a criminal, the nation-state system is not a criminal system and power test is not a criminal offense. Historically, it has been proved that state is more important than the individual and the whole world. Modern state system is not sacrificed at the altar of the whole mankind. Today, the whole mankind is for the modern state system not vice versa. But, the nation-state system is for whole mankind not vice versa. The Cuban Missile Crisis also proved that nation is more important than the whole world. Consequently, modern state system has continued till today.

2. Failure of UNO in Prison Reformation

The UNO is an association of sovereign states. It is merely an inter-state cooperation for the achievement of certain common ends by joint international action. No National Sovereignty is conceded to the United Nations. It has neither any direct jurisdiction over individuals nor any financial resources of its own, and therefore, it falls short of a Government. It is more like an assembly of diplomats. Hence the efforts of the UNO towards prison reformation have failed to bear fruit. However, the United Nations has the germs of the World Government.[3] But, Albert Einstein rightly opined: "The only step towards World Government is World Government itself."

Comparing to modern governments, in power hierarchy, the religious heads of organised religions and wealth concentrators never acquired such a worst, dangerous and destructive capacity of mankind. Yet, organised religious heads and wealth concentrators are now outdated powers. Because, power of punishment must be vested only with governments including the World Government. This becomes an ammunition to establish "Prisonless and Crimeless World System."

The modern prison system is drawing to its close and the old ideas about prison administration ought to be discarded under the influence of new world system. Today, there is a clarion call for the abolition of the prison itself throughout the world. One Sudanese exiled singer Mohammad Wardi strongly advocated the abolition of prison itself in Sudan. One of his most popular pieces is one in which he sings that there should be no prison in Sudan, that prisoners should be freed and the penitentiaries turned into schools and hospitals, since, when people struggle for independence, they do not want to live in prisons.[4]

Prison is neither a part of human nature nor it is natural. Prison is artificial. It continues so long the human being wants to continue. The moment the whole world decides to eliminate prison, it will not be there.

3. Crime is a Global Problem

Crime is eternal—as eternal as society. Crime cannot be abolished except in a non-existent Utopia. No way of drawing the scheme of the good life has yet been discovered which will fulfill the needs of all human beings at all times.[5]

In the modern state system opportunities for crime abound and impunity is assured at a time when humanity, having lost its moorings, is still groping for some new methods of social control. S.Venugopal Rao, former Director of the Institute of Criminology and Forensic Science, says "When it is difficult to define crime or explain it coherently; it is equally difficult to find ways and means of controlling it when criminolo gists make revolutionary suggestions to eliminate the prisons and reorient the concepts of punishment, they are merely expressing their continuous search for the ideals." Sir Leon Radzinowicz, Director of the Institute of the Criminology, Cambridge, observed: "No national characteristics, no political regime, no system of social welfare or criminal law, of police or justice, of punishment or treatment has made any country exempt from crirne in the modern world and scarcely any can claim to have saved off its relentless increase.[7] The truth is that crime is part of human nature. Crime rate has continued an upward trend. Crime being a global problem requires global remedy.

4. The Future of Punishment

The question is whether alternatives to punishments may exist which can be implemented in a social order that falls short of Utopia. There is existence of alternatives. The history of punishment in the past century and a half shows that punishment has always been excessively used. But punishment has been in retreat during the past century. Prisons which prescribed silence, solitude, and hard labour for their captives have been replaced by probation, parole, and correctional facilities which subject their inmates treatment, training and idleness.

There are many indications that modern societies are at the beginning of a significant transformation in their penal systems. Imprisonment as a principal method of handling the convicted criminal has proved to be costly, and its effectiveness has been increasingly questioned. Theories of the causation and prevention of crime now place less stress on moral factors that might be dealt with by awakening penitence or fear in the criminal. The segment of the population from which the majority of convicted criminals are drawned has ceased to be regarded as an alien, sub-human lower class and the demands for just and humane treatment have increased.

The need for professionally trained people in the field of correction is recognized; there is a growing demand for the services of social workers, psychologists, sociologists and persons with a background in public administration. Humanists, rationalists, scientific temperists etc. are inevitable and the hope of the future. In the near future penal institutions will come to be used as rationalist, diagnostic and classification centres rather than as places of long-term confinement. The variety of institutions will continue to grow, there will be more use of temporary detention homes and half-way houses where custody and security no longer take first precedence. Finally, institutional treatment will diminish in importance in comparison with supervision in the community.[9]

It must be observed that the solutions to the problems of prison and prison itself do lot lie only in prisons but in the larger socio-economic fields as well. These problems can be solved neither by making the system of punishment more deterrent nor by making the system of punishment too weak and diluted.

5. Suggestions for Prisonless and Crimeless World System

Prison population and crime rate in many parts of the world continued an upward trend. The following broad suggestions lead to the establishment of the "Prisonless and Crimeless World System" throughout the globe including India.

International Measures

UNO should take the following measures:

(i) The UNO should frame the "World Prisonless and Crimeless Policy" so that all nation-states join the world mainstream.

(ii) UNO should pass World Prisons Act.

(iii) World Standard Minimum Rules for the Treatment of Offenders and Maintenance of Prisons should be passed.

(iv) Prisons should be renamed as Rationalist Centres.

(v) The leading note struck by the resolution of the International Prison Congress held in London in 1872., viz., that "moral regeneration should be the primary aim of prison discipline and that hope should always be a more powerful agent than fear" should be taken into consideration. After 2000 years, we are coming back to the old Roman definition of prison viz., ad contindos, non-ad puniendos. Prison will be primarily for safe custody and there will be no penal infliction beyond deprivation of liberty, which is after all, the only and the greatest punishment.[10]

(vi) A new Rationalised Universal Declaration of Human Rights and Duties law should be passed. Outdated rights like right to nationalism, right to organized religion, right to wealth concentration and such other rights should be excluded from it. In the list of duties rationality, development of scientific temper, broad mentality, service mentality etc. should be included. Rationalised Universal Human Rights and Duties Commission should be set up for its implementation.

(vii) Global Declaration of Rationality for Prisonless and Crimeless World System should be adopted. Global Rationalist Commission should be set up. It should direct all the Member States to change their national practices accordingly. Prison Administrations of All Nations and International Prison Administration must join the mainstream of the World Rational Prison Administration.

(viii) United Nations Convention on Torture should be modified and renamed as the World Convention on Torture and world standard requirements should be added in it.

(ix) International Criminal Court is established. History has endorsed the idea of a World Criminal Court. When the dust finally settles on the 20th century, realisation will dawn that most of its heinous crimes have gone unpunished. The great irony of our times is that while the assassins of individuals have been meticulously arrested and charged, the annihilators of whole communities of people, the mass murderers of the times, have eluded punishment. It is to make some amends for this that representatives from 150 countries have congregated in Rome in June 1998 to explore the possibilities of setting up World Criminal Court, with the world's mandate to investigate, prosecute and try those guilty of genocide, crimes against humanity and war crimes. The vision is valuable in an era that has seen an estimated 170 million die at the hands of tyrants in the post-Second World War years. The biggest obstacle towards realising it lies in a force that has come to replace religion in the power it has been able to exert on people's lives and emotions-nationalism. One of the most bitter lessons of the 20th century is that tyrants and tyrannical regimes don't disappear, they reinvent themselves and perpetrate their outrage in another corner of the world, on another helpless community. A World Criminal Court of Justice could be the international community's last chance to stop the holocaust clock.[11]

The United Nations negotiations that culminated on 18 July 1998, in Rome with the world getting its first permanent international court to try war crimes. 113 countries applauded its birth. India abstained for the treaty's failure to include use of nuclear weapons as war crimes but did not oppose the treaty because New Delhi upheld its basic principles. The new International Criminal Court (ICC) which will operate out of the Hague in Netherlands and will bring individuals to justice for genocide, crimes against humanity, war crimes and aggression. The new ICC which could take up to five years to become truly operational will be independent of the UN and will be able to act even when the international community is divided as was in the Balkans and Africa. This treaty is a milestone towards world justice. It is the five weeks strenuous United Nations negotiations that has bore the fruit.[12]

(x) Establish Economic Equality. There is a big gap between the rich and poor people and countries. The combined wealth of the world's seven richest men could wipeout poverty and provide access to basic social services for the quarter of the world who live in severe need, according to a United Nations study published in June 1997.

In a call for urgent action to attack global deprivation, the UN called for a new Marshall Plan to rid the world of extreme poverty by early in the next century. Its annual Human Development Report indicated the growing disparity between rich and poor—with the net wealth of 10 billionaires worth 1.5 times the combined national income of the 48 least developed countries. The UN said that an $ 80 billion anti-poverty programme providing access to basic social services, and income transfers to the poverty-stricken would be less than the net wealth of just seven Billionaires.

Richard Jolly, the reports main author, said : "What is needed is a 20-year Marshall Plan. Without that sort of big thinking we are still going to be struggling with the problem of Africa in the middle of the next century". "It is an ethical scandal that we do not provide the basics of education and health for everyone in a world with a $ 25 trillion economy", Dr. Jolly noted that there had been "a worrying slowdown in the battle against world poverty." The report shows that, for the first time since 1990, in the last year 30 countries have shown a decline in the Human Development Index (HDI)—the reports key measure of poverty.

Extreme poverty could be banished from the globe within one or two decades", Dr. Jolly said that the gap between the poorest fifth of the world's population and the richest fifth has increased from 30 to 1 in 1960 to 78 to 1 in 1994.

The report found wide degrees of income inequality both within and between countries. Mexico's richest man had net wealth of $ 6.6 billion in 1995, equal to the income of the 17 million poorest Mexicans.[13] To bring economic equality the only remedy is to abolish right to wealth concentration. This measure helps to reduce crime rate. Mere abolition of poverty cannot reduce crime rate.

(xi) Lord Acton rightly said: "Power tends to corrupt and absolute power corrupts absolutely. The great men are almost always bad men even when they exercise influence and authority. Among all the causes which degrade and demoralize man, power is the most constant and the most active". Today, it is the limited power of police functions, not welfare functions of the modem governments which has threatened the annihilation of mankind. The worst love is the love of power and the best love is the love of global humanity should be taken into consideration while framing global level measures. UNO should start a global movement to replace the politicians, monks and businessmen by rationalists.

(xii) Prisons must be owned and managed by the governments. Privatisation of Jails first commenced in Britain in 1992. It entered Germany in 1996. Germany unveiled its first privately-owned prison in July 1996.[14] Privatisation of prisons first commenced at the national level in Europe. In the Asian continent, India explored the possibility of privatisation of prisons in 1996. This makes quite clear that nationalisation of prison has led to the privatisation of prison. This leads to more crimes. To curb crimes inside and outside the jail, prisons must be owned and managed by the governments. It must be remembered that it is not the institution of prison which threatened the annihilation of mankind itself. Family prisons like Aranjuez Prison in Spain should be constructed. The general public should be allowed to stay in prisons as in the London Jail. Diversify prison institutions and classify prisoners.

The number of closec jails should be reduced. The number of open air jails should be increased. The concept of open air colonies will help the jail inmates to have better psychological conditions and their families to accompany them in these colonies.[15]

(xiii) Juvenile delinquency is a worldwide problem. There are divergencies in magnitude of the problem consistent with socio-cultural and socio-political differences within and between countries. Prevention of juvenile delinquency must be the starting point of any crime control programme. Already there is United Nations Carcas Declaration regarding juvenile delinquency. To tackle this problem, it requires global efforts. To prevent juvenile delinquency Global Prevention of Juvenile Delinquency Convention to be adopted.

(xiv) Women prisoners are a very small percentage of prison population in the whole world. Children often accompany their mothers to jail or may even be born in prison. The immediate fact that there is no one else to look after the child, outweighs long-term considerations such as permanent psychological scars left on the child as a result of its having spent the formative years in prison. The only way to solve the special problems of women prisoners is to provide jails exclusively for them. A separate jail would bring all women prisoners under one roof, ending isolation of those in undeserved solitary confinement in distant jails. It would also enable a study of problems of women prisoners and the patterns of female crime.

(xv) World Rationalised Penal Policy should be framed. Capital, corporal and torture punishments should be banned. All the religious punishments should be stopped. Private property of the criminals should be seized as a punishment.

(xvi) Global Rationalisec Rights and Duties of Prisoners should be drawn up. Provision should be made for separate jails for undertrials.

(xvii) Enhanced medical facilities should be provided. There should be speedy disposal of cases. Corruption should be rooted out etc.

(xviii) Non-Governmental Organisations like Amnesty International, Human Rights Watch, International Red Cross Society, anti-nuclear groups etc. should be strengthened further and made more popular. To rationalise prison administration more NGO's should come up. NGO's are a means of public opinion to create a world level movement.

(xix) Financial and other assistance should be given for rationalisation of prison administration to all those countries which are not in a position to spend on it, and for the construction of global standard jails.

(xx) Prisons should have the following holidays:
   - (a) Weekly two holidays.
   - (b) National Independence Day of the respective country.
   - (c) UNO Day and all International days, months and years should be celebrated.
   - (d) World Government Day. The same model should apply to other fields also.

(xxi) International peace keeping forces, Interpol etc. should be strengthened further.

Remedies to Solve the Problems of Prisoners of War

The only remedy to solve the problems of Prisoners of War is to abolish war itself. The UNO seriously direct all its energy to abolish war itself. All the nuclear weapons should be destroyed. Universal Disarmament should be made a reality. The PoWs held in different parts of the world should be released under UN supervision. Prof. Arnold Toynbee rightly said: "Man's number one enemy is nationalism, pick its teeth." The UNO should start universal movement for the surrender of sovereignty to establish a new world system so that it can be realised in the beginning of the 21st century. Surrender of national sovereignty of all modern states to the UNO, or to a new world system is the beginning of the end of the problems of Prisoners of War.

Indian Measures

Prison Administration in India is a legacy of the British rule. There has been a very slow growth of prison administration. Instead of paying lip sympathy, India must join voluntarily the world main stream to create a new global system. India must adopt rational approach and press the UNO for a new universal system and make changes accordingly in its national practices. To rationalise prison administration in India, major amendments in the Constitution of India should be made or it is better to draft a new Constitution of India.

At the root of a continuous pattern of neglect is the problem of the continuously neglected area of prison reform. As Kiran Bedi, former I.G. (Prisons) says: " Prison reform has never been on the national agenda. It has been a highly individualized concern—that of social reformers or criminologists. It has never been an institutional concern." M.B. Kaushal, says, who is Additional Director-General, Central Reserve Police Force: "I wrote to the Delhi Administration a number of times during three years as Commissioner asking them to declare some premises as temporary prisons to reduce overcrowding in jails, but there was no response".

India need not wait till the world community takes initiative. It should take the following measures:

(i) Within the framework of the World Prisonless and Crimeless Policy the Government of India should frame the National Prisonless and Crimeless Policy.

(ii) The Government of India should pass new Indian Prisons Act, Indian Prisoners Act and other related Acts.

(iii) World Standard Minimum Rules for the Treatment of Offenders and Maintenance of Prisons should be implemented. Adopt a common jail manual. Classify prisoners, separate custodial executive and correctional functions. Involve NGO's in jail activities. Allow visits by authorised NGO's, lawyers and accredited journalists under a specified procedure.

(iv) Prisons should be renamed as Rationalist Centres.

(v) The important decision of the International Prison Congress held in London in 1872 should be followed.

(vi) Rationalised Universal Declaration of Human Rights and Duties list should be included in the Constitution. Indian Human Rights and Duties Commission should be set up for its implementation. State governments and district governments should set up such commissions.

(vii) Global Declaration of Rationality for Prisonless and Crimeless World System should be followed. Indian Rationalist Commission should be set up. State governments and district governments should be set up such commissions.

(viii) World Convention on Torture should be adopted.

(ix) First India should join the International Criminal Court and continue its efforts for World Criminal Court.

(x) Since the inception of the Constitution of India, Right to Religion is a fundamental right. The organized religions have enormous wealth. Property of these organized religions must be nationalised. The power of punishment of the religious heads should be abolished. All the religious places should be nationalised. In future construction of any religious place should be declared as outdated practice.

Right to Property was a fundamental right and now it is a legal right. Right to Wealth Concentration should be declared as a practice against humanity. This leads to economic equality in India and reduces crime rate. India should join the global mainstream to establish economic equality. Mere abolition of poverty cannot lead to the reduction of crime rate.

(xi). Global humanity should be taken into consideration to reduce the thirst for power among Indians. Now, struggle for power is going on between the natural born citizens of India and the artificial citizens of India. All the top public offices should be held only by the natural born citizens of India who have stayed in this country for a long time. Only the natural citizens of India should be qualified in the name of India to hold public offices in the International forums or UNO or in the world mainstream. Private armies should be banned. India should start a movement to replace the politicians, monks and businessmen by rationalists. This reduces the thirst for power and becomes easy to join the universal mainstream. This also abolishes the abuse of power.

(xii) Prisons must be owned and managed by the governments in India. Prisons exclusively was a State subject with the Centre exercising only a co-ordinating function. Today also it is a state subject with the Centre exercising only a co-ordinating function.

All India Committee on Jail Reforms, 1980-83 recommended that the subject of Prisons and allied institutions were to be included in the Concurrent List of Seventh Schedule of the Constitution of India. But this does not suit to a big country like India. In future also prisons and allied institutions should be continued as a State subject. So that burden of Central Government can be reduced. Moreover, it prevents the concentration of more power in the Central Government. The Centre should exercise only a co-ordinating function and give financial and other assistance to the States.

There is a scarcity of after-care organisation for the rehabilitation of juveniles. Special efforts should be made in this field. To solve the problems of women prisoners and children who accompany them, there should be jails exclusively for them and other facilities as recommended by the Committee on Women Prisoners, 1986-87.

Rationalised penal policy of India should be framed. Capital, corporal and torture punishments should be abolished. New Indian Penal Code, Criminal Procedure Code and allied codes should be passed. Private property of the criminals should be seized as a punishment.

(xiii) The NHRC Chairman M.N. Venkatachaliah rightly observed that 60 per cent of all the arrests made by the police were "unnecessary and unjustifiable". At least 43 per cent of the prison's total expenditure was incurred on accommodating the innocent persons arrested, without evidence. The rate of acquittals, particularly in heinous crimes, is also at increase. It is almost 80 per cent and the delays in trials have now become proverbial. The NHRC further claimed that of all the arms of the state, it is the police in which the average citizen has least confidence.[18] Unnecessary and unjustifiable arrests should end. Heinous criminals must be punished. There should be speedy trial. Government should create people's confidence in the police. Corruption should be rooted out.

Rationalised Rights and Duties of Indian Prisoners should be framed. Enhanced medical facilities should be made available. World standard prisons should be constructed.

With the introduction of modern prison system in India, the Committee of 1836 was not in favour of giving education to prisoners. The prison education underwent a change from "No education in prison" to "Education for all". In future "Rationalised Education for all" should be followed. Prisoners should be encouraged to join for higher education etc. free of cost.

The jail holidays should be as under:

(a) Weekly two holidays.
(b) National Independence Day.
(c) UNO Day and all International days, months and years should be celebrated.
(d) World Government Day. The same pattern should apply to other fields also.

(xiv) The continued detention of persons who might eventually be proved innocent is illegal and constitutes a violation of the fundamental right to personal liberty. Poor people who cannot give a surety or engage a counsel are caught in the grip of a monstrous judicial machinery. The immediate result of this injustice is that prisons have been turned into squalid slums run by veteran convicts and cruel wardens. To rectify this defect except grave offenses bail should be liberalised.

(xv) In countries like Swedan, Denmark, and Finland, there is a 'Prison Ombudsman'. The prisoners have unrestricted right to move to Ombudsman regarding their grievances against jail authorities. There is need for such 'Ombudsman' in Indian States.[19]

(xvi) India should pass resolutions for transferring its sovereignty, surrender and destruction of nuclear weapons, renounciation of war etc. to the UNO or to the new world system. Under UN supervision, exchange of PoW and other detainees held in other countries should take place. This solves the problems of Indian PoW.

Individual Measures

Every prisoner should rationalise himself and try to change other prisoners. He should not escape from this responsibility in the name of present imperfect social system.

Historical Development and Future of Social Hierarchy

Sl. No.	*Name of Age*	*Social Hierarchy*			*Year*
I	Primitive Age		Nil		Before 4000 BC
	Beginning of Power Agesim				
II	Ancient	1. Head	2. Brain	3. Brain	4000 BC onwards
		Body	Mouth Neck Arms Stomach Waist & Below	Mouth Neck Arms Stomach Thighs Knees Feet	
III	Feudal		Religious (Caste) Heads Kings (Rulers) Wealth Concentrators		423 AD
IV	Modern		Rulers Religious Heads Capitalists		1522
			End of Power Ageism		
V	World		World Government Provincial Governments Sub-Provincial Governments District Governments Taluka Governments Village Governments		2000 AD onwards

The modern system has moved towards world unity, liberty, equality and fraternity, the formation of the prison administration is replaced by the reformation of the prison administration. The reformation of the prison administration must be replaced by the rationalisation of prison administration. Such a change is necessary in the interest of the whole world. Man being a rational animal, must sacrifice the modern state system at the altar of the World Government. During the third and the last epoch "In the beginning of the World Governmental System and in the end of the Modern Governmental System all national and international efforts must lead to the Prisonless and Crimeless World System."

References

1. Amrendra Mohanty and Narayan Hazary: *op. cit.*, p. 18.
2. Encyclopaedia Britannica, Vol.18, p. 515.

3. Tyagi, A.R.: *Public Administration*, Atma Ram & Sons, Delhi, 1975, p. 100.
4. *The Indian Express*, 26th May 1997, Bangalore, p. 17.
5. Sirohi, J.P.S.: *Criminology and Criminal Administration*, Allahabad Law Agency, Allahabad, 1983, p. 17.
6. *Ibid.*, pp. 17-18.
7. *Ibid.*, p. 18.
8. John P. Conrad: Crime and its Correction—An International Survey of Attitudes and Practices, University of California press, California, 1965, pp. 301-02.
9. Encyclopaedia Britannica, Vol. 14, 1977, p. 1103.
10. *Ibid.*, 14th ed., Vol, 18, p. 518.
11. *The Indian Express*, 19th June 1998, Bangalore, p. 8.
12. *Ibid.*, 19th July 1998, Bangalore.
13. *Ibid.*, 13th June 1997, Bangalore.
14. *Ibid.*, 3rd July 1996, Bangalore.
15. *The New Indian Express*, 6th April 1999, Bangalore, p. 3.
16. *The Indian Express*, 6th August 1995, Bangalore.
17. *The Times of India*, 15th March 1999, Bangalore, p. 9.
18. *Ibid.*, p. 12.
19. Amrendra Mohanty and Narayan Hazary: *op. cit.*, p. 202.

8
Case Study of Prison Management in Karnataka

"Karnataka is within India. What is applicable to India regarding prison system is also applicable to Karnataka". Prison administration in Karnataka is a legacy of the British rule. There has been a very slow growth of prison administrative system here. The administration of prisons in Karnataka is the outcome of developments in the areas, which the new State had inherited.

1. Before Unification of Karnataka State

(i) Old Mysore Area

During the non-regulation period (1831-56) there were eight jails in former Mysore State. In 1863, Bangalore Central Jail was constructed, which served as an institution mode to other prisons in the State but was widely known as second to none in India. The accommodation was intended for one thousand prisoners. The Mark system was introduced in 1879 by which convicts of good conduct could earn appointments as Warders and Work-Overseers with some remission of sentences.

The Prisons Act (The Act of XXVI of 1870) was introduced in Mysore in 1879. At the time of Rendition, there were nine jails in the State. After the revision of districts and taluks in 1882-83, there were changes in the number of jails. In 1882, the practice of sending prisoners to Andamans was stopped and they were kept in Central Prison, Bangalore. Female prisoners were separated from male prisoners. Educating the convicts was done in the Central Jail, Bangalore and Jail at Mysore. To improve the social and moral condition of the convicts in the jails, arrangements were made for instructing the prisoners on religious and moral subjects.

The jails in Mysore were controlled by the ex-officio Chief Judge of Mysore under the designation of Inspector-General of Prisons till 1897, after which the control of jails was transferred to the Senior Surgeon. In stations where there were Munsifs, the charge of lock-ups was entrusted to them and in other places. The Amildar or the Deputy Amildar retained charge of them.

In 1899, the charge of lock-ups under Munsifs was transferred to Medical Officers and above the rank of Sub-Assistant Surgeons. At the headquarters of taluks without Assistant or Sub-Assistant Surgeons, Sub-Registrars were appointed as a tentative measure in 1904-05 to be incharge of lock-ups, the Amildars and the Deputy Amildars in such places being thereby relieved of such duties as lock-up officers.

In addition to official visitors to jails, i.e., District Magistrates, Sessions Judges, Inspector-General of Police, Inspector-General of Education and others, there were a number of non-officials appointed as visitors of jails. During 1910-14, discourses on religious and moral subjects to the prisoners were arranged. The jails were provided with good libraries for the benefit of prisoners.

In 1923, there were one central jail, one district jail and 78 lock-ups in the Mysore State. At the Central Jail, Bangalore, the industries like carpet, kambli making, cloth weaving, tent repairing, gunny and coir work, carpentry, smithy, pottery, ratten work and basket making were introduced. At the Mysore District Jail also some industries were started. In 1925, the Government accepted that the articles manufactured in jails should not compete with articles of private enterprise or industries. The Prisoners' Aid Societies were formed to release the convicts.

In the old Mysore region different Acts such as the Prisons Act of 1870 and the Prisoners Testimony Regulation Act of 1894 were in force before 1956. The Mysore Jail Manual and Mysore Lock-up Manual were also in operation in the old Mysore region. The Abolition of Whipping Act, 1949 (Mysore Act No. XIII of 1949) was passed by Mysore State. It abolished the sentence of whipping.

(ii) Madras Karnataka Area

When the Ceded Districts were taken over by the East India Company, there was not a single prison in Bellary district. Sir Thomas Munro wrote to the East India Company's Board in 1806, of his difficulties in confining convicts in open choultries and forts. There were nine subsidiary jails and a district jail at Bellary in 1905.

The Madras Prisons and Reformatory Manual (Volume II) was in force in the district. In 1926, there were six sub-jails in the Dakshina Kannada district and a District Jail at Mangalore. Convicts were also taken to Cannanore Central Jail in Malabar.

In the Madras Karnataka region various Acts enacted by the Madras Presidency Government such as the Prisons Act of 1894, the Prisoners Act of 1871 and 1900, Evidence and Appearance Act of 1869 and the Reformatory Schools Act of 1897 were in force before 1956. The Madras Jail Manual was in force in the jail, which were under direct control of Madras Provincial Government before 1956. The Madras Prisons Reformatory Manual was in force in Bellary, Dakshina Kannada and Kodagu districts.

(iii) Kodagu Area

There are no records to show that there was a Central Prison in Kodagu during Raja's time. After the British occupation also, the only jail that served for convicted prisoners was at the Madikeri Fort. The bulk of the jail population was confined in the Madikeri district jail, the taluka lock-ups, being reserved for undertrial prisoners and others sentenced to short terms of imprisonment. In 1824, the Madras Jail Manual was adopted for the administration of Kodagu jails. At that time, besides the Central Jail at Madikeri, there were four sub-jails located in various parts of Kodagu.

Prisoners of Kodagu domicile sentenced for ten years or less were retained in the Madikeri Jail and others were sent to Cannanore. The Chief Commissioner of Kodagu was the ex-officio Inspector-General of Prisons. The woman convicts were sent to Vellore in North Arcot district. The State Medical Officer of Kodagu was the ex-officio Superintendent of the Madikeri Jail and the Subedar of Virajpet Taluk was the ex-officio Superintendent of the sub-jail at

Virajpet. Kodagu had one Central Jail at Madikeri, one sub-jail at Virajpet and nineteen lock-ups in 1956.

(iv) Bombay-Karnataka Area

As early as in 1883, there were jails at each Mamlatdars' offices of taluks of Bombay-Karnataka area and one District Jail at Kaladagi (later shifted to Bijapur) and a subordinate jail at Basavan Bagewadi of Bijapur District. Also there were District Jails at Karwar, Dharwa and Belgaum and a subordinate jail at Athni. The chief jail industries were cane work, weaving and carpentry. There was a Borstal School at Dharwa and a Central Jail at Hindalga near Belgaum.

In The Bombay-Karnataka region, the different Acts enacted by the Bombay Presidency such as the Prisons Act of 1894, the Prisoners Act of 1990, the Transfer of Prisoners Act of 1950, Whipping Act of 1909, the Indian Lunacy Act of 1912, the Bombay Borstal Act of 1929 and other Acts commissioned by the Bombay Provincial Government were in force before 1956. The Bombay Jail Manual was also in force in the Bombay-Karnataka area before 1956.

(v) Hyderabad-Karnataka Area

Before 1897, the Department of Prisons in Hyderabad State was in a very backward condition. Hankin, the Director-General of Prisons in the Hyderabad State in 1897 compiled a Jail Manual and organized District Prisons wherever needed. Gulbarga town had a jail, as it was the capital city of Bahumani Sultans for some time. Raichur and Bidar towns had one jail each. Formerly, District Surgeons were the ex-officio Superintendents of District Jails. Several reforms were introduced in the management of prisons during Hankin's regime. The prisoners were provided evening recreation, and a system of parole was introduced in favour of convicts.

The Imperial Gazetteer of India, 1908 states that Hyderabad State had the district police and jails under an Inspector-General of Police, who was also the Inspector-General of Prisons. Each of the outlying Central Jails was incharge of a Superintendent controlled by the First Talukdar in his capacity by Nazim-i-Mahabis or Inspector of Jails. The Third Talukdars or headquarters tahsildars, supervised

District Jails. Central Jails at Gulbarga and district jails at Raichur and Bidar were maintained. Lock-ups and subsidiary jails were located in some of the taluks.

In 1903, there were five Central Jails, twelve District Jails, ninety five lock-ups, four thousand seven hundred forty two male prisoners and ninety female prisoners in the Hyderabad State. Tents, rugs, carpets, cotton tweeds, checks, shirting and police clothing and dress for office were made in the jails.[1] The Hyderabad Jail Manual was in force in the Hyderabad-Karnataka region till the Karnataka Prison Manual, 1978 was introduced in Karnataka State.

Dr. G. Reckless, United Nations Expert in Criminology, visited the Mysore Jail on 11th November 1951 and held a joint meeting of both the police and jail officials. This further encouraged the Karnataka Government to improve prison administration. After Independence, the Government of India took some interest in prison reformation.[2] A model Prison Manual was prepared and circulated by Government of India. As a result of this, the Karnataka State was also keeping pace with the modern concepts of prison administration.

In India, all institutions for the confinement of prisoners convicted, unconvicted, civil and security are owned by the State Governments and controlled by the Minister for Jails. Until the Government of India Act, 1919, the jail department formed a part of the Central Government. Under the said Act it was transferred to provincial control as a reserved subject. The Act of 1935 abolished dyarchy in the provinces and transferred the department to the ministers control. The minister is assisted by secretaries taken from the senior cadre of the Indian Administrative Service.[3] The Inspector-General of Prisons is the executive head of the jail department, entrusted with carrying out the policy framed by the minister.

2. After Unification of Karnataka State

The new State of Mysore (later renamed as Karnataka) as envisaged in Section 7 of the State's Reorganization Act, 1956 comprising of erstwhile States of Mysore, Coorg and some parts of former states of Bombay, Madras and Hyderabad, came into existence on 1st November 1956. Since then, there was no common Manual for Prison Administration in the State of Karnataka and the

Manuals that were in force in the respective areas were followed for day to day administration. It was essential to have uniform rules applicable to all the jails in the State.

After the Karnataka Prison Rules were brought into force with effect from 1974, the existing manuals had to be gone through carefully with reference to the Karnataka Prison Rules and a new uniform manual had to be framed. The Model Prison Manual prepared and circulated by Government of India, was also kept in view to make the manual up-to-date and useful for day to day work in the department. The manual is brought out with a broader view in consonance with modern trends in the field of correctional administration.[4]

The State has an area of 74,861 square miles with a population of 1,94,01,193 as per 1951 Census. The new State stood eighth among the fourteen States of the Indian Union, both in size and in population and it accounts for 5.9 per cent of the total area of India and 5.4 per cent of the total population of India. With the Re-organization, the new Mysore State owns a sea coast of 200 miles studded with 21 ports.[5] Thus, Karnataka State has all the land, water and air routes of transport and communication. At present, the State is divided into 27 districts.

(i) Classification of Prisons in States in India

The classification of prisoners cannot be practically effective if all types of prisoners are huddled together in the same institution or institutions of the same type. The different types of criminals are led to crime by different forces and need individual treatment, which they cannot receive in one type of institutions. In India the states have classified their prisons differently. But, classification of prisons on the basis of numbers to be accommodated is the common feature in all the states. Thus, there are large prisons called Central Jails and small prisons called District Jails.

(ii) Prison Institutions

According to Section 2(j) of the Karnataka Prisons Act, 1963, "Prison" means any jail or place used permanently or temporarily under the general or special orders of the State Government for the detention of prisoners and includes all lands and buildings appurtenant thereto, but does not include—

(a) Any place for the confinement of prisoners who are exclusively in the custody of the police;

(b) Any place specially appointed by the State Government under Section 541 of the Code of Criminal Procedure, 1898;

(c) Any place which has been declared by the State Government, by general or special order, to be a subsidiary jail.[6]

When the new State was formed in 1956, there were six Central Jails at the headquarters cities and four District Sub-Jails at district level. Apart from these, in addition to the District Jails, there were two Special Sub-Jails and two Borstal Schools. Besides these prisons, there were two agricultural-cum-industrial farms one at Bijapur and another at Khanapur for prisoners. The prison population in the beginning of 1956 was 6,365 convicts and 554 undertrials and there were 599 Borstal lads in the two Borstal Schools.

As usual, the policy of prison administration in 1957-58 was one of reformation and rehabilitation of the convicts. During the year, 24,616 prisoners were admitted to the prisons. The prisoners were engaged in the manufacture of carpet, kambli and also other industries like carpentry, weaving, tailoring, smithy, rattan and coir industry and agricultural farming.

A scheme for settling of well-behaved convicts in an agricultural farm near Gangavathi in Raichur District was sanctioned and steps were taken to implement the scheme. Under the Probation of Offenders Act, those persons who were offenders and who were above 16 years of age, who by reason of their home conditions, character and antecedents were fit to be given a chance to show improvement on their release on probation, were spared harmful experience of jail and were given a chance to improve their behaviour in their own home surroundings.[7]

In 1958, there were five Central Jails at Bangalore, Bellary, Belgaum, Alipuram and Gulbarga; three District Jails at Mysore, Bijapur and Mercara; four Special Sub-Jails at Raichur, Bidar, Mangalore and Karwar; two Special Lock-ups at Davangere and KGF; and seven District Lock-ups at Kolar, Tumkur, Mandya, Hassan,

Chikmagalur, Shimoga and Chitradurga. The total number of lock-ups continued to be the same as in the previous year, i.e. eighty-six.

There were two Borstal Schools at Dharwar and Alipuram, Bellary. The Alipuram Jail at Bellary was closed in 1958. During the year, two lock-ups at K.R. Nagar and Shikaripur were closed. There were five thousand seventy-one prisoners of all classes at the beginning of 1958 and twenty-three thousand four hundred fourteen prisoners were newly admitted during the year 1958 and twenty-three thousand two hundred thirty three prisoners were discharged, leaving five thousand two hundred fifty two at the end of the year. The daily average number of prisoners in all the prison institutions in the State was 4,763.42 (4796.39).[8]

(iii) Organisation of Prisons in Karnataka

The Prisons and Jails in Karnataka State are constituted under the Karnataka Prisons Act 1963 (Karnataka Act 33 of 1963). The Inspector-General of Prisons is appointed under Section 3 of the said Act and he exercises, subject to the orders of State Government, general control and superintendence over all Prisons, Jails, the Borstal School and the Training Institute in the Karnataka State. He is in immediate charge of the Office of the Inspector-General of Prisons in all its branches and conducts all routine work.

According to Section 5 of the Karnataka Prisons Act, the State Government provides accommodation for the prisoners in the State in prisons constructed and regulated in such manner as to comply with the requisitions of this Act in respect of the separation of prisoners.

Section 6 of said Act says that whenever it appears to the Inspector-General that the number of prisoners in any prison is greater than can conveniently or safely be kept therein, and it is not convenient to transfer the excess number to some other prison, or whenever from the outbreak of epidemic disease within any prison, or for any other reason it is desirable to provide for the temporary and safe custody of any prisoners provision shall be made by such manner as the State Government may direct for the shelter and safe custody in temporary prisons of so many of the prisoners as cannot be conveniently or safely kept in the prison. At present, temporary prisons are not there. Temporary prisons may be opened whenever necessary for confinement of such class of prisoners as the State Government may from time to time direct.

Classification of Prisons

In Karnataka also, prisons are classified on the basis of number of prisoners be accommodated. They are:

1. Large Prisons: Central Prisons
2. Small Prisons:
   - (i) District Prisons:
     - (a) Class and
     - (b) Class II
   - (i) Sub-Jails:
     - (a) District Headquarters Sub-Jails and Special Sub-Jails
     - (b) Taluka Sub-Jails and Taluka Special Prisons

According to Rule 3(1) in Chapter II of the Karnataka Prisons Rules, 1974, all prisons situated in Karnataka are classified as under:

1. Large Prisons:
   - (a) Central Prisons
2. Small Prisons:
   - (b) District Prisons, Class I
   - (c) District Prisons, Class II
   - (c) District Headquarters Sub-Jails and Special Sub-Jails
   - (e) Taluka Sub-Jails
   - (f) Juvenile jails
   - (g) Open air jails

Under Sub-rule (2), the names of various prisons under the different classes of prisons are as follows:

1. Large Prison:
   - (a) Central Prisons are at Belgaum, Bangalore, Gulbarga and Bellary.
   - (b) District Prisons Class I are at Bijapur and Mysore;
   - (c) District Prisons, Class II are at Raichur, Bidar, Mercara, Mangalore, Shimoga and Karwar;
   - (d) District Headquarters Sub-Jails are at Chikmagalur and Bijapur;

(e) Special Sub-Jails are at Kolar Gold Fields and Davangere;

(f) Taluk Sub-Jails in

(i) Bangalore District are at Doddaballapur, Ramanagaram and Open Air Jail at Koramangala;

(ii) Mysore District at Nanjangud, Hunsur, Kollegal and Chamarajanagar;

(iii) Hassan District at Holenarasipur and Arasikere;

(iv) Shimoga District at Sagar;

(v) Tumkur District at Madhugiri, Tiptur and Pawagada;

(vi) South Kanara District at Udupi, Karkal, Puttur, Coondapur and Bantwal;

(vii) Bidar District at Bhalki, Humnabad and Aurad;

(viii) Mandya District at Srirangapatna;

(ix) Chickmagalur District at Tarikere and Narasimharajapur;

(x) Kolar District at Chikkaballapur;

(xi) Bellary District at Hospet, Harapanahalli and Kudligi;

(xii) Raichur District at Deodurga, Gangavathi, Koppal, Kushtagi, Lingasugur, Manvi, Sindhanur;

(xiii) Gulbarga District at Aland, Chincholi, Chitapur, Sedam, Shorapur and Yadgir;

(xiv) Belgaum District at Athani, Hukeri, Khanapur, Parasagad (Savadatti), Bailhongal, Gokak, Ramdurg, Raibhag, Chikodi;

(xv) Dharwar District at Gadag, Hangal, Hubli, Hirekerur, Haveri, Ranebennur, Ron, Shirahatti, Kundagol, Navalgund, Shiggon, Juvenile jail at Dharwar, Kalaghatta;

(xvi) Bijapur District at Badami, Bagalkot, Bagevadi, Hungund, Indi, Muddebihal, Sindgi and Jamakhandi;

(xvii) Karwar District at Bhatkal, Honnavar, Kumta, Haliyal, Ankola, Siddapur, Sirsi and Mundagod;

(xviii) Coorg District at Virajpet.

According to Sub-rule (3), special prisons may be opened whenever necessary for confinement of such class of prisoners as the State Government may from time to time directs. Under Sub-rule (4)(i), the following kinds of prisoners are ordinarily confined in Central Prisons:

(a) Prisoners sentenced to death;
(b) Life imprisonment prisoners of all classes;
(c) Prisoners of imprisonment exceeding 10 years of all classes;
(d) Civil prisoners;
(e) Prisoners awaiting trial in the local courts;
(f) Female prisoners;
(g) Military prisoners; and
(h) Juvenile prisoners.

A Central Prison also serves as the prison of the district in which it is situated and of the adjoining districts where there are no district prisons.

Under Sub-rule (5) the following kinds of prisoners are ordinarily confined in District Prison, Class II:

(a) Prisoners of all classes sentenced to a term of imprisonment not exceeding 10 years;
(b) Female prisoners;
(c) Civil prisoners;
(d) Prisoners awaiting trial before the local courts;
(e) Military prisoners; and
(f) Juvenile prisoners.

According to Sub-rule (6) the following classes of prisoners are ordinarily confined in the district headquarters sub-jails, special sub-jails and taluka sub-jails and taluka special sub-jails:

(a) Prisoners sentenced to a term of below three months in case of headquarters sub-jails and upto 15 days in case of taluk sub-jails;
(b) Female prisoners;
(c) Persons awaiting trial before the local courts; and
(d) Civil prisoners.

Place of confinement of certain types of prisoners:

Rule 4 deals with the place of confinement of certain types of prisoners. Under Sub-rule (1), prisoners sentenced to death or life imprisonment or for a term exceeding ten years by courts situated in the districts specified in column (1) of the table below are confined in the jails specified in the corresponding entries in column (2) thereof:

1	2
Bangalore, Mysore, Mercara, Mangalore, Hassan, Mandya, Chikmagalur, Shimoga, Chitradurga, Tumkur and Kolar Districts.	Bangalore Central prison.
Bellary District.	Bellary Central Prison.
Raichur, Gulbarga and Bidar Districts.	Gulbarga Central Prison.
Bijapur, Dharwar, Belgaum and Karwar Districts.	Belgaum Central Prison.

Under Sub-rule (2) all convicted juvenile prisoners whose term of imprisonment exceeds six months are confined at the Juvenile jail, Dharwar. Under Sub-rule (3), habitual prisoners sentenced to imprisonment for more than three months are confined at Bellary Central Prison.[9]

According to Chapter I of the Karnataka Prison Manual 1978, all prisons situated in Karnataka State fall under the following classes, viz.:

(i) Central Prisons
(ii) District Prisons Class I
(iii) District Prisons Class II
(iv) District Headquarters Sub-Jails and Special Sub-Jails
(v) Taluk Sub-Jails
(vi) Juvenile Jails
(vii) Special Prisons
(viii) Open Air Jails
(ix) Borstal Schools.

The Central Prisons are at Belgaum, Bangalore, Gulbarga and Bellary.

The District Prisons Class I are at Bijapur and Mysore. The District Prisons Class II are at Raichur, Bidar, Mercara, Mangalore, Shimoga and Karwar. These kinds of prisoners are confined in District Prison Class I:

(i) Prisoners of all classes sentenced to a term of imprisonment not exceeding 10 years.
(ii) Female Prisoners.
(iii) Civil Prisoners.
(iv) Prisoners awaiting trial before the local courts.

(v) Military Prisoners and
(vi) Juvenile Prisoners.

In District Prisons Class II, the following kinds of prisoners are confined:

(i) Prisoners of all the classes sentenced to a term of imprisonment not exceeding or unexpired portion of sentence not exceeding 6 months.
(ii) Female Prisoners.
(iii) Civil Prisoners.
(iv) Prisoners awaiting trial before local Courts.
(v) Military Prisoners.
(vi) Juvenile Prisoners.

The District Headquarters Sub-jails and Special Sub-Jails and Taluk Sub-Jails.

The following kinds of prisoners are confined in District Headquarters Sub-Jails, Special Sub-Jails and Taluk Sub-Jails:

(i) Prisoners sentenced to a term of imprisonment upto 3 months in case of headquarters sub-jails and upto 15 days in case of Taluk sub-jails.
(ii) Female Prisoners.
(iii) Prisoners awaiting trial before the local courts, and
(iv) Civil Prisoners.

All Juvenile prisoners convicted by the Courts in the State whose term of imprisonment exceed 3 months are confined at the Juvenile Jail, Dharwar. Habitual prisoners sentenced to imprisonment for more than 3 months are confined at Central Prison, Bellary.

Open Air Prison at Koramangala is established with two fold objectives, viz., (i) Imparting training to the inmates in Agriculture and Horticulture as a reformative measure with no heavy guards. (ii) To rehabilitate them in their original profession of Agriculture with training in modern methods. Only well behaved long term prisoners are kept in this institution.

Prison Training Institute, Mysore imparts training to the Head Warders and Warders of the Department in correctional administration.[10] In 1969, the population of the entire jails in Karnataka was seven thousand eight hundred forty convicts and one thousand eight hundred eighty nine undertrials.[11] The police guards at the District Jails of Bijapur and Raichur were replaced by prison guards in 1971.

The Prisons Department was reorganised in pursuance of the recommendations of the Pay Commission creating one post of Deputy Inspector-General of Prisons, two posts of Senior Superintendents of Prisons for toning up the administrative efficiency in the Department. The post of Superintendent, District Jail, Bellary was upgraded to that of a Superintendent, Central Jail.

A Research and Planning Unit headed by a Research-cum-Statistical Officer (Class I–Gazetted) with a Research Assistant (Class II–Gazetted) were created for attending to the following aspects:

(a) Development of facts concerning the operation of Correctional System from the Institutional data;
(b) Maintenance of a Central Index Card file of such offenders;
(c) Preparation of reports of the operations of the Department including information on the programme and activities of the Department and tabulation of other significant data;
(d) Preparation of Annual Statistical Report of Correctional Administration;
(e) Forwarding Statistical information to Central Bureau of Correctional Services;
(f) Study of the type of data collected from the forms prescribed and the registers maintained to simplify the manner of collecting, analysing and interpreting data.

Open Air Jail

Establishment of an Open Air Jail, (Agricultural-cum-Industrial Farm) on an extent of 144 acres of land near Bangalore (Koramangala village, Devanhalli Taluk) was sanctioned, after the successful implementation of the Open Air Jail at Ugargol in Belgaum during 1968-71. Establishment of the Farm was to be implemented in three stages utilising prison labour. The first stage of this project was commenced. The intention was to train prisoners in modern methods of cultivation as ninety per cent of the long-term prisoners belong to the agricultural community and the training given to them will go a long way in their rehabilitation after release.[12]

(iv) Prisons Institutions in 1981-82 to 2000-2001

Prison Institutions in 1981-82

In course of time, the status of some of the prisons was changed. In 1981-82 there were four Central Prisons at Bangalore,

Belgaum, Gulbarga and Bellary; two District Prisons (Class I), one at Mysore and another at Bijapur; six District Prisons (Class II), at Raichur, Bidar, Madikeri, Mangalore, Shimoga and Karwar; two special Sub-Jails at Davangere and Kolar Gold Fields; seven Sub-Jails one each in the remaining district headquarters and 75 Taluk Sub-Jails.

In all major jails and 32 Taluk Sub-Jails, guarding was done by the prison staff and in 43 Taluk Sub-Jails guarding was done by police personnel and the Revenue Sheristedars were working as ex-officio Superintendents. One Open Air Jail at Koramangala in Devanhalli Taluk, Bangalore District and one Borstal School at Dharwad and one Juvenile Jail at Dharwad were functioning. Thus, there were 99 prison institutions in the State.

The District-wise numbers of jails in the State in 1981-82 were: Bangalore–5; Belgaum–10, Bellary–4; Bidar–3; Bijapur–10, Chitradurga–2; Chikmagalur–3; Dakshina Kannada–6; Dharwar–15; Gulbarga–7; Hassan–3; Kodagu–2; Kolar–3; Mandya–1; Mysore–5; Raichur–6; Shimoga–2; Tumkur–3; Uttar Kannada–10 and the total was 99. There has been a reduction in the population as in 1981-82, the total prison population was 4,073, out of which 1,911 convicts and 2,162 undertrials were there.[13]

Prison Institutions in 1992

As in 1992 (March) the following were the prisons in the State:

(1) Central Prisons (6) at Bangalore, Bellary, Gulbarga, Belgaum, Mysore and Bijapur, with a total accommodation for 3,679;

(2) District Prisons (6) at Mangalore, Madikeri, Raichur, Bidar, Shimoga and Karwar, with a total accommodation for 844;

(3) District Central Sub-Jails (7) at Mandya, Chitradurga, Kolar, Hassan, Chikmagalur, Tumkur and Dharwad, with a total capacity for 558;

(4) Special Sub–Jails (2) at Davangere and KGF with a total capacity of 113;

(5) Twenty Six Taluk Sub-Jails under the direct control of the Prisons Department and 44 Taluk Sub-Jails under the control of ex-officio Superintendents of Police Department and Revenue Department, in the State with a total capacity of 1,669;

(6) One Open Jail at Koramangala accommodating 80 prisoners;

(7) One Jail for youth prisoners (Taruna Bandikhane) at Dharwar with a capacity of 250 inmates; and

(8) One Borstal School at Dharwad for 133 inmates. In total there were 94 jails to accommodate 7,376 persons.

Table I. Jail Organisation, Types and Inmates Capacity in 1992

Nature	*Sl*	*Types of*	*No.*	*Total*
	I	Central Jails	6	3,679
	II	Dist. Prisons	6	844
	III	Dist. Central Sub-jails	7	558
Traditio -nal	IV	Special Sub-jails	2	113
	VI	Youth Prisoners Jail	1	250
	VII	Borstal School	1	133
Open	VIII	Men's Open Air Jail	1	80
		Total	**94**	**7,376**

The total number of undertrials was on the increase and in order to avoid delay in the disposal of cases, Government constituted a State level committee in 1979, under the Chairmanship of the Chief Justice of Karnataka, to review the cases of undertrial prisoners and to suggest measures for speedy disposal of cases.

In 1991-92, there were 1,136 staff as against 1,438 sanctioned posts. The details were as here under: Group A–16 (14 males, 2 females), Group B–17 (16 males, 1 female) Group C–1,042 (1,006 males and 36 females) and Group D–81 (61 males and 20 females).[14]

Table II. Prison Institutioins in 1994-95

(i)	Central Prisons at Bangalore, Belgaum, Bellary,	06
(ii)	District Prisons at Mangalore, Madikeri, Raichur, Bidar,	06
(iii)	District Headquarters Sub-Jails at Mandya, Chitradurga,	07
(iv)	Special Sub-Jails at Davangere and KGF	02
(v)	Taluk Sub-Jails	73
(vi)	Open Air Jail, Koramangala	01
(vii)	Juvenile Jail, Dharwar	01
(viii)	Borstal School, Dharwar	01
	Total	**97**

Table III. Prison Institutions from 1997-98 to 2000-01

1. Large Prisons		
(i)	Central Prisons at Bangalore, Belgaum, Bellary,	06
2. Small Prisons		
(ii)	District Prisons at Mangalore, Madikeri, Raichur, Bidar	06
(iii)	District Headquarters Sub-Jails at Mandya, Chitradurga	07
(iv)	Special Sub-Jails at Davangere and K.G.F.	02
(v)	Taluk Sub-Jails	72
(vi)	Open Air Jail, Koramangala	01
(vii)	Juvenile Jail, Dharwar	01
(viii)	Borstal School, Dharwar	01
	Total	**96**

Borstal School, Dharwar

At the beginning of the year, there were 2 lads. No lad was admitted and no lad released during the year and at the end of December 1997 as no lads were remanded by the courts.[15]

Prisons have also been Organised, Classified and Controlled on the following bases:

According to Sub-rule (2) of Rule (3) of the Karnataka Prisons Rules of 1974, Special Prisons may be opened whenever necessary for confinement of such class of prisoners as the State Government may from time to time direct. At present, special prisons are not there.

Areawise: All areas of the State have been given representation. There are other bases like family-wise prison, exclusive open air jail/camp/minimum security jail for women etc. are not taken into consideration.

Prisons have irrationally been organised, classified and controlled:

First, all jails are not manned by Department. Forty-three taluka sub-jails are under the control of the Sheristedars of Revenue Department and the remaining twenty-nine taluka sub-jails are manned by Department Staff.

Secondly, prisons have been unnecessarily classified into District Jails, District Headquarters Sub-Jails and Special Sub-Jails.

Thirdly, Taluka Sub-jails have been brought under the control of the Head Office through District Prisons.

Fourthly, different types of sub-jails category has been unnecessarily added.

Fifthly, the total number of ninety six prisons is not required.

Sixthly, Policy of freezing prisons is not there.

Seventhly, most of the jails are convict-cum-undertrial jails.

Eighthly, Open Air Jails/camps are neglected.

Totally, there is no scientific organisation, classification and control of prisons, which should be simple and easily understandable even by the general public.

(v) Administrative Staff

At the helm of the Department, there is the Inspector-General of Prisons. The Inspector-General of Prisons is appointed under Section 3 of the Karnataka Prisons Act, 1963 and he exercises subject to the orders of State Government, general control and superintendence over all prisons, jails, the Borstal School and the Training Institute in the Karnataka State.

He controls the expenditure of the Prisons Department, submits annual budget to the Government, distributes the total budget allotment among the several jails and authorises all expenditure, inspects the prison institutions, submits to Government a special report regarding any jail which is in unsatisfactory state, and submits to Government a detailed annual administration report etc. For list of Inspector-General of Prisons.

The Deputy Inspector-General of Prisons appointed by the State Government assists the Inspector-General in the management of prison institutions and attends to such other duties prescribed by The Inspector-General of Prisons. During the absence of the Inspector-General of Prisons, he performs the current duties of the Inspector-General of Prisons, exercises administrative and financial powers delegated to him by the Government, supervises the prison institutions within his jurisdiction, conducts enquiry into all cases of accidental and unnatural deaths of prisoners in jails or any serious injury to prisoners endangering their life or any outbreak of violence or neglect of duty by the prison staff and any negligence on the part of the superintendent, etc.

There is Research Unit attached to the Inspector General of Prisons at the Headquarters with Research Officer and Research Assistant. The duties of the Research Unit are the development of facts concerning the operations of the correctional system from the institutional data, maintains a Central Index Card File of such offenders, preparation of reports of the operations of the Department, preparation of annual statistical report of correctional administration, forwarding of statistical information to the Central Bureau of Correctional Services and study of the type of data collected from forms prescribed and the registers maintained to simplify the manner of collecting, analysing and interpreting data.

There is a Superintendent for every prison to manage the prison in all matters. Superintendent of a prison other than a Central Prison, has to obey the District Magistrate respecting the prison. The superintendent is the officer in charge of a prison. The superintendents of all Central and District Prisons are officers specially appointed by name. In the absence of a superintendent, his powers and duties are exercised and performed by the Assistant Superintendent or Jailor. The Superintendent thoroughly acquaints himself with the rules and acts and regulations related to jails and is responsible for carrying out all such rules and statutory provisions, execution of all such sentences of prisoners committed to his charge.

He visits the prison once in the forenoon and once in the afternoon on every working day, Sundays and Prison Holidays and also whenever special circumstances demand. At least once a week he visits all parts of prison at night at odd hours to satisfy himself that everything is in order. He maintains a Journal to record his daily activities and a copy of the Journal is forwarded to the Inspector-General of Prisons on or before 5th day of the month.

The Superintendent, Central Prisons/District Prisons inspects Taluk Sub-Jail twice in a year and sees that Sub-Jails in his jurisdiction function smoothly and efficiently. He conducts all jail business within its prescints, and holds weekly inspection parade and listens to the grievances of the prisoners. He controls the receipt and expenditure of the jail and submits the annual budget to the Inspector-General of Prisons. He maintains records and responsible for submission of reports and returns.

The Assistant Superintendent appointed in certain prisons assists the superintendent in administration of the prisons. The Assistant Superintendent visits all parts of prisons daily, secures safe custody of prisoners and enforces discipline amongst the subordinates and prisoners will be present at the time of unlocking and locking-up of prisoners.

He has no power to punish a prisoner, enforces greatest economy, gives attention to the management of the prison, supervises the prison factory in prisons, collects social history of offenders, prepares case histories and writes index cards of prisoners, looks after the proper functioning of the judicial section of the prison, inspects the jail to carry out field inspection etc.

The District Surgeon/District Medical Officer of the District in which a Central Prison or District Prison or District Headquarters Sub-Jail is situated is the Visiting Medical Officer of the Prison. He visits the prison twice a week to hear complaints of sickness and arranges for medical treatment. His duty embraces every matter of the prisoners and the general hygiene of the prison; especially as regards diet as well as the treatment of the sick.

In each Central Prison and District Prison Class I and Borstal School, Dharwar a member of Medical Department of the rank of Assistant Surgeon Grade II is appointed as Medical Officer. The Medical Officer of Taluka Government Hospital in which a Taluka Sub-Jail or Special Sub-Jail is situated is the Medical Officer of the Taluka Sub-Jail and Special Sub-Jail. He visits the Sub-Jail at least twice a week or oftener in case of emergency to attend to sick prisoners.

The Medical Officer visits and sees the sick daily except on Sundays and on those days also whenever necessary and inspects the jail at least once a week and enters the same in his journal. The duties of the Medical Officer generally are to attend to the health and cleanliness of the prisoners, the treatment of the sick and the hygiene of the prison especially as regards diet, raw and cooked. He attends to the fortnightly weighment of prisoners and all other matters connected directly or indirectly with the health of the staff and the inmates of the jail. He also examines all newly admitted prisoners.

Compounders and male nurses are deputed from the Department of Health and Family Planning Services to the prison. They are subordinate to the Superintendent, Assistant Superintendents, Assistant Surgeon and Chief Jailor. They help the Medical Officer in the maintenance of health of the staff and prisoners.

Wherever the Chief Jailor is appointed, he performs the duties of a Jailor. The Jailor gives notice of death to the Superintendent and Medical Officer and is responsible for safe custody of records. Jailor would not be absent from the prison for a night. He keeps prisoners' admission registers and prisoners' properties and responsible for the search of prisoners and reports all cases of illness to the Medical Officer and puts a prisoner under irons. The Jailor is the Chief Jailor's immediate Assistant, whose duty is to take his place or whatever portion of the Chief Jailor's duties are delegated to him. He maintains his report book.

The Jailor supervises the admission and search of prisoners, custody of clothing store, issue of new clothing and maintenance of clothing registers, custody of prisoner's private clothing, storage of all grains and other articles of diet, weighment and issue of rations; maintenance of ration accounts and ration registers; mustering of jail guards at morning and evening parade; maintenance of extra articles purchased by civil debtors. The jailor performs all duties, powers and responsibilities of the Chief Jailor. The Jailor visits the prison at night once a week. He discharges the duties assigned by the Superintendent.

Subordinate Officers

All subordinate officers obey the Superintendent and officers subordinate to the Jailor performs the duties imposed on them by the Jailor. Section 8 of the Act provide that no officer of a prison should have business dealings with prisoners.

Warders Establishment

The following Grades of Warders are on the establishment of the Prisons Department–

(i) Chief Warders

(ii) Head Warders; and Female Head Warders

(iii) Warders (Male and Female).

The Chief Warder or senior most Head Warder where there is no post of Chief Warder subject to the general control of the Jailor; is the Head of the Warder Establishment. He is responsible for its work and for the due carrying out of all rules relating to it and to the guarding of the jail.

He assists the Jailor at unlocking and locking-up. He visits the guards and sentries on duty frequently by day and at least twice a week at night and makes entry of the hours of their visits and of any irregularities he may discover in his report book which he maintains in a form similar to that of the Jailor and submits it daily to the Superintendent through proper channel. He keeps the attendance and duty rosters and prisoners punishment book and the register of the warders establishment. He performs such other duties as the Superintendent may by order to be recorded in the Jail Order Book assigned to him.

The Chief Warder/Head Warder assists the Chief Jailor/Jailor with regard to allotment, handing over and taking over of staff quarters. He is incharge of maintenance of quarters, sanitary conditions, water facility of staff quarters. The Chief Warder has charge of the whole arms, ammunition; uniform and equipment of every description of the warder establishment and of the accounts relating thereto. He supervises drill and practice in Musketry of the men; the attendance of the standing guards; the mounting of sentries relief etc. He is responsible for the smartness and cleanliness of the warders and for their being at all times properly dressed.

In the event of any attempt by the prisoners to break out of the jail or any other disturbance occurring the guard communicates with the Chief Jailor or Assistant Superintendent. If however the prisoners assault the prison officers or subordinates or attempt to break out of any particular ward or yard and the Chief Warder considers dangerous will order to open fire.

The Inspector-General of Prisons may sanction the entertainment of such temporary staff in addition to permanent establishment provided, according to circumstances. Every warder is assigned to him from time to time particular duty by the Chief Jailor under orders of the Superintendent.

Women Officers

The following categories of Women Officers are in the Department:

1. Woman Jailor.
2. Woman Head Warder.
3. Woman Warders.

They perform duties of Jailor, Head Warder and Warders respectively. In every prison in which woman prisoners are confined there are such number of woman officers of such class. The Woman Jailor or the Head Warder or the Woman Warders as the case may be have the entire care and superintendence of the woman prisoners and discharge the following duties; she is present at the opening of wards and mustering of woman prisoners every morning. She is also present at locking-up and see that every prisoner is present.

During day she has the custody of key of the wards, cells and yards in which women prisoners are confined and at night after locking-up she hands over them to the Chief Jailor; she sees that the wards are thoroughly cleaned as soon as the prisoners turnout in the morning at which time also the latrines, bathing places and all other parts of the woman ward are swept and cleaned; she also allots tasks to woman convicts, sentenced to labour and sees that they are duly performed; she sees that the woman prisoners are clean in their persons and clothes etc.

She searches all woman prisoners on admission and may search any woman prisoner at any time; she takes care that no male prisoner enters the woman yard unless accompanied by an authorized jail officer; she supervises the distribution of food to the woman prisoners. Woman warders have the same duties in regard to woman prisoners as male warders have in relation to male prisoners.

A woman warder invariably forms part of the escort of woman prisoners sent to appear before courts or under transfer. Woman officer believes that any woman prisoner is pregnant reports the facts to the Superintendent or the Chief Jailor. In jails where there is a woman jailor or woman head warder, the woman officer keeps a diary in the prescribed form in which she records all occurrence of importance within her department.

Gatekeeper

The officer acting as gatekeeper or any other officer of the prison examines anything carried in or out of the prison, may stop and search or caused to be searched any person suspected of bringing any prohibited articles into or out of the prisons or carrying out any property belonging to the prison and if any such article or property be found, gives immediate notice thereof to the Chief Jailor. In every jail there is a gatekeeper who is constantly on duty as a gatekeeper at the main gate by day and by night. He is under the general control of the Chief Jailor. A Jailor in the case of Central Jails and Head Warders in other District Prisons and District Headquarters Sub-Jails and Special Sub-Jails are posted as gatekeeper. An additional warder and another for opening the doors and wickets may with the sanction of the Superintendent be employed to assist the Gatekeeper.[16]

At present, the administrative set up of jails is headed by the Director General /Inspector General of Prisons. The Director General of Police and IG of Prisons is the executive head of the Jail Department. The IG of Prisons is assisted by a DIG of Prisons, a Research Officer, a Headquarters Assistant and a Gazetted Manager of the Headquarters. All the central prisons, district prisons, district headquarters sub-jails are managed by departmental staff. Of the 73 taluk sub-jails in 1994-95, 28 were managed by departmental staff and 45 by revenue and police staff. In 1997-98 and at present, of the 72 taluk sub-jails, 29 are managed by Departmental staff and 43 by Revenue and Police staff.

An officer of the rank of superintendent of central jail is the Principal of Prison Training Institute at Mysore. The services of psychiatrists are available for inmates at Bangalore and Belgaum Central Prisons. Superintendents are in-charge of Central and District Prisons, District Headquarters Sub-jails and Taluk Sub-jails. In addition to these officers, there are Assistant Superintendents, Chief Jailors, Jailors, Chief Warders, in the Prison Department. All Central Jails and Borstal School at Dharwar have regular medical officers to look after the health of the inmates.

In Prison Department, there are in all 1792 posts existing in different cadres as on 31-12-99. Out of which 1,318 posts are filled and 474 posts are vacant. Details are as under:

Table IV. Posts Existing in Different Cadres

Group	*Sanctioned Strength*	*Working Strength*	*Vacant*
A Group	35	14	21
B Group	31	15	26
C Group	1, 624	1, 207	417
D Group	102	82	20
Total	**1,792**	**1,318**	**474**

Table V. Prison Institutions in Karnataka on 30-9-2000

otal No. of Types of nstitut-ions	*No. of Type of Institutions*	*No. of Institutions*	*Total Accommodation Capacity*			*Total Actual Strength*		
			Male	*Female*	*Total*	*Male*	*Female*	*Total*
(i)	Central Prisons	6						
(ii)	District Prisons	6						
(iii)	Dist. Headquarters Sub-jails	7						
	Special Sub-jails	2						

Cont....

Total No. of Types of Institut-ions	*No. of Type of Institutions*	*No. of Institu-tions*	*Total Accommodation Capacity*			*Total Actual Strength*		
			Male	*Fe-ma le*	*Total*	*Male*	*Fe-ma le*	*Total*
(iv)	Taluka Sub-jails (29 are managed by Prison Dept. Staff and 43 are managed by Revenue Dept. in the grade of Sherestedar / Tahsildar as superintendent and guarded by Police Personnel)	72						
(v)	Open Air Jail	1						
(vi)	Juvenile Jail	1						
(vii)	Borstal School	1						
	Total	**96**	**7,296**	**422**	**7,718**	**9,032**	**270**	**9,302**

Table VI. Strength and Category-wise Staff of Prison Department on 30-9-2000

Sl. No.	*Category-wise*	*Strength*
1.	Correctional Executive	1,276
2.	Technical	280
3.	Ministerial	246
	Total	**1,802**

The proposal of revision of the Cadre and Recruitment Rules of the Department has already been submitted to Government and the orders of the Government are awaited.[17] Recently, organization of the Prisons Department commenced on modern lines. The Karnataka Prisons Act, 1963, was implemented in 1974 only. Even here onwards also it was not organized in a systematic way. Totally, Prisons Department is unscientifically organized. Now, it is a neglected department from all angles.

The Prisons Department is headed by an individual with the designation of the Inspector General of Prisons. The Inspector General of Prisons previously was also taken from the Indian Administrative Service and Indian Police Service. At present, The Inspector-General of Prisons is from the Department of Police.

The Deputy Inspector-General of Prisons and below officials belong to the Department of Prisons. All jails are not managed by the Department. Police and revenue departments are mixed with the prisons. The lower level jails i.e. taluka sub-jails even today are managed by revenue and police staff. Of the 73 taluk sub-jails in 1994-95, 45 taluk sub-jails; from 1997-98 of the 72 taluk sub-jails 43 taluk sub-jails are managed by revenue and police staff. This shows the Department of Prisons is not bifurcated from other departments like police and revenue.

The Government has not made any provision for the appointment of Special Officer for the Rationalization of Prison Administration in Karnataka on statutory basis. Rationalists are not appointed to rationalise the prisoners and the staff.

(vi) Modernisation of Prison Administration

In order to implement the recommendations of the All India Jail Reforms Committee, Government of India and the State Government with their matching shares from the years 1989-90 to 1997-98 in a phased manner have so far granted Rs. 389.37 lakh (Government of India Rs. 256.965 lakh and State Government Rs. 132.405 lakh).

These amounts have been spent for construction of High Security Jails with provision CC TV surveillance at Central Jail at Belgaum and Bellary. Repairs, improved water supply and sanitation to some selected jail buildings and female blocks were also effected. Metal detectors, diesel generator sets, vehicles, ambulance, mini clinical laboratories, X-ray equipments etc., at jail hospitals, games and sports articles, television sets etc., have also been provided under the scheme.[18]

For imparting vocational training in agriculture and horticulture, tractors, sprayers, sprinklers and drip irrigation facilities have also been provided. Furniture, xerox machines, fax machines, vehicles, intercom, ICD video projector etc., have also been provided to Prison Training Institute.

Sewing machines, tape-recorders and television sets have also been provided to female prisoners. Solar water heating system has been installed for providing hot water to female, old and sick prisoners at Bangalore Central Jail. It is proposed to extend all the above facilities to the remaining jails in the coming years. Efforts are being made to provide better facilities to prison officials in terms of quarters, transport etc., for improvement of efficiency and morale.

The construction of jail building and staff quarters under Five-Year Plan was started in the year 1976–77. A sum of Rs. 263.87 lakh and 231.73 lakh was spent during the year 1995-96 and 1996-97 under these works. A sum of Rs. 118.74 lakh was spent during the year upto September 1997.

(vii) Budget and Related Matters

The following are the budgetary provisions made for the year 1999-2000 of the Department:

Table VII. Budget for 1999-2000

	Head of Account	*Non-Plan allotment during the year 1999-2000 (Rs. in lakh)*	*Expenditure upto December 1999 under Non-Plan (Rs. in lakh)*
1.	Direction and Administration	82.46	66.97
2.	Jails	1791.57	1485.50
3.	Jail Manufactures	57.02	34.92
4.	Other Expenditures	73.02	52.16
5.	Borstal School	73.63	71.86
	Total	**2077.70**	**1711.41**

Population of the prison is on the increase. Thereby the expenditure towards diet, medicines etc., are also proportionately on the increase.

Buildings

Most of the jail buildings and staff quarters constructed during the British Regime are old and are deprived of timely repairs and renovations due to perennial paucity of funds and hence, are in dilapidated conditions. Efforts are on to get adequate funds under the PWD Budget Head for carrying out of these works. Proposals have also been submitted to Government of India for the Eleventh Finance Commission under the scheme of Modernisation of Prison Administration.

Construction of jail buildings and staff quarters have been taken up in a phased manner under State Plan Scheme. An amount of Rs. 151.10 lakh has been earmarked during1999-2000 for sub-jail buildings at Aland, Narasimharajapura, Nanjangud and Hadagali have since been completed. Construction works are completed at New Central Prison, Parappana Agrahara (II phase), and District Head Quarters sub-jail, Chikamagalur. An amount of Rs. 77.73 lakh has been spent up to December 1999.

Men's Open Air Jail

Another reformative measure is the establishment of a Men's Open Air Jail at Koramangala village in Bangalore Rural District. Prisoners work here under minimum security. The prisoners are being trained in modern methods of agriculture, horticulture, sericulture, sheep rearing, soil conservation and water utilization in irrigation. Steps have been taken to provide drip irrigation system under the scheme of Modernisation of Prisons in Karnataka. The authorized accommodation of the Open Air Jail is eighty.

The population in 1997-98 was only thirty. But in 1999-2000 increased to fifty-two. Though there is a single Open Air Jail in whole State, this too is under utilized. Well-behaved long-term prisoners are lodged in this Open Farm. They look like farmers on agricultural lands. There is not even a single open air jail/camp/minimum security jail exclusively for women prisoners. Even, construction of such a prison is not under the consideration of the Government.

Director-General of Police and Inspector-General of Prisons Mr. L. Revannasiddaiah, on October 8, 2000 in Chikmagalur said that it would take long time to solve the problem of wall jumping. Construction of new jails and repair of old jails in the State would cost around Rs. 70-80 crore. Hence, instead of this, priority would be given to complete the works being undertaken at once. The construction work of new jails in Bangalore, Nanjangud and Narsimharajapur was almost complete.[19]

(viii) Karnataka Acts and Rules

The Prison Administration is conducted under the provisions of the following Acts and Rules:

1.	Karnataka Prisons Act	1963
2.	Karnataka Prisoners Act	1963
3.	Karnataka Prison Rules	1974
4.	Karnataka Prison Manual	1978
5.	Borstal School Act	1963
6.	Borstal School Rules	1969
7.	Juvenile Justice Act	1987
8.	Criminal Procedure Code	

The whole prison administrative staff including clerical, police guards, escort parties etc., are not involved in reformative activities. Reformative culture is not there in the prison administration.

References

1. Karnataka State Gazetteer, Part II, ed. by Kamath Suryanath U., Parishree Printers, Bangalore, 1983, pp. 438-40.
2. Report on the Administration of Mysore for the year 1951-52, Part I, printed by the Director of Printing, Stationery and Publications at the Government Press, Bangalore, 1953, p.60.
3. Bhushan Vidya: *op. cit.*, p. 39.
4. Karnataka Prison Manual 1978, Vols. I and II, prescribed by the Government of Karnataka, Bangalore.
5. Report on the Administration of Mysore for the year 1957-58, Part I–General Summary, Published by Order of Government, Government Press, 1960, pp. 12, 16.
6. Sathpal Puliani: The Guide to Police Laws in Karnataka—Karnataka Prisons Act 1963, Karnataka Law Journal Publications, Bangalore,1999, p. 302.
7. Report on the Administration of Mysore for the Year 1957-58, Part I–General Summary, *op. cit.*, pp. 33-34.
8. Report on the Administration of Mysore for the Year 1958-59, Government of Mysore, Government Press, Bangalore, 1961, p. 34.

9. Sathpal Puliani: *op. cit.*, pp. 330-35.
10. Karnataka Prison Manual, 1978, *op. cit.*, pp. 4-5.
11. Karnataka State Gazetteer, Part II, *op. cit.*, p. 441.
12. Working of The Departments of Government of Mysore (from March 27, 1971 to October 31, 1971), Prisons Department, Government Press, Bangalore, pp.137-39.
13. Karnataka State Gazetteer, Part II, *op. cit.*, pp. 441, 447- 48.
14. Gazetteer of India—Karnataka State Gazetteer, Decennial Supplement (1983–93), Kamath Suryanath U., Lakshmi Mudranalaya, Bangalore, 1994, pp. 448, 450.
15. Prisons Department Annual Reports 1994-95, 1997-98 and 1999-2000, Department of Prisons, Government of Karnataka, Bangalore, pp. 1, 13.
16. Karnataka Prison Manual, 1978, pp. 34–60.
17. Prisons Department Annual Reports, 1994-95, 1997-98 and 1999-2000, Department of Prisons, Government of Karnataka, Bangalore.
18. Prisons Department Annual Reports, 1997-98 and 1999-2000, Department of Prisons, pp. 4-19.
19. Annual Reports 1994-95, 1997-98 and 1999-2000, Department of Prisons, Government of Karnataka, Bangalore.

Bibliography

Agarwal, K.M.: *Kautilya on Crime and Punishment*, Kanchan Publications, Bodh Gaya, Bihar, 1983.

Agarwal, K.M.: *Prevention of Crime*, Radiant Publications, New Delhi, 1997.

Altekar, A.S.: *State and Government in Ancient India*, Jainendra Press, Delhi, 1958.

Amnesty International Reports, 1997, 1998.

Bar Carl I Von: *A History of Continental Criminal Law*, Boston, Little Brown, 1916.

Bartollas Clemens: *Introduction to Corrections*, Harper & Row Publishers, New York, 1981.

Basham, A.L.: *The Wonder That Was India*, Third Edition, Rupa & Co., Calcutta, 1997.

Bhattacharya, B.K.: *Prisons*, S.C. Sarkar and Sons, Calcutta, 1958.

Bhuniya Niranjana: *International Organisations*, Associated Publishing House, New Delhi, 1970.

Bhushan Vidya: *Prison Administration in India* (with special reference to Uttar Pradesh), S. Chand and Company, New Delhi, 1970.

Billy S. Wayson, Gail S. Funke, Sally F. Familton, Peter B. Meyer: *Local Jails—The Correctional Dilemma*, Lexington Books, Lexington, Massachusetts, Toronto, 1977.

Blackwell Encyclopaedia of Political Thought: Janet Coleman, William Connolly, Alan Ryan; Rasil Blackwell Inc., New York, 1987.

Bombay Jail Manual: 1955.

Britannica Book of the Year: 1994.

Ibid.: 1958.

C.S. Malliah: Prison System in India— Past & Present- Future Vision: Paper presented at Sri K.L.N. Reddy Memorial Lecture, and also articles in '*Jaana*' a Kannada Monthly Magazine, July,

August, October, 1997; March 1998, May, June, August, September, October, 1999.

'CBI BULLETIN' 2: Open Prisons in India, May, 1994.

Chadha, Kum Kum: *The Indian Jail*, Vikas Publishing House, New Delhi, 1983.

Chandradeo Prasad: *Political Ideas of Ram Manohar Lohia*, Janaki Prakashan, Patna, 1989.

Chris Cook: *World Political Encyclopaedia*, Jaico Publishing House, Bombay, 1993.

'Civil and Military Journal' 18; Education in Prisons, by Punjab Riyaz; July- September 1982, pp. 198-201.

Clarence Darrow: *Crime—Its Cause and Treatment*, First Indian edition, Logos Press, New Delhi, 1990.

Clifford W.: *Regional Developments in Corrections*, Australian Institute of Criminology, ACT, Australia, 1982.

Contribution to Indian Sociology (N.S.) 27, Sage Publications, New Delhi, 1993.

Cressey R. Donald: *The Prison—Studies in Institutional Organisation and Change*, Holt Rinehart and Winston Inc., New York,1961.

Datar, H.B.: *Karnataka Acts and Rules*, Vol.17, Lawyer's Law Book, Bangalore, 1993.

Datir, R.N.: *Prison as a Social System* with special reference Maharashtra State, Popular Prakashan, Mumbai, 1978.

Das, R.M.: *Manu on Crime and Punishment*, Janaki Prakashan, Chouhatta, Patna, 1987.

Datar, H.B.: Karnataka Acts and Rules (1956-92) Vol.16, Lawyers Law Book, Bangalore, 1992.

David Crystal: The Cambridge Encyclopaedia, 1994.

Deccan Herald, State Daily Newspaper, Bangalore.

Devendra Chandra: *Open Air Prisons* (A Sociological Study), Vohra Publishers & Distributors, Allahabad, 1984.

Dodge R. Calvert: *A World Without Prisons—Alternatives to Incarceration Throughout the World*, Lexington Books, Lexington, Massachusetts, Toronto, 1979.

Donald R. Cressey: *The Prison—Studies in Institutional Organisation and Change*, Holt, Rinehart and Winston Inc., New York, 1961.

'Economic and Political Weekly' 27, Bharthi Indu: End of News Censorship for Prisoners in Bihar,13-20 June, 1992, p. 1242.

Encyclopaedia Britannica: Vols. 9, 10, 13, 14, 17, 18.

Encyclopaedia of Police in India: Vol. 3, ed. by Ghosh, S.K., Ashish Publishing House, New Delhi, 1997.

Encyclopaedia of Social Work: ed. by Shukla, K.S., Vol. II, Ministry of Welfare, Government of India, 1987.

Engels F.: *The Origin of the Family, Private Property and State* Progress Publishers, Moscow, 1977.

Fitzgerald, P.J.: *Criminal Law and Punishment*, Oxford University Press, London,1962.

Fredrick L. Schuman: *International Politics*, McGraw-Hill Book Company, Inc., New York, 1958.

Gate Lodge, The Voice of the POA, February 2000, a monthly magazine, Edmonton, London, N9 9HW.

Gazetteer of India: by Chopra, P.N., Vol., *The Ministry of Education and Social Welfare*, Government of India Press, New Delhi, 1978.

Gettel, R.G.: *Political Science*, World Press, Calcutta, 1956.

Goodman, R. Elliot: *Soviet Design for a World State, Studies of the Russian Institute*, Columbia University Press, New York, 1960.

Guha Roy, Jayatilak: "Role of Voluntary Agencies in Prevention of Crime and Treatment of Offenders; Indian Journal of Public Administration, The Indian Institute of Public Administration, New Delhi, Vol. XXXIII, No. 3., July-September 1987.

Hans Toch: *Peace Keeping: Police, Prisons, and Violence*, Lexington Books, Lexington, Massachusetts, Toronto, 1979.

Harold Wheeler: *International Encyclopaedia of Facts*, Vol. II, Castle Books, New Delhi, 1992.

Hartman H. Fredrick: *The Relations of Nations*, Macmillan Company, New York, 1963.

The Hindu, National Daily Newspaper, Bangalore.

The Hindustan Times, National Daily Newspaper, New Delhi.

Howard Jones and Paul Cornes: *Open Prisons*, Routledge & Kegan Paul, London, WCIE, 7DD, 1977.

Illustrated World Encyclopaedia: Bobley Publishing Corp., Woodbury, New York.

India Annual, A Reference: Research, Reference and Training Division, Ministry of Information and Broadcasting, Government of India, New Delhi, 1990.

India 1995, A Reference Annual : *op. cit.,* 1996.

India 1998, A Reference Annual: *op. cit.*

India 2000, A Reference Annual: *op. cit.*

India 2001, A Reference Annual: *op. cit.*

India Today, A National Monthly Magazine, by Sumit Mitra, January 31, 2000.

The Indian Express, National Daily Newspaper, Bangalore.

India Journal of Public Administration; Indian Institute of Public Administration; New Delhi, October-December; 1985.

Indian Journal of Public Administration; *op. cit.*, Oct-Dec.; 1989.

Indian Journal of Social Work, 1993.

Jangam, R.T.: *An Outline of International Politics*, Allied Publishers, New Delhi, 1981.

Jeanne Hersch: *Birth Right of Man*, UNESCO, 1968.

Jogan Shankar: *Social Problems and Welfare in India*, Ashish Publishing House, New Delhi, 1992.

Jonna Kelley: *When the Gates Shut*, Longman, London, 1967.

Joy Cameron: *Prisons and Punishment in Scotland from the Middle Age to the Present*, Canongate Publishing Ltd., Edinburgh, 1983.

Kane, P.V.: History of Dharmasastra—Ancient and Medieval Religions and Civil Law,

Bhandarkar Oriental Research Institute, Poona, 1946.

Karl Lewis: *Justice is the Crime*, KAT, 1972.

Karnataka Prison Manual 1978: Government of Karnataka, Bangalore, 1978.

Karmaveer: A Kannada State Weekly Magazine, 6th October 1996, Bangalore, p.19.

Karnataka Prison Department Reports: Report on the Administration of Mysore, 1938-39; 1939-40; 1940-41; 1941-42; 1942-43; 1945-46; 1950-51; 1951-52; 1952-53; 1954-55; 1955-56; 1956-57; 1957-58; 1959-60; 1962-63; 1963-64; 1964-65; 1965-66; 1966-67; Eleventh Administration Report of the New State of Mysore (Now Karnataka) 1966-67; Report on The Administration of the State of Karnataka 1974-75; Prisons Department Annual Report

1975-76; Report on the Administration of the State of Karnataka 1975-76; 1976-77; 1977-78; 1978-79; 1979-80; 1980-81; 1982-83; 1983-84; 1984-85; 1985-86; Annual Report on the Working of the Prisons Department 1986-87; Report on The Administration of the State of Karnataka 1987-88; 1988-89; 1989-90; 1990-91; Annual Report on the Working of the Prisons Department 1989-90; 1990-91; 1991-92; 1992-93; 1993-94; 1994-95; 1997-98; 1999-2000; 2000-01.

Karnataka Prisons Act, 1963: Government of Karnataka, Bangalore.

Karnataka Prisons Website Number; WWW. Karnataka Prison.org., Office of The Inspector General of Prisons, Bangalore.

Tihar Jail http://Tiharprison.nic.in/.;

Kiran Bedi http://Kiranbedi.com/.;

Prison Fellowship http://www.differentindia.org.;

Pfi.html; Prison wall http://www.Prisonwall.org/.;

Prison zone http://www.prisonzone.com/.;

Prison Activist Resource Centre http//www.prisonactivist.org.;

Others:http://www.the week.com/99april/events6.htm;

http:www.federalprisonconsultant.com/;

http:www.freeworldfriends.com;survivalguide.html.

Karnataka State Gazetteer, Decennial Supplement (1983-93): Chief Editor-Kamath U. Suryanath, Lakshmi Printing Press, Bangalore, 1994.

Karnataka State Gazetteer, Vol. II: Karnataka State Government, Lotus Printers, Bangalore, 1985.

Karnataka State Gazetteer, Part II : Kamath U. Sryanath, Government of Karnataka, Bangalore, Parishree Printers, 1983.

Khera, R.C. Central Criminal Minor Acts: The Identification of Prisoners Act, 1920; The Juvenile Justice Act, 1986; The Mental Health Act, 1987; The Prisoners Act, 1900; The Prisoners (Attendance in Courts) Act, 1955; The Prisons Act, 1894; The Probation of Offenders Act, 1958 (Central Act No. 20 of 1958); The Protection of Human Rights Act, 1993 (Central Act No. 10 of 1994); Allied Book Company, Delhi, 2000.

Madan, G.R.: *Indian Social Problems*, Vol. 1, fifth edition, Allied Publishers Limited, New Delhi,1997.

Madan, G.R.: *Indian Social Problems*, Vol. 2, fourth edition, Allied Publishers Limited, New Delhi, 1995.

Manorama Year Book 1994: ed. by Mathew, K.M., Kottayam, Kerala.

Margenthau Hans J.: *Politics Among Nations*, Scientific Book Agency, Calcutta, 1996.

Marx and Engels: *Manifesto of the Communist Party*, Progress Publishers, Moscow, 1975.

Mathiesen Thomas: *Prison on Trial—A Critical Assessment*, Sage Publications, New Delhi, 1992.

Mohanty Amrendra and Hazary Narayan: *Indian Prison System*, Ashish Publishing House, New Delhi, 1990.

Myril E. Alexander: *Jail Administration*, Charles E. Thomas, Spring Field, US, 1957.

Mysore Borstal School Act, 1963, and Mysore Borstal School Rules,1969: Government of Karnataka, Government Press, Bangalore.

Narula, R.K.: *Justice Jounder Trials—Jail or Bail*, Himalaya Publishing House, Bombay, 1979.

The New Indian Express; National Daily Newspaper, Bangalore.

The New Indian Express; National Daily Newspaper, Shimoga, Karnataka State.

Norval Morris: *The Future of Imprisonment*, The University of Chicago Press, Chicago, 1974.

Orland Leonard: *Prisons-Houses of Darkness*, The Free Press, Macmillan Publishing Co., Inc., New York, 1978.

Palmer and Perkins: *International Relations*, Scientific Book Agency, Calcutta, 1970.

Pandey, J.N.: *Constitutional Law of India*, Central Law Agency, Allahabad, 1989.

Park E. Robert: *On Social Control and Collective Behaviour*, Phoenix Books, University of Chicago Press, Chicago, 1969.

Parmesh Dangwal: *"I DARE" Kiran Bedi—A Biography*, UBS Publishers, New Delhi, 1996.

Prajavani, A Kannada Provincial Daily Newspaper, Bangalore.

Protection of Civil Rights Act, 1989: Central Law Agency, Allahabad.

Radley, Neil S.: *The Treatment of Prisoners Under International Law*, Clarendon Press, Oxford, 1987.

Ramji Lall: *Bertrand Russel—Unpopular Essays*, Seventh Edition, Rama Brothers, New Delhi, 1999.

Rani Dharam Shankar Dass: *Prisons and Punishment*, Seminar, 4439-March 1996.

Report of the All India Committee on Jail Reforms, 1980-83, Vols. I & II, Government of India Press, New Delhi.

Report of the Sixth United Nations Congress: "On the Prevention of Crime and the Treatment of Offenders".

Report of the Working Group on Prisons in the Country, 1973-73: Government of India, Ministry of Home Affairs, New Delhi.

Revel Francois Jean: Without Marx or Jesus, 1972.

Robertson Ronald: *Globalisation—Social Theory and Global Culture*, Sage Publications, New Delhi, 1992.

Roy Jayatilak Guha: Role of Voluntary Agencies in Prevention of Crime and Treatment of Offender, Indian Journal of Public Administration, Vol. 33(3), July-September 1987, New Delhi.

Roy Jayatilak Guha and Yatish Mishra: Criminal Administration in India—Emerging Trends and Futuristic Introspection, Indian Institute of Public Administration, reprinted from Indian Journal of Public Administration, July-September 1997, Vol. XLIII, No. 3, pp. 794-803, New Delhi.

Roy, R.G.: *Prisons and Society—A Study of the Indian Jail System*, Gyan Publishing House, New Delhi, 1989.

Rukmi Basu: *The United Nations*, Sterling Publishers, New Delhi, 1993.

S. Ghosh: *Open Prisons and the Inmates* (A Socio-psychological Study), Mittal Publications, New Delhi, 1992.

Sandhu, H.S.: *A Study of Prison Impact*, Publication Bureau, Punjab University, Chandigarh, 1968.

Sathpal Puliani: *The Guide to Police Laws in Karnataka*, new edition: The Karnataka Prisons Act, 1963 (Karnataka Act No. 33 of 1963); The Karnataka Prisons Rules, 1974; The Karnataka Prisoners Act, 1963 (Karnataka Act No. 25 of 1964); State Service Cadres in respect of the Karnataka Prisons Service; The Karnataka Prisons Service (Recruitment) Rules, 1976; The Probation of Offenders (Karnataka) Rules,1960; The Juvenile Justice (Karnataka) Rules, 1987; Karnataka Law Journal Publications, Bangalore, 1999.

Index

A

D

E

N

O

U

V

W